Balls

BALLS

Men Finding Courage
with Words, Work, Wine, and Women

RON JOHNSON and DEB BROCK
Foreword by Dan Feaster

WIPF & STOCK · Eugene, Oregon

BALLS
Men Finding Courage with Words, Work, Wine, and Women

Copyright © 2025 Ron Johnson and Deb Brock. All rights reserved. Except for brief quotations in critical publications or reviews, no part of this book may be reproduced in any manner without prior written permission from the publisher. Write: Permissions, Wipf and Stock Publishers, 199 W. 8th Ave., Suite 3, Eugene, OR 97401.

Wipf & Stock
An Imprint of Wipf and Stock Publishers
199 W. 8th Ave., Suite 3
Eugene, OR 97401

www.wipfandstock.com

PAPERBACK ISBN: 979-8-3852-3258-1
HARDCOVER ISBN: 979-8-3852-3259-8
EBOOK ISBN: 979-8-3852-3260-4

VERSION NUMBER 011025

Contents

Foreword by Dr. Dan Feaster | vii

Introduction | 1

SECTION I: MEN AND FEELINGS | 15

Chapter 1
The Nature of Feelings | 17

Chapter 2
Men and Fear | 28

Chapter 3
Men and Anger | 46

SECTION II: WORDS, WORK, AND WINE | 59

Chapter 4
Men and Words | 61

Chapter 5
Men and Work | 79

Chapter 6
Men and Wine (Addictions) | 98

SECTION III: THE BIG W: WOMEN | 119

Chapter 7
Men and Women: Different Creatures | 121

Chapter 8
Men's Fear of Women's Disapproval | 135

Chapter 9
Finding the Right Woman | 155

SECTION IV: MATURE MANHOOD | 167

Chapter 10
The Emotionally Mature Man | 169

POSTSCRIPT: DOS AND DON'TS | 193

Chapter 11
Dos and Don'ts for Women | 195

Chapter 12
Don'ts and Dos for Men | 212

Bibliography | 229

Foreword

I have known Dr. Ron Johnson for more than two decades. I first met Ron when he worked for me and with me at the Samaritan Counseling Center as a psychologist, where he provided counseling and psychological testing. I have personally consulted with Ron and have sent countless individuals to him for psychological and neurological testing. I have enjoyed spending time with Ron and his wife Dr. Deb Brock, also a psychologist, on many occasions.

On occasion, Ron and I get together for breakfast. During our last breakfast meeting, Ron asked if I would be willing to write the foreword for his book about men called *Balls*. I was honored to write this foreword. My initial response to hearing the title of this book, *Balls*, was a chuckle that led to my asking Ron why he would want to use a term such as "balls," given the public reaction that it might bring. I suggested it is not politically correct and might be offensive to some people. As Ron explained his rationale for the term "balls" and why he wanted to use it, it started making sense to me. By the end of our breakfast, he convinced me why the title, *Balls: Men Finding Courage with Words, Work, Wine, and Women*, actually made sense.

Many years ago Ron told me that early in his counseling practice he would work with anyone who came through his office door, including men, women, and parents wanting him to see their children. Ron noted that most of the women spoke of the troubles they had with their husbands or boyfriends, finding these men challenging, offensive, or even abusive. He began to have a picture of men that was largely negative, namely the lack of maturity that these men seemed to display. Slowly, Ron started seeing and working with some of these same men who were related to the women who didn't know how to deal with them. He was surprised to get a very different perspective of these men. He began to understand how men operate in the world, as well as how they struggle with "words, work, wine, and women," as the subtitle of this book suggests. The more Ron worked with men, the more he understood them. He also saw the troubles they have in the world but without a primary orientation towards seeing what was wrong with them. Instead, he developed an understanding the basic psychological structure of men, as well as the personal and interpersonal challenges that most men have in life. Ron has focused his practice on seeing, understanding, and helping men understand themselves so that they can more adequately communicate to the people in their lives, particularly the women in their lives. Conjointly, Ron's wife and colleague, Deb, came to work primarily with women. While Ron and Deb work with different clientele, they share a passion for seeing strengths of people more than their weaknesses, helping people mature personally and interpersonally. Some of Ron's work includes working with couples, with a primary focus on communication based on deeper understanding of personality differences, gender differences, and differences in maturity.

As you read this book, you will come to see that Ron and Deb have this positive approach to counseling that tends to be unique in the psychological community. The traditional medical model of mental health is based on an examination of the individual to identify problems and pathology that lead to a diagnosis, treatment, and "cure" for these problems. While Ron and Deb are fluent with mental health diagnoses, their focus is on understanding "what is right about people," as they say, rather than what is wrong. They find it more useful to help people understand themselves first and understand other people second, an understanding that is based partly on gender differences. Their approach to psychology and psychotherapy is consistent with positive psychology, which has been espoused by many psychologists this century.

In my more than forty years of psychotherapy practice, I have learned much from Ron and Deb and continue to learn from their work and knowledge. Their earlier works, *The Positive Power of Sadness*, *I Want to Tell You How I Feel*, and *What's Your Temperament?: Identifying and Enhancing Your Personality Strengths*, bring a wealth of knowledge of understanding ourselves and other people. The present volume adds a new dimension to this understanding, with the focus primarily on Ron's interest in how men operate and how they can mature in the various aspects of their lives. You will find that elements of their previous books are rephrased from the perspective of what it means to be a man and how men can find deeper and more fulfilling lives.

It is clear that men and women are different, physically, emotionally, relationally, and chemically. The authors identify some of these differences, as well as how the brains of men and women work differently. It is no surprise that there are so many unhappy relationships and divorces today,

FOREWORD

many of which are due to a lack of understanding of these differences. There are a number of books that examine some of the differences between men and women. In *Balls* Ron and Deb attempt to identify how men and women communicate quite differently and provide practical tools in addressing the challenges that these differences often present.

This book is a how-to book about becoming a healthy man, which essentially means a mature man. Many men have not had the luxury of healthy and mature male role models in their lives. Deb and Ron use the very term "balls" to convey the courage it takes men to understand themselves, value themselves, and communicate themselves, particularly their feelings. A major focus of this book is helping men develop valuable skills to improve their relationships with the women in their lives as well as in their friendships, their work relationships, and their parenting skills.

I can say with certainty that Ron Johnson has balls. In this book he honestly shares his own failures and weaknesses, together with some of the successes helping men avoid his mistakes. He demonstrates the courage to be honest in examining his feelings and his life. He shows how to put this honesty into practice by becoming the best man, partner, father, friend, worker, and leader that men can become. Deb is also a great model of what it is like to be the healthy woman in the life of a man. She displays herself as a person willing to be patient as the man in her life often struggles to find the right words to express his feelings.

I invite you to read, study, and think about what Ron and Deb have presented in *Balls: Men Finding Courage with Words, Work, Wine, and Women*. You will learn, agree, disagree, and otherwise challenge some of what these authors have written. It is my hope that you can find ways to combine what you learn, what you feel, and what you already know to enhance your lives, particularly your relationships. It has been a passion of mine for forty years to improve relationships based on self-understanding and personal maturity in order to help people communicate better. I hope you can do this as well by reading this book and learning from its contents.

Dr. Dan Feaster,
MSW, MDiv, DMin
Psychotherapist and Director of Samaritan Counseling Center

Introduction

Nobody Taught Us How to Be Men

Who taught you how to be a man?

- Who taught you how to deal with the mistakes you make?
- Who taught you how to deal with female criticism?
- Who taught you how to deal with any criticism?
- Who taught you how to find your profession in life?
- Who taught you how to deal with not liking your job?
- Who taught you how to have fun as an adult?
- Who taught you about the dangers of alcohol and drugs?
- Who taught you about the dangers of gambling, promiscuity, and overeating?
- Who taught you how to take care of your adult body?
- Who taught you how to deal with money?
- Who taught you how to be alone without being lonely?
- Who taught you how to raise children?
- Who taught you how to take care of your adolescent?
- Who taught you how to reconcile your own adolescence, to deal with your early life's wounds and mistakes?
- Who taught you how to deal with being humiliated in school by some bully?

- Who taught you how to deal with feeling stupid because you didn't read well?
- Who taught you how to deal with feeling inadequate because you weren't good at sports?
- Who taught you when you can swear and when you shouldn't?
- Who taught you how to deal with your sexual feelings?
- Who taught you about masturbation?
- Who taught you how to swing a hammer, do the vacuuming, or draw a picture?
- Who taught you how to deal with male competition?
- Who taught you how to understand spirituality and religion?
- Who taught you how to make money, spend money, and save money?
- Who taught you to use all of these skills in your relationships with women?

Most likely, you learned these things primarily on your own or with the inadequate direction of your male friends or enemies.

Who taught you how to deal with these real-life responsibilities that are a part of every man? Your father? Stepfather? Uncle or grandfather? Other adult men? Quite possibly no one taught you these things, so you entered adult male life pretty unprepared to meet the challenges of these responsibilities all alone. Then you got into a job you didn't like, a woman you didn't like, and a life you didn't like. So, here you are in this life with no one's direction but everyone's opinion of what you should do. You're a good man, but somehow being good isn't enough. You crave for something more, but what is it? Perhaps you want to be great. You want to do great things, have great fun, have great relationships, and have a real positive impact on the world. How can you do that?

Because we haven't had much help in learning how to be a male, we men tend to fall into one of three things: avoidance, addiction, or anger, but there is a deeper phenomenon that underlies these things: anxiety. We men feel a great deal of anxiety because we often feel overwhelmed by what lies before us. A central task in this book is to help you identify this anxiety and then to find ways to end it, which consequently ends avoidance, addiction, and anger. Before we do that, we have to help you find yourself, find your feelings, express your feelings, and then feel capable of facing the responsibilities of your life. If you do that, you will be a great man.

INTRODUCTION

Good to Great

I see many men in my practice who are good men, but I don't see any of them being great, at least not yet. I have many friends who are good men but not yet great men. I am not great. Greatness isn't about power, wealth, influence, authority, or fame. It isn't about what people think of you. Greatness for a man is about having *balls*. If you want to be a better man who has a meaningful and productive life, you need to have balls. But what does it mean to have "balls"? How dare we say such a thing, you might ask? Isn't "having balls" some kind of power move, some macho-man thing, some superiority thing, some kind of dominance or "don't give a shit" attitude? Does having balls mean a guy can do whatever he wants? None of the above. Being ballsy has nothing to do with genitals, much less any kind of personal power or social superiority. Certainly, the term may be offensive to many quarters of life including women, many men, people of certain religious persuasions, the LGBTQ community, and many more. We apologize forthrightly to any and all whom we offend with the term "balls," and yet we must use the term for many reasons, not the least of which is the shock value that it may have. We want to direct men into finding a way to be courageous in their lives. Different phraseology might be more palatable, but palatability would soften what we want to say about men and what we think they need to do in life to be happy, content, and of service to the world. We have decided to stick with the street term "balls" because finding a more culturally acceptable term would whitewash the phenomenon that most men struggle with: *feeling, thinking, speaking, and acting courageously in service to humankind.*

Aside from its possible offensive nature, "balls" is one of many body-based expressions that are quite common in English like, "having heart," "using your head," "having backbone," or "standing on your own two feet." These physical expressions all derive from emotional and social situations and behavior. "Having backbone" graphically describes what is meant by having courage in the face of adversity. "Standing on your own two feet" references making decisions and having courage to face what comes your way in those decisions. Likewise, "balls" suggests a different kind of courage that is primarily associated with men who are faced with challenging situations and finding ways to accept those challenges. As there is an intrinsic fear that all men have of being assaulted in their genitals, there is a more important fear that most men have of failure, mistakes, and criticism. It is our hope that we can help men overcome these fears so that they can be better men: better to the people in their lives, better to the work in their lives, better to themselves, and better for the world at large. To overcome their fears men have to have courage. *They have to have balls.*

The term balls, which we have chosen as the main title of this book, is largely synonymous with courage. But courage to do what? The foundation of our concept of balls is courage is to be *honest*. When a publisher read a blog that I wrote some time ago entitled "Why Good Men Lie," she said that I should write a book about it. This is the book. You will see that the basic theme of this book is being honest: first honest with oneself, then honest with trusted others, then selectively open with other people. Being honest does not mean saying everything to everyone. Honesty is one of those very basic human elements that cannot be easily defined because it is so central to good living. The fact that we cannot explicitly define honesty does not mean that we can't understand such concepts. An honest man needs to use discretion to whom he speaks and use great care in how he speaks.

Finding Courage to be Honest

Note that the subtitle of this book is "men finding courage with words, work, wine, and women." Men find one or more of these important elements challenging, and many men find them all challenging. By far the most challenging thing for men is to find words, especially when men are emotional—and more so when they engage an intimate woman in their lives. Men are usually caught with a paucity of words in their emotional vocabulary that then leads to the other difficulties that men have, namely women, wine, and work. Men's general inability to find words for their feelings leads to tremendous difficulty with women and consequent dishonesty with women. If that weren't enough fodder for failure, men are very inclined to addictions, which I have summarized as "wine" for alliterative purposes. If men can't be honest with themselves, can't find words to express themselves, and can't be honest with the women in their lives, they will fall into some kind of addiction and will not succeed in a man's greatest purpose in life: meaningful and productive work.

You want to grow a pair? You want to have balls? You want to develop the courage it takes to grow a pair? Be *honest*. That's the beginning of becoming ballsy. Many men are simply not honest: not with themselves, not with the women in their lives, not with their children, not with their colleagues at work, not with their friends. It is extremely difficult for men to be honest when they don't know *what* they feel or *how* to express their feelings. If you don't know how you feel and don't have words to express these feelings, you will not be very good at understanding how *other people feel*, which is ultimately what leads to successful relationships.

I must quickly add that being honest doesn't necessarily mean talking. We will deal with how we can be honest in our actions and communicate our feelings through actions. We will deal with how to be honest as well as when to be honest, especially with what we say. Most of the classical philosophers, particularly the groups called Cynics and Stoics, suggested that being honest was the center of *virtue*, which was itself the cornerstone of success in the world. I define success in the world as being *a force for good* in the world.

I mostly see men in my psychological practice, something that I have done for many years, perhaps to a total of having seen about ten thousand men. What do men present as their primary concern? Depression? Yes, some. Financial challenges? Yes, many. Vocational challenges? Yes, many. Addiction? Yes, most. Anxiety? Yes, almost all. Challenges with women? Again, almost all men. Difficulty finding words? Every one of them. The difficulties that men have in life begin with words, namely not having words to describe what they think, what they value, and most importantly, how they feel. If I can help men identify their feelings, I may be able to help them communicate their feelings. A man has to do a lot of work between *knowing* how he feels and *communicating* how he feels. Men do all kinds of things to keep from using words that actually communicate how they feel. I remember a very outgoing and expressive man who would sometimes just open his mouth, spread his arms widely, and then make a kind of nonsense syllable seemingly with the expectation that the listener could understand how he feels. Instead of words, many men simply go quiet, leave the room, and avoid any conversation about feelings. Most men get angry easily because they don't know how to communicate their feelings. Men tend to speak in anger, react in anger, and a few will take anger to an extreme becoming physically harmful to the people in their lives, particularly their family members.

When a man truly begins to understand how he feels, he then has the task of accepting his feelings, valuing his feelings, and thinking about his feelings before he is ready to start the process of communicating these feelings. However, in order to successfully *communicate* his feelings, a man has to begin by *expressing* his feelings. There is a huge difference between expressing feelings and communicating feelings. The odd phenomenon for us men is that we really know how we feel, but we aren't usually skilled to successfully communicate how we feel in words. For most men it is nearly an impossible task to communicate how they feel. Later in this book we will discuss the fact that *words are not men's primary means of communication*. If men are to have balls and overcome the challenges that women, addictions, and work present to them, they will have to improve in their use of words, especially when they speak about their feelings.

Once men understand how to communicate how they feel, they then have an even harder task: to listen and understand how other people feel. Men can do this very difficult task only if they know how they feel, value how they feel, express how they feel, and ultimately communicate how they feel. Good psychotherapy begins with self-understanding and self-acceptance, but it is not sufficient to only "know thyself," as Socrates suggested. Socrates's suggestion is that knowing oneself is the *beginning* of wisdom. Men have to start with knowing themselves and then go beyond themselves, first into understanding other people and then finding ways to serve the world. If men are really to serve the world, they will need to have many things in their psychological toolbox:

- First, men need to have what we call "self," which means one's personal essence.
- Secondly, men will need to have a good understanding of other people, namely how other people think, feel, act, and value.
- Thirdly, men will need to have a broad understanding of the world at large, which means how relationships work.

Some men are particularly good at understanding how the world works, but they may not be as good at understanding people. Some men are good at understanding other people, but they may not be as good at understanding themselves. There are also men who might be quite psychologically sophisticated in understanding themselves and other people, but they don't do anything with this understanding. My intention in this book is to help men do all three of these ingredients so they may be of service to the world: understanding oneself, understanding other people, and understanding how the world works. Then men will be ready to do what they were made to do: engage in meaningful, creative, and productive work.

Finding Courage with Words, Women, Wine, and Work

Finding words is distinctly the hardest thing for most men, especially words that describe how they feel. Almost always the next thing that men deal with is the challenge of relating successfully to the women in their lives. Too often men fail to have a grasp of the effective use of emotional words when they relate to women and fall into the third category, addictions ("wine"). Very few men have avoided becoming addicted to something, whether chemical like alcohol and pot, or behavioral, like gambling or video game playing. Before we even tackle words, women, wine, and work, we will start our study by an examination of feelings, specifically how all people feel.

If men truly find ways of dealing with words, women, and addictions, they will be able to do the real task in life: work. Work is not necessarily making widgets, selling widgets, or making new widgets but rather doing something that needs to be done and something that you can get really good at doing. The world needs men to do good work. In order for men to do meaningful and valuable work, they will need words, which is much of our discussion in this book, and ultimately men will need to deal effectively with women. There are many other characteristics that define a good man including being kind, gracious, humble, courageous, and wise, but these characteristics all erupt from self-understanding, understanding of other people, and understanding how the world works. The underlying concept is still honesty, something I have been working on with men for decades. In the forthcoming pages we will discuss the possibilities, the challenges, and the opportunities for men to be great men if they can find a way to be honest. Honesty remains the cornerstone of having balls.

Finding Courage to Be

Philosopher/theologian Paul Tillich wrote a book with this exact title: *The Courage to Be*, in which he suggested that the central ingredient in life is to be true to oneself and then to communicate oneself. Having balls means having this kind of courage. A good portion of this book is devoted to this task of *being* and understanding yourself. We will discuss how being yourself doesn't mean that people will understand you or like you. Being yourself has nothing to do with other people. Being yourself means being courageously honest, which naturally leads to saying something and doing something. It is in the realm of *being*, which is the realm of self-understanding, where most men establish courage in life and find their balls.

Speaking Courageously

If a man can courageously be himself, which requires a depth self-understanding, his second task is to *speak* courageously. Speaking courageously means that a man is willing to be misunderstood in what he says, to be criticized for what he has said, or simply to be wrong with what he has said. Most men have great difficulty in this area of life because they are afraid of being misunderstood or being wrong. Men tend to move from good words to bad words, especially when they try to communicate their feelings to women. Because words are not the preferred means of communicating for most men, men often stumble with words when they are dealing with women (as well as with wine and work). They would much rather *do* something, *think* something, or *feel* something than *say* something. Nothing wrong with doing, thinking, and feeling, but eventually men have to be courageous to put their thoughts, feelings, and actions into words. Failing to put their thoughts, feelings, and actions into words puts them at a tremendous disadvantage in the world, particularly with women. This failure leads to their being misunderstood, judged, and disregarded in their female relationships. It takes courage for a man to learn how to speak, then when to speak, and eventually how to listen. We will discuss in depth the significance of words in a man's life, especially as they relate to women.

Avoiding Addictions

If a man can courageously *be* himself and *speak* himself, he will be less inclined to *avoid* his feelings by being addicted to something. When men fail to know what they feel and successfully communicate what they feel, they avoid the whole process of expressing feelings by finding a coping mechanism that becomes addictive. Addictive behaviors include buying, working, playing, gambling, promiscuity, and pornography, working out, TV-watching, cell phone use, and many other behaviors. Chemical addictions include food, alcohol, street drugs, prescription drugs, sleeping, and even working too much. We will discuss the various forms of addiction later.

Serving the World

If a man has mastered the *being* part of manhood, the *speaking* part of manhood, and has avoided or corrected the *addictive* tendencies, he is then ready to *do* something. This doing needs to be some form of serving the world. Doing is where many men are most courageous. Most people in the military are men, and many of them have been very courageous in military affairs putting themselves in harm's way as needed. Men can be courageous off the battlefield by working fourteen hours a day, if necessary, in order to make ends meet for their families, and other men might work the same amount in an occupation that is life-saving, like cancer research. Other courageous men work simply "doing their work," whatever it might be, because they find a purpose in it and that purpose requires of them courage to be faithful to their chosen task.

There are many forms of working that are important in the world, some of them physical, some intellectual, some theoretical, and some practical. Some people like philosophers, mathematicians, and theologians do a great deal but they may not be able to swing a hammer or fix a computer. There are scientists who work all their lives looking carefully at the structure of cells or working diligently to find a way to contain nuclear fusion. There are poets, writers, and musicians who might spend hours, days, or years constructing good poetry, fiction, or music that truly profit humanity. The key to doing is using the gifts and passion that you have without fear. But to be without fear, you really have to have a pair.

When I speak of men making a contribution to the world, I am suggesting that men can be much more effective in their whole orientation to living, something that is not only beyond their own personal satisfaction but also beyond the satisfaction of their intimate partners. A ballsy man is someone who first cares deeply for himself, then cares deeply for the people in his circle of friends and family, and finally cares just as deeply for the world at large. The people who have made the greatest marks on the world, equally men and women, are generally people who first love themselves, then love their intimate contacts, and then come to love the world at large. You cannot have a positive and meaningful impact on the world if you have not first had a positive and meaningful view of yourself and a positive impact on those in your intimate circle.

Courageously Relating

If a man can *be* himself courageously and *speak* himself courageously, and *do something* significant, he can then *relate* courageously. Relationships are built on self-knowledge, saying something, and doing something. Too often, men (and many women) think that they can succeed in a relationship with someone if they are just good people. Many very fine people have failed in relationships because they were remiss in being, speaking, or doing. A meaningful relationship does not come out of the blue: it comes out of the hard work of knowing something, speaking something, and doing something. As a child born in the 1940s and raised primarily in the 1950s, I remember the time when the word "relationship" actually entered the American vocabulary. The word relationship became popular during the American cultural revolution in the 1960s. For adults younger than me, which is most adults, the word relationship is used so frequently that people think they know what this word actually means. The word relationship means many different things to many different people. Some people equate the word relationship with intimacy, and many more people equate the word "intimacy" with sex. If men are to be courageous in their relationships, and even more so in their intimate relationships, they need to have an understanding of what a relationship means to them and to other people. You can't throw around the word relationship and expect people to have the same definition of that word that you have.

Relationships are not just among intimate partners. We have relationships with our children, our friends, our relatives, our employers, our employees, and even our enemies. If we are to succeed in these many relationships, we have to be courageous in our relating. Relationships with a supervisor at work, a child at home, a friend on the golf course, or a sexual partner are substantially different, but men need to be courageous in all of these relationships in the aspects of being, speaking, and doing. Then we can have a positive impact on the people in our lives.

Finding Ways to Display Courage

Being courageous, being ballsy, has nothing to do with a man becoming controlling, dominating, or authoritative. Having balls has to do with his being honest, forthright, and clear in his actions, which can only happen when a man is ever deeper in his self-understanding. This is no small task. It is no easy task. It is a task that is essential if a man wants to be happy and to bring happiness to his intimates, his family, his friends, his community, and the world.

When a man understands his own feelings and the feelings of others, he can tackle the problems that plague almost all men: fear of mistakes and fear of disapproval, especially disapproval from women. These fears inhibit a man from becoming a force for good with the people around him, and perhaps the world in general. To get to a place where a man is not afraid of mistakes and disapproval does not remove the hurt that everyone experiences with such things. We spend a whole chapter on the fear of female disapproval and an equal amount dealing with the feeling of hurt.

Many men come to my office never having had genuine understanding, acceptance, and encouragement together with appropriate challenge and limits. Rather, they have been criticized, threatened, shamed, or indulged. It is often my task to be the father figure that they have not had who is understanding, accepting, encouraging on the one hand and challenging and limiting on the other. It is a challenge for most men to trust me enough to render these basic ingredients of good parenting. My psychologist wife and I have a standing joke about how men come into my office: they come in with a female handprint in their backs. This means that some woman, usually a female partner, has pushed the man into seeing a therapist to "work on what is wrong with him." No man in his right mind wants to admit to having something wrong with him.

I often tell men that there is nothing wrong with them. Nothing wrong with him? How dare I say that? Certainly, there is something wrong with men who are angry too much, work too much, play too much, drink too much, or do nothing but watch football and drink beer. Right? Wrong. No, there is nothing wrong with *them* even if there is something terribly wrong with what they *do*. The reason men seem so unwilling to admit to their errors and mistakes in life is because to do so brings up their low self-esteem that was established many years beforehand. It would be great if a man would come to my office with a genuine interest in self-understanding and self-improvement, but seldom does that happen. It takes a great amount of courage for a man to walk into another man's office and explore the rights and wrongs in his life, the ups and downs of his life, and the successes and failures of his life.

I would much rather skip the whole "what's wrong with you" part of psychology together with all the diagnoses that are rendered in favor of seeing therapy as self-understanding, self-enhancing, and self-improvement. Coming in for therapy takes courage: courage to examine what you have done right and what you have done wrong, rather than there being something wrong with you. The poet Rudyard Kipling said, "If you can meet with Triumph and Disaster and treat those two impostors just the same . . . You'll be a Man, my son" (Kipling, circa 1895, stanzas 2, 4). Good therapy is not about "fixing" men or resolving their "issues" but rather should start with understanding one's strengths and abilities. Then, men can begin to deal with their challenges with words, work, women, and wine. It is very hard for men to look deeply at themselves and it is costly.

Courage Is Costly

Having balls in life is costly. It may cost money, recognition, visible success, property, job, or house. It may even cost friendship, family relationships, or marriage. But it is well worth the cost because the cost of doing life without balls, i.e., without courage, is life-draining and leads to a life that is not worth living. Sadly, the lives of many men are not worth living . . . and they know it. This is why many men in their 50s and 60s are frequently depressed. This is why many men fail in their marriages. This is why many men fall into addictions. This is why many men fail as fathers. This is why so many men are riddled with anxiety. This is why men are five times more likely to commit suicide than women.

This book is composed of a number of chapters forged together in four sections and a postscript. In the first section we will discuss the nature of feelings, including the nature of emotion. We suggest that the most important emotions are joy and sadness because they are love-based and the two emotions of fear and anger that are defense-based. We deal with how the emotions of fear and anger dominate most men's lives often because they haven't learned how to accept the necessity of sadness in life.

In Section II we discuss the first three of the W's in the subtitle of this book: words, work, and wine. We begin this discussion noting the centrality of words in a man's life and how most men fail to develop a meaningful emotional vocabulary. We then discuss how men often settle for work that is unsatisfying to them. This is followed by a discussion of how men tend to fall into chemical or behavioral additions when they have failed to develop words to deal with work and women.

Section III is devoted to the fourth W: women. We begin by examining some of the significant differences between males and females. This is followed by a discussion of the most potentially devastating element in many men's lives: fear of female disapproval. We close this section by suggesting how if a man can be the right man, the honest man, the courageous man, and the ballsy man, he can find the right woman.

Section IV is entitled Mature Manhood, composed of chapter ten: The Emotionally Mature Man. This chapter amounts to a summary of what it means to be a mature man, including examples of how a man can be ballsy with both words and action in various aspects of his life with illustrations of how many men have successfully communicated themselves. We close our book with a postscript with simple, practical suggestions of do's and don'ts for both women and men.

Pronouns. To say the least, it is a challenge to find the right English pronoun when writing and speaking these days. We have done our best to be inclusive in our use of pronouns. Given the fact that this book is mostly about men, we have chosen to use the masculine pronoun in most of our discussions. Deb and Ron have co-written this book, which has led to our using the collective pronoun "we" most of the time. However, most of the examples of people we have discussed come from Ron's clientele, so frequently we have chosen to use "I" when Ron is writing specifically about a client.

We express deep appreciation for the many men who have comprised the bulk of Ron's practice and have contributed to our understanding of men and how to help them mature in life. We also express our equally deep appreciation for our primary editors: John Ganahl, Dr. Dan Feaster, Tim Jorgensen, Scott Savage, and Joséph Hastreiter for the suggestions and corrections that have been so essential in our completing this book. Equally, a special thank you to Mal Jeffris for his unending encouragement.

SECTION I

Men and Feelings

It is in the realm of feelings where men tend to lose their balls, often because they don't have words to adequately express their feelings. In this section we will discuss the very nature of feelings, which we describe as the basic psychological foundation of all people and best described as *spiritual*.

In chapter one we discuss this elusive concept of feelings and how feelings erupt and how they are expressed: physically, emotionally, cognitively, actively, and verbally. We then discuss the most problematic element of feeling expression: emotion. We examine the four basic emotions: joy, sorrow, fear, and anger, noting that joy and sorrow are "love-based" emotions, while anger and fear are defense-based emotions. We discuss the feeling of hurt, namely how to experience hurt, express hurt, and hear others' hurt. We close chapter one with a discussion of how to hear feelings and how to govern the expression of feelings.

Chapter two is devoted to the most misunderstood and potentially the most damaging emotion: fear, as well as the anxiety and worry that erupt from fear. We suggest that fear and its cognates are the primary basis for all psychological and interpersonal challenges that men have. We note how fear tends to migrate into anger, avoidance, and addiction in many men.

Chapter three is devoted to a study of anger, including how potentially harmful anger can be in a man's life, particularly with relationships. We examine how men come to anger quickly and frequently with devastating interpersonal effects. We close chapter three by describing how both anger and fear can be prevented by having a deeper understanding of sadness that always precedes anger.

CHAPTER 1

The Nature of Feelings

BEFORE WE CAN TALK about words, work, wine, and women, we need to deal with how men experience and express feelings. Feelings and words are not the same thing. Words can be an excellent vehicle for the expression of feelings, but they are never feelings themselves. In fact, we can communicate our feelings in many other ways, like art, music, work, play, and maybe just staring at a sunset. When we talk about feelings, we are not necessarily talking about the words that express these feelings. This is an especially important distinction to make with men because their ability to verbally articulate their feelings falls way short of the quantity of feelings that they have. When a man truly discovers the depth and breadth of his feelings, he is on the road to communicating them. First, he has to recognize what feelings are. Then, he has to work diligently at expressing them verbally, usually failing on his first attempts. Only then can he develop a skill to communicate himself successfully. Having used the term "feelings" several times already, I need to explain how feelings are experienced and expressed. In short, we experience our feelings in four different ways, and we express our feelings in four different ways. To understand your feelings, communicate your feelings, and understand other people's feelings, you need to know how feelings erupt inside of you.

The Four Expressions of Feelings

In *I Want to Tell You How I Feel* we explain more fully the essence of feelings, so we won't belabor the point here, except to note some very essential matters related to feelings. When we use the term feelings, we do not mean emotions exclusively. Emotions are a subset of feelings. The distinction between feelings and emotions is an important one to make because when people hear the word feelings, they tend to immediately think that feelings = emotions. While the phenomenon of feelings is undefinable, it is a central element of what it means to be a human being. Note that many central elements of life are also undefined, like love, God, or even life itself. Even basic elements of our human experience such as time are functionally undefinable. We understand love, life, time, and God by observation and experience. Likewise, our feelings are defined by our experience of them. We must be content with understanding that feelings erupt from our core selves and are experienced as indisputable.

If we are to understand human beings in general, and men specifically, we have to understand how feelings erupt in a human being. Four things happen when I feel something: I feel some physical sensation, I feel some emotion, I think something, and finally, I say something or do something. The physical and emotional elements of feeling are reactive, meaning they are unconscious and occur nearly instantaneously, if not simultaneously. Thus, we all begin our feeling experiences though physical and emotional sensations before we ever think something, say something, or do something. We may not fully recognize the physical and emotional experiences, but they are always there before we think and before we say something.

While everyone experiences feelings in this four-part process, people differ on how they recognize and express their feelings. We all tend to have a certain propensity of recognition towards one or more of the four components of feeling. For instance, people whose strongest experience of feeling is physical and/or emotional express their experience in phrases such as "I just have a feeling about . . ." or "I just know what I feel." In other words, it is seemingly sufficient for them to just experience the feeling, and they may or may not cognitively evaluate their feeling or have a drive to do anything about the experience. Other people tend to ignore the physical or emotional and go right into what they think, this followed by saying something or doing something. People who think something when they feel something usually want to explain what they think and why they think it. Other people might want to take immediate action after feeling something. Those of us who register feelings cognitively might say, "I have thought about this a lot and I believe . . ." Note that the very word "feeling" can have very different meanings to people according to how they experience feelings. Consider how you tend to experience your feelings, whether physically, emotionally, cognitively, or with action or words.

In human communication and in the overall phenomenon of relationships, men get in trouble because they don't attend to the physical and emotional aspects of their feelings. In other words, they think something quickly and they say something or do something quickly without knowing that there is an important emotional aspect of their feelings. Having explained a bit about feelings, we want to take a closer look at emotions.

The Four Emotions

We have just noted that there are four experiences and expressions of feelings. Likewise, there are four basic emotions that all human beings have. These four emotions are joy, sadness, fear, and anger. These four emotions all have to do with love in some way. We call joy and sadness "love-based" emotions, while we call anger and fear "defense-based emotions." The emotion of joy occurs when I have something that I love, and the emotion of sadness when I lose something that I love. The "something" can be person, property, or even an idea or possibility. It is valuable to think of these emotions as connected by love:

Joy--------------------------Love----------------------Sadness
(I have something)   (I lose something)

The importance of thinking of joy and sadness as being about love is immensely important. I cannot feel joy unless I have something that I love, and I cannot feel sadness unless I lose something that I love. It is important to note that I cannot feel sadness without joy because the only reason I am sad is that I have had some joy beforehand. I have to love something first in order to feel sadness at having lost it.

The other two basic emotions are fear and anger. These are feelings that erupt when I feel the need to defend myself. These emotions also lie along a spectrum:

Anger----------------------Defense--------------------------Fear
(fight)   (flight)

Note that a human response to some kind of threat usually leads to some kind of "flight or fight," which are reactions to some kind of danger. Importantly, I always feel fear first when feeling some kind of danger and come to anger when I feel the need to defend myself. While we suggest that joy and sadness are "love-based" emotions and anger and fear are "defense-based" emotions, we must admit that when I am afraid or angry, these two emotions have also erupted because of love:

- I get angry when I *have lost* something that I have loved in the *past*.
- I get afraid when I consider that I *might lose* something that I love sometime in the *future*.

Men are socially allowed the expressions of joy and anger much more than the emotions of fear and sadness. The cultural or anthropological origins of this phenomenon are beyond the scope of this work. There is no doubt, however, that American boys are not generally permitted the fear and sadness that girls are. This fact probably causes the higher incidence of heart disease among men compared to women, much more incarceration, and certainly leads to more depression in later life for men. Males commit suicide about three to five times more frequently than women, although interestingly, women make more suicidal threats than men. Because men may not have access to the important emotions of sadness and fear, they may develop feelings of hopelessness and helplessness, which are precursors to suicide. Because women have been allowed to feel fear and sadness as more acceptable, they tend to talk more about these emotions. Men generally attempt suicide in much more violent ways than women, and so the likelihood of rescue is diminished with men. Perhaps the most important explanation is simply and sadly that men do not know how to feel, express, and resolve the emotions of fear and sadness, emotions that are essential for personal and interpersonal survival and growth. This apparent fact is of profound significance because if men can't admit to feeling sad, they do not know how to lose something that they love, grieve the loss, recover, and love again. Sadness is hard for anyone to express. Who *wants* to be sad? No one. But it is essential for people, including men. Men need to be able to feel sad in order to cope with loss, restore, recover, and go on with life. Instead of feeling sad, men tend to run to anger, avoidance, or some form of addiction.

Sadness is not only normal in life; it is necessary. An ideal childhood is one where the child is allowed to have any feeling and slowly learn that it is not always good to express these feelings. This is a delicate balance where a good parent allows children feelings but does not indulge them with complete freedom to say whatever they want, much less have everything they want. Male children are often given permission to express the emotion of anger but not the expression of sadness. When a man is unfamiliar with how to experience and express sadness he will access some other expression, usually anger, avoidance, or action. Most of men's anger is really sadness, so when a man is angry, it is most likely that he has been hurt in some way and feels sad. He may not even know that he is sad. Men tend to get angry so quickly that they override the underlying feeling of hurt, which is perhaps the most identifiable cause of sadness.

The Experience of Hurt

The phenomenon of hurt is of profound importance in human relations. Like so many concepts of science and life, hurt is *undefinable* like the other undefinables we mentioned above. We understand hurt by the way we experience it, express it, feel it, or repress it. When I am emotionally hurt, something has wounded my core in some way, very often in a way that I cannot readily explain. When I am hurt, it is as if I am unable to think, feel, or move. Hurt may last for a second or for hours but rarely more because hurt tends to either be *finished* or *changed in its form*. When my hurt is "finished," I will have allowed hurt to migrate into the emotion of sadness, and then sadness runs its course until I am no longer sad. If hurt lasts more than hours, it tends to migrate into avoidance, anger, or addiction, the areas where men tend to divert their feelings of sadness.

I am hurt when I have been *assaulted* in some way. I use the term "assault" with some caution because the word sounds like someone is physically hitting you. While physical assaults do occur, you can also be assaulted emotionally, cognitively, or verbally. Regardless of the manner in which you have been assaulted, you will feel hurt, and this hurt will immediately be experienced physically and emotionally, which, recall, are the first two experiences we have when we feel something. Then, depending on your feeling experience, you might move into thinking about your wound or doing something about your wound. Emotional assaults usually come to us verbally, but they can come in some kind of action or inaction. All assaults violate our value system in some way, namely what is important to us. Verbal assaults hurt you because something you value has been denigrated in some way. You are hurt, for instance, when someone says you are stupid. You can also be hurt when you are criticized for something that you did or didn't do, which the other person thought you should have done or not done. You are hurt when you have assaulted yourself, perhaps by making a small mistake like misspelling a word, spilling your coffee, or hitting your thumb with the hammer. The way most men experience hurt and the emotional cascade that follows hurt is always the same: get angry. We will focus primarily on verbal assaults and consequent hurts that occur from these assaults because it is in the realm of words where we men are most undeveloped in effective response to hurt. We do much better when we have been assaulted in an athletic competition or even in a physical fight than when we have been assaulted verbally.

The entire experience of verbal assault and hurt normally follows this course:

- You experience the feeling of hurt both physically and emotionally . . .
- You try to make sense of what has been said to you, and then . . .
- You try to justify yourself instead of feeling hurt.
- Experiencing emotional hurt often leads men into one of three actions:
  - Getting angry,
  - Engaging in some kind of addictive activity, or
  - Avoiding the whole feeling situation.

The progression from physical to emotional to cognitive to active usually occurs in a split second, so fast that we do not know that we have been hurt, much less how what has been said to us has wounded our core self in some way. When people are hurt, whether in a small or a large way, they actually feel *helpless* in the moment. They are helpless because they can't turn back the clock and un-hurt themselves. They can't change history. This is a very important element in understanding the phenomenon of hurt, especially for men. No one likes to feel helpless, but due to cultural expectations of men and the lack of a breadth of emotional expressions in their lives, they do not know how to handle the helpless aspect of being hurt.

Men usually are not aware of the process of hurt → anger → action. In his experience a man: (1) says or does something that causes someone to say something to him that hurts him; (2) is hurt but is not aware that he is hurt; (3) is scared of being hurt again but only marginally aware of being afraid; (4) thinks of something to say to defend himself; (5) gets angry as he avoids the feeling of hurt; and finally, (6) says something angrily. The man has quickly skipped over the hurt, the helplessness, and the fear that always happen when someone is hurt. He is not able to figure out what to say and ends up just getting angry in some way, possibly speaking defensively, possibly yelling, possibly damaging property, and often looking or sounding dangerous.

Remember that anger is a *defense*-based emotion and is utilized when the love-based emotion of sadness cannot be accessed. Whether by culture, family, or school, most men have learned to express hurt by being angry. Addiction and avoidance often come in conjunction with anger but only after a man has had years of being hurt and failing to recognize hurt for what it is: a deep feeling of wound, together with the very difficult feeling of helplessness that always accompanies hurt. There is no *cure* for anger, much less any "anger management." Anger doesn't need to be cured or managed. It needs to be prevented. A man can prevent expressing anger by learning about the underlying feeling of hurt and the accompanying emotion of sadness. I am not suggesting that men need to be "soft" and "tender" to be sad. They simply need to be in touch with the real essence of sadness, which is always based on love.

If you are to prevent anger, addiction, and avoidance, you will need to be aware of hurt and helplessness. If you had this kind of awareness, you would know that:

- You love something.
- You have been assaulted.
- You are hurt.
- You feel helpless to undo the assault and hurt.
- You allow yourself to feel sad.
- The sadness communicates to the other person that you are a loving person because sadness only comes from something loved and lost.
- You may be the recipient of comfort from the other person.
- Your sadness ends.
- You are a better person for having loved and lost.
- Now you can love again.

Can you see how better it would be for you to know that you are hurt (and helpless to unhurt yourself), however crazy that sounds? It takes real balls to feel hurt and helpless. When you feel sadness instead of anger, avoidance, or addiction, you are a better person because you know that you love things, that you lose things, and that you can recover from these losses by learning the value of sadness.

The Value of Sadness

The real key in this highly emotional process of being hurt is sadness. We wrote an entire book entitled *The Positive Power of Sadness*, in which we suggested the centrality of sadness in the human experience, as well as how we can profitably use sadness to prevent anger, anxiety, and depression. If a man can find his way through the maze of hurt, helplessness, and fear to the feeling of genuine sadness, he will become an emotionally mature man and ultimately a productive man. Most men don't mature to this level. Rather, they become angry easily, get stuck in anger, spend years being angry, and then find some kind of compensation for their inner unhappiness, often in some kind of addiction. Later in life many men experience profound depression that is directly related to the fact that they have not allowed themselves to feel hurt and sad. Their failure to allow themselves to feel helplessness ultimately leads to anxiety.

Recall that both emotions of sadness and joy have to do with love: I feel joyful when I love something and sad when I lose something that I love. When I have been assaulted, I first feel this undefined important feeling of hurt. If I would follow the most natural progression of feeling and emotion, I would feel sad. I feel sad because I have lost a part of myself. If I have lost an arm in some battle, I would naturally feel sad about the loss. The same is true of emotional assaults: the man should feel sad at having lost some part of him. But what "part of him" has he lost? He has lost a sense of self-value or he has lost a sense of what he values outside of himself, like an idea or someone's approval. I need to feel sad whenever I have lost anything, whether a portion of my physical self, my property, my ideas, or my inner spirit.

Let me be clearer about what is *lost* after an emotional assault. For example, when I have been criticized, I have lost the sense of success, value, or productivity in my eyes—and possibly in the other person's eyes. When I am criticized, I might even think something like "everyone thinks I'm an idiot" or some other form of feeling inadequate. Any kind of loss naturally makes me sad—not angry, just sad. The mature man, the ballsy man, is the man who has found a way to feel sad when he is hurt. This awareness and acknowledgement give him great power: power in himself, power in his feelings, power in his emotions, and ultimately power in his words or actions. This is not power over anyone else. Balls has nothing to do with having power over other people. The true power of balls is grounded in knowing and honoring oneself in order to know and honor others. If a man has this kind of personal grounding, he will know how and when to communicate his feelings while governing his emotion in the process.

It may sound counterproductive to say that hurt, helplessness, and sadness can empower a man, but such is the case. When I allow hurt to lead to sadness, I can find a way to restore what is lost. When I feel sad, I need to immediately realize that I have a "love problem," which means that I have suffered because I have lost something that I love rather than a "defense problem" that causes anger. I have used the term "love problem" quite successfully with men to help them prevent anger with sadness. When my core self is wounded, I need to find what the wound is and then find ways to restore myself. I am not restored by being angry, much less finding some kind of addiction or some way of avoiding the feeling altogether. I am restored by allowing myself to feel sad, to let sadness run its course, and then to see the overall package of love, loss, hurt, and sadness. If I allow this process to unfold, difficult as it is to do, I will be a better man, a deeper man, a softer man, and a more powerful man. I will be a man with balls. I will be able to look at the statement that feels critical and perhaps see that there is some truth in what was said. I will see that what he or she said is honest but not perfect. I will see that I am a good person but not perfect. I will see that I can improve. I will also see that someone has attacked me because he was hurt in some way, possibly by me, possibly by someone else. Importantly, a man with balls realizes that people usually hurt him *unintentionally*.

Unintentional Hurt

Almost all hurt is unintentional. When I am hurt by someone, it is rare that this person was trying to hurt me. All hurt is difficult to manage, but intentional hurt is easier to experience because I am immediately aware of the nature of the assault and perhaps the nature of my antagonist. You can see both the attack and the attacker and then defend yourself if need be. In fact, when someone hurts you intentionally, you might actually need to be angry to forestall further attack.

Intentional attacks are difficult, and they can be managed forthrightly, but most assaults are not intentional, which make them hard to detect and harder to process. Furthermore, most unintentional assaults come from friends and loved ones. Most of these "friendly assaults" come from people who actually want to help you, but their "help" comes in the form of telling you what you should do. Functionally, they are criticizing you erroneously, thinking that they have the right to tell you what you should do or what you should feel. Sadly, they are assaulting you in the process of trying to help you, and they are not usually aware that their comments are an assault. They think of their criticism as helpful or "constructive." Recently a good friend told me he thought I was "stubborn" because I chose not to go to a doctor when I had a mild illness. He happens to be a guy who regularly goes to doctors, something that I do not do. He did not intend to hurt me, and while I was hurt and then sad about the encounter for a day or two, I know that Fred loves me and was trying to help me stay well. However love-based his telling me that I was stubborn might have been, I could not profit from his assault of me. I knew that it was not valuable for me to explain how I deal with physical illness, and it was not profitable for me to tell him that I was hurt because it wouldn't have made any sense to him. The mature man realizes that any criticism is hurtful, however well-intended it might be. Most people do not recognize that they have unintentionally hurt you. This creates a delicate situation because if you are ballsy, you will be aware of your hurt. In order to come to grips with feelings, hurt, and sadness, the ballsy man needs to realize that his friend did not intend to hurt him and allow for the natural process of sadness to run its course. Realizing that you are hurt but choosing to keep the hurt to yourself is what we call *containment*.

Containing Feelings

Emotional maturity is knowing what you feel, valuing what you feel, and keeping this feeling to yourself. Containment is not repression, and it is not failing to be in touch with one's feelings. This *ability* that men tend to have to keep their feelings to themselves is based upon a man's knowing that words come to him slowly, particularly emotional words. A mature man knows that it is not always wise to express feelings, it is not always appropriate, and it is not always safe. It is not wise for an athlete to tell his coach that his critique has hurt him, nor is it wise to tell a neighbor that her screaming four-year-old is irritating. Likewise, to avoid anger, avoidance, and fruitless arguments, it is often wise to keep your feelings to yourself, like when my friend told me to go to the doctor. There are many times in day-to-day life that it is wisest to keep your feelings to yourself. Ideally, a man knows when to speak feelings and when to contain them. This is true at home, at work, in social settings, and especially true in intimate relationships. The real key to containment, however, is first knowing what it is you feel so that you can gauge if what you feel should be expressed or not. The danger we men have is to never speak our feelings even when we do know what they are. This is avoidance, not containment. Avoidance leads to resentment and addiction. Containment is an act of love.

When you choose to contain your feelings, you will be hurt and you will be lonely, at least for a period of time. Most of the time when I am hurt, I contain this feeling and find that I can allow a simple process of sadness to run its course. Sometimes, the hurt that I experience is only slightly painful, and I find the emotion of sadness waning. Other times are harder, which tend to be times when a friend or family member has hurt me in some unintentional way, and it seems inappropriate that I say anything about it. Most men have not matured to the place where they can profitably contain their feelings because they haven't learned to value feelings in the first place.

It is no small task for men to add awareness of sadness to their relational toolbox, but I ask a lot when I suggest men need to do that exact thing. A ballsy man is a man with access to all his emotions and the deeper feelings that erupt into emotions; he is a man ready to serve the world. However central the emotion of sadness is for men, the really difficult emotion that men have to deal with is fear, which is our next study.

Summary

- Feelings are the most basic element of human psychological functioning.
- Feelings are experienced and expressed physically, emotionally, cognitively, actively, or verbally.
- There are four basic emotions: joy, sorrow, fear, and anger.
- Joy and sorrow are love-based emotions. I feel joy when I have something I love. I feel sadness when I lose something I love.
- Fear and anger are defense-based emotions. I feel fear when I might lose something that I love. I feel anger when I have lost something that I love.
- Sadness is the most important emotion in human psychological functioning because I eventually lose everything that I love.
- Sadness ends if it is fully felt.
- Hurt is a feeling that naturally leads to sadness, but it is not generally a part of a man's expression.
- We need to learn to contain our emotions in order to more adequately communicate our feelings and thoughts.
- Fear is the most basic of all emotions. It is meant to keep us alive, but it can migrate into anxiety, avoidance, anger, and addiction.

CHAPTER 2

Men and Fear

WITHOUT A DOUBT, FEAR lies at the source of all the troubles men have in life. Fear is the source of an invisible anxiety that most men suffer, an anxiety that ultimately creates a myriad of problems in their lives. The anxiety that men suffer is not particularly obvious. Rather, people see the anger, avoidance, and addiction that erupt from a man's anxiety. It is easier for a man to be angry, avoid life, or find some addiction than it is to face this underlying phenomenon of anxiety. Because anxiety is not particularly obvious in most men's lives, no one really knows how we men are plagued with nearly constant worries that come with anxiety. I have just begun to see a man who presented with depression, marital dissatisfaction, and job insecurity. He did not show any physical or emotional symptoms of anxiety, but when asked him about it, he said, "I feel anxious all the time." I think I am the only person in his world who knows how he suffers with anxiety. Everyone else in his life sees him as successful in his profession, bright, and a person of character. They see what he *thinks* and what he *does* but they don't ever hear how he *feels*. He just doesn't know how to communicate his feelings, especially fear and anxiety. Nobody taught him how to express his feelings, especially the feeling of anxiety and the emotion of fear that lies beneath.

Fear affects how men deal with words, how they approach their work, and how they fall into addictions, all of which affect their relationships, particularly their female relationships. In the following chapters we will also discuss how fear and its most common representation, anxiety, is the source of the maladies that men tend to have. Only in the recent years have I acknowledged to myself how much I have felt some kind of anxiety. It has been of immense help for me to talk about the fear, anxiety, or worry that I might have, but talking about anxiety came only after I admitted to myself how I feel. I recall a therapist once saying to me that I exuded "palpable anxiety," something that I had never really noticed, much less acknowledged. When my therapist stated this, I thought, "What, me? Anxiety?" Then as I began reflecting on it, I realized that I did feel a lot of anxiety. Now, I take the privilege of talking to Deb about worries or fear that I might have. Most men have no one to talk to. If we men can admit to feeling this very basic emotion of fear and its subsequent symptom of anxiety, we can not only deal with the anger, avoidance, and addictions that we are inclined to have, but more importantly, we can approach with courage the matters of words, women, and work.

If we can understand how all men have some basic fears, we will understand a central experience that men have, something that men rarely admit to until later years of life when fear has caused so much anxiety that they deteriorate emotionally and physically. What causes this anxiety in men? What are they afraid of? Answer this question, and you will understand one of the basic ingredients of maleness and the lack of balls that most men suffer. The most important fear that all men have is generated by the natural feeling of responsibility. Whether young or old, wealthy or impoverished, disabled or fully abled, successful or unsuccessful, men have this natural feeling that they are the ones who have to do something.

The Fears That Men Have

1. Fear of failure:
    a. Of academic failure
    b. Of not succeeding physically in some task
    c. Of not succeeding in vocation or profession
    d. Of not making enough money

2. Fear of disapproval
    a. Primarily of female disapproval
    b. Disapproval from work associates
    c. One's physical appearance

3. Fear of making mistakes

a. Mistakes at work

b. Mistakes at play

c. Mistakes in relationships

d. Mistakes with words

4. Fear of the display of emotion, particularly

    a. Sadness

    b. Fear

5. Fear of loss of one's physical abilities

    a. Loss of physical ability

    b. Loss of energy or ability to do something

    c. Dying

The essence of all of these fears is men's failure to own up to how they feel, value how they feel, and selectively tell someone how they feel. As you peruse this list of typical fears that men have, note that the crux of all of these fears is some kind of loss, namely:

1. Loss of female approval
2. Loss of anyone's approval
3. Loss of self-esteem
4. Loss of others' respect
5. Loss of a sense of equality with other men
6. Loss of life's dream of vocational success
7. Loss of ability to pay bills
8. Loss of physical stability

Before we carefully examine the cause and cure of fear and anxiety in men's lives, read about a few men who have come to me for assistance. Note what they present is often external, like wife, girlfriend, job, kids, or money. Then note that the essence of their anxiety is a feeling of being overwhelmed by the responsibilities they have in life.

José's Fear of Failure and Criticism

José: José is a young Latino gay man who graduated from college a few years ago and just married a few months ago. He and his husband recently jumped right in and bought a house. He came to me because he has been suffering increasing anxiety and has had three or four panic attacks, usually in the morning before he goes to work. These became more frequent after he married, and then after they bought their house increased to nearly a daily event. He had some struggles when he immigrated with his family a number of years ago, but he has adapted well. His main challenge appears to be dealing with his job. He has had several jobs over the recent years, but he hasn't seemed to be able to find work that fits him well. He doesn't like his current job which is described as customer service but this "service" is entirely remote and involves a good deal of administrative work. He is concerned that if he leaves this position, together with his work record of having stayed with previous jobs for just a few months, it will adversely affect new offers. Complicating his current work is the fact that his supervisor thinks he is a good worker, which has led to José being straddled with more and more responsibility that he does not enjoy. José reports that he is very unhappy with what he is doing and feels stressed every time he wakes up in the morning knowing that he will have to do a job that he doesn't like.

The dilemma for José is twofold: (1) he is afraid of quitting this job and having yet another black mark on his work record, and (2) he hasn't been able to find work that is satisfying. He speaks with great distress that he isn't sure what profession might be best suited to him and worries over how he will ever find "the right profession." With much reflection he knows that he wants "to be of service" and wants to value his introverted nature, which suggests that he is best one-on-one. José feels caught in not liking what he is doing while not knowing what he wants to do.

José is a good person, a good worker, and an intelligent person, but he doesn't have balls. His perspective is that the external world needs to change rather than he finding his balls. In simple terms, José wants to do what he wants and get paid for it, even though he doesn't really know what he wants to do in life. The result of his being unable to know what he wants to do, do what he wants to do, and get paid a lot of money to do this unknown thing, José finds himself in a state of anxiety almost all the time. Additionally, he is concerned that his husband will be critical or disapproving of him in considering living on less and possibly going back to school. He is deathly afraid of not making enough money. He told me recently that he "couldn't live the style of life he and his husband have become accustomed to" without making a certain amount of money. It means that he *wants it both ways*. He wants to keep the security of his present job and income but then somehow not be required to do the work that he is employed to do. He wants the opportunity and freedom to do something meaningful, but he also wants to have the security of a high income so he can continue to spend money the way he spends it . . . all without doing anything about changing his work. All of these wants are "wanting it both ways" and not having the balls to see that he can't have it both ways. He doesn't have the balls to face up to the real problem: fear—fear that he will do something wrong, fear that his partner will disapprove of him, and fear that he won't have the money he wants. I have to help José find a way to face, feel, and finish the anxiety he has in life. This is not a problem of his job, money, or his partner. It is a problem of having no balls. To have balls means facing up to choices, losses, disappointments, failures, and criticism. Most importantly, it means learning how to want something, love something, and lose something, all of which lead to the central ingredient in emotional maturity: sadness.

Everyone wants it both ways. This is not something that is pathological. This is not something to be afraid of or ashamed of. There is a way out of this dilemma. When we want it both ways, we have to *admit* that we want it both ways without criticizing ourselves for wanting. At the same time, we must see there is a difference between *wanting* and *needing*. José doesn't *need* to have it both ways. He, like many of us men, hasn't grown up emotionally and grown a pair in order to face the necessary choices that we have to make in life. No one is going to knock on José's door offering him the perfect job, the perfect salary, and the perfect security. I hope to help him carefully navigate through these complex waters, weighing the importance of financial security but also finding a job, and hopefully a profession, where he can shine. I'm not suggesting that he throw caution to the wind and just up and quit his job but rather find the balls to consider what is really important to him and then find a path to take in order to have a life of meaning that ultimately will also be a life with financial security.

Money, security, status, and success in life often bring on a lot of anxiety and fear for men. The pressure of success based on an income level is nearly unavoidable in our American culture. It takes great courage . . . balls . . . to face a high paying job and admit that it isn't what you want to do and let it go for something more satisfying that has a lesser income attached. I have two people in my practice, one fifty-three and one forty-nine, who have given up their six-figure jobs to pursue psychology-based master's degrees where they most certainly will not make six figures. They have found the balls to trust their inner instincts that lead to a meaningful life by taking a risk and facing the disappointment of how much time it might take to establish themselves and settle into the contentment of a preferred profession, as well as facing the reality that a professional life as a therapist isn't going to pay the same as their current CEO jobs. I have a way to go with José, but I think I can help him do the same. José is in the ugly place of giving in to the fear-based complaining of wanting something to happen without taking the initiative to bring it about.

I hope I can help José move from fear to sadness. What does that mean? It means that he will most certainly have to consider losing something in order to gain something better. He might have to lose his work reputation to give him time to find his best profession. He might have to give up having the money he wants to have. He might have to give up the approval of his husband. Most importantly, *he will have to give up anything related to what someone might think of him.* It took José twenty-two years to come out to his parents about being gay. That took balls, so I know he "has a pair." It would be wonderful if he could use the pair in his professional development before he turns fifty like the guys I just mentioned.

What other people think of us does play a role in our lives. We are not islands to ourselves. Other people affect us, especially their opinions of us or their *possible opinions* of us. Furthermore, we affect other people. Men with balls do not dismiss the effect that people have on one another. In fact, a ballsy man is one who acknowledges that he is affected by other people and their opinions, whether these opinions are favorable or unfavorable. I do not suggest that we dismiss the importance of criticism and disapproval. Rather, I suggest we admit to it and take the consequences of these two elements of any relationship, whether the relationship is intimate, professional, familial, or friendship. The task we have is to avoid being dominated by the fear of disapproval or the seeking of approval.

Many people tell me that they are "people pleasers." In fact, these people are not so much seeking to please others but seeking to *avoid their criticism*. More accurately, they are afraid of *potential* criticism. People spend way too much time worrying about what he, she, or they might think of them. Actually, most people don't care what you might do, and the people who really care about you are probably more accepting than you think they are. It is a delicate matter that takes more than balls to distinguish when, how, why, and with whom we should allow ourselves to be examined by others. Most importantly, however, we need to avoid the danger of governing our behavior according to fear of criticism. *Men with balls govern their behavior and their words according to what is right to do or say and take the consequences.* Hard as it is for us men to find what they want to do, examine it, and perhaps do what they think is right to do, our fear of potential criticism looms largest, especially when it comes from women.

Frank and Jason's Fear of Female Criticism

Having our parents' approval, our friends' approval, or even our colleagues' approval is all important . . . yet our biggest fear is their potential disapproval. For men, it is the potential disapproval of the intimate women in our lives that is so terrifying. Let's look at how a few men have lost their balls with this fear and consequently have lost time, energy, and confidence, being afraid of a woman's potential disapproval. It is what women might say to us, more than what they actually say to us, that stirs men to being afraid of women.

Frank and Jason are two of the many men I have heard use the word *terrified* when considering what the women in their lives might say to them. When I first heard "terrified" from these men, I was a bit stunned because the word terrified is not in my active vocabulary. I have since learned that it is very much in the hearts of many men, especially in regards to women's disapproval. When Frank used the word terrified, I was engaged in marital work with his wife, Sarah, and him. Frank is a very successful musician who has worked diligently, effectively, and successfully for more than twenty years and is well respected in his professional community. When I asked Frank how he felt when he considered what his wife might say to him about something he had done, he immediately said that he was terrified. In the moment of my hearing the word, I was nonplussed to hear a person who was very confident on stage be terrified of what his wife might say to him. I have since learned that he is not the only man who is terrified of female disapproval.

Jason is soon to retire from a very successful career in sales. He originally came to me a few years ago, also presenting with relationship difficulties stemming from underlying challenges from his childhood, as well as the suicide of his first wife a few years prior to our meeting. Despite the fact that he has been exceedingly successful in his sales work, largely because of his naturally ingratiating personality, he was *terrified* of his girlfriend's potential judgment. In the early stages of therapy, he admitted that he frequently lied to her about various things for fear of her potential disapproval. He would lie about the smallest things for seemingly no reason. He was perplexed as to why he lied to his girlfriend because he is a man of his word and would never lie to anyone else, even in his sales work. Why would a person of such integrity lie to someone who possibly could be the most important person in his life? He couldn't tolerate the possibility of his girlfriend's disapproval.

What we have with these two men is the rather odd combination of high intelligence, success in vocation, and personal integrity, together with a deep-seated fear of female disapproval. They are, in fact, not nearly so fearful of criticism that might come from the people they work with or from their family members. As with many men, these two guys had fathers who were angry all the time while equally afraid of the wrath of their wives. Frank reported in one session how his father would simply cower when his mother criticized him. Frank said when he saw his father cower, especially as a young child, he began to fear for himself that "something must be very dangerous about Mommy if Daddy backs up and turns his head away." Similarly, Jason related that his father was "a wimp" with his mom and that it was "always mom" who had the say in their house. Jason confesses that every day he is afraid of how his girlfriend might call him a wimp if he would actually say how he feels, or more importantly, he would display any level of tenderness to people, what he calls his "softer side." While seemingly all men are unduly afraid of female disapproval, some men bring to their female relationships an even larger amount of emotional baggage than Frank and Jason.

Clint's Fear of Losing Everything

Clint is afraid of losing the little that he has in life. He has been unhappy in his twenty-five-year marriage from the very beginning, a marriage that started with his getting his girlfriend pregnant and feeling compelled to marry her. Naturally, this situation came about because of his irresponsibility in some way, perhaps in his failing to use contraceptives, failing to deal with feeling seduced by his girlfriend, or perhaps by his unmanaged sexual desires in general. Regardless of the reason he got into this situation, he felt compelled to "do the right thing" and marry his girlfriend, even though he didn't love her and may not even have liked her. When Clint came to me, he was still married to the women he got pregnant as a young man. Clint told me that he had been having an affair for the past four years. He was afraid to admit to what his feelings were to his lover, to his wife, or any of his friends. In Clint's case, which is not so different from many other cases of unfortunate marriages, his way of coping with his fear was to drink too much and avoid saying what he was feeling to anyone. When he even came close to finding a way to be honest in his life, he became almost completely overwhelmed with fear, a fear that no one understood. A fear that is based on shame.

Shame

Clint was afraid of ending his marriage because of the disruption a divorce would make in his life, a disruption that would potentially affect his vocation, his finances, his relationship with his children, his relationship with his church, and his self-esteem. When we examine all of these fears, we discover that Clint has a fear of feeling ashamed. However harmful anxiety is for men, the fear of shame is even worse. *When I feel shame, I think there is something wrong with me.* Shame is much different from the feeling of *guilt*, which is the awareness and consequent sadness having done something that is wrong. The potential shame that Clint feels comes from a childhood that included having been humiliated. Clint is an evangelical Christian, which often includes a feeling of shame for doing something that is contrary to God's desire. Interestingly, Clint is not honest with himself, much less with his wife, family, and church because he can't bear the shame associated with being a divorced man.

Clint is an honest man as so many men are, but he doesn't have balls to be honest with his feelings. Why are good men so afraid? What can men do to be honest with themselves and other people and consequently find their balls? Before we find answers to these questions, we have to study a bit of neuropsychology, namely what happens in the brain when a man suffers from fear and anxiety.

Fear Is a Brain Problem

How is fear a "brain problem"? Your brain is a wonderful machine, but it is a machine, and it is also "stupid" in many ways because it has only the two functions, both of which are primal: safety and pleasure. The most important operation of your brain is to keep you alive, which means keeping you safe, while the second function of your brain is to maximize your pleasure. While a wonderful machine that keeps us alive every second of our lives, the brain does not know what the mind knows. Your brain does not know the future or the past, only the present. If your brain hears from your mind that you are in some kind of danger, it will create a protection for you in the form of vigilance. These two functions, safety and pleasure, often operate jointly, which then gives the brain tremendous power over how you think, how you feel, and what you do. Your brain is doing what it is designed to do, keep you happy, but most importantly, keep you safe. Your brain keeps you safe by keeping your body functioning in a multitude of ways, primarily through regulating your breathing and blood flow and secondarily through the secretion of certain hormones. If your brain determines that you are not getting enough oxygen, it will automatically increase your breathing; if your brain determines that you are not getting enough blood flow, it will increase your heart rate. For the most part, you are not aware of your brain taking care of you and protecting you. If you could talk to your brain, you could say, "Thank you for keeping me alive with breathing and blood flow." The pleasure-seeking part of the brain is also very important and will be discussed when we deal with addictions in chapter six. Our present interest is in the safety operation that the brain does for you.

Not only does your brain function entirely in the present, it doesn't know about anything in your life, like whether you are male or female, whether you live in Wisconsin or Canada, whether you love something or someone. Your brain is a machine that your mind uses to think and do things, but it doesn't know about your life aside from how your feelings suggest safety or pleasure or the lack thereof. The brain concludes that when you worry about some potential loss in the future, there is danger and hence the need for hypervigilance and fear, which then turns into anxiety. What you experience as anxiety is what the brain interprets as necessary hypervigilance to protect you from imminent danger. What happens is this: a man considers what might happen in the future and sees the future as unknown and distressful. His mind is considering something that might happen in the future, but when the brain gets this message of potential loss or distress, it immediately translates the potential loss as *immediate* danger and creates faster blood flow and breathing. Remember, the brain does not have an operation that can separate the future from the present. So, if you think that you *might* lose your job your brain interprets this feeling like there is an immediate danger and that you are already penniless. Anytime your brain gets the message from your mind that something dangerous might happen, it concludes something like, "There is a lion coming over the hill towards you right now." Because the brain thinks that there is some immediate danger, some lion, it increases your breathing and heart rate so you can be vigilant in the face of this lion. In your mind, you might just be thinking of what you would do if you lost your job and concern about how the rent might get paid, while your brain thinks the lion is about to pounce. Anxiety is *anticipation of danger* and loss in the future, but the brain doesn't know that. It thinks there is *immediate danger*.

In addition to your brain increasing your breathing and heart rate, it secretes the hormone cortisol, which causes you to be quite aware of your surroundings, something that we call hypervigilance. Likewise, when you think of something that was dangerous or harmful to you that happened in the past, your brain churns up the emotion of anger. Note that anger is about real past losses and fear is about future potential losses, but your brain doesn't know future and past because it is only wired for the present. The feeling of fear that the brain creates about future losses and the anger it creates about past losses are emotions that are necessary for survival. Your brain is keeping you alive by creating these emotions. We will discuss the brain function in anger in the next chapter.

All the men we have discussed in this chapter have experienced some kind of anxiety as they examined their lives. José is afraid of being unemployed and consequently losing his partner's approval. Frank and Jason are terrified of the potential disapproval of the women in their lives and showing their deeper emotions. Clint is afraid of being judged, shamed, and abandoned, perhaps by people, perhaps by God. All of these men are afraid of something untoward that might happen in the future, but because their brains don't know what the future is, their brains stir up cortisol in order to protect them from the nonexistent lion coming over the hill. The brain is doing what it does best: protect you. You can't blame your brain for doing its job. You have to find a way to get your mind in control of your brain, which is no easy task.

We want you to appreciate your brain for taking care of you, protecting you, keeping you from danger, and helping you be prepared for danger. Additionally, we want you to help your brain distinguish between genuine real danger in the present and thoughts about potential future losses. We also want you to get your mind in control of your brain in this matter, which is no small task because the brain works so instantaneously. We would like you to face the smallest of concerns without anxiety and face the larger concerns with patience. Too often, men fall into the results of anxiety: worrying, general agitation, fretting, and even panic attacks. Additionally, men can fall into anger, avoidance, and addictions if they do not find ways to cure anxiety and ultimately prevent it. How can men get their minds in control of their brains so that their minds can do what minds are designed to do and allow the brain to do what it should be doing? Learn to feel sad.

The Solution to Anxiety: Anticipatory Sadness

When I am anxious or worried, I am afraid that I might lose something. We call anxiety *anticipatory loss*. Anticipatory loss is a valuable term because it gives us permission to know that losses in life are natural and that they will come our way. No one can avoid loss, whether those losses are of people, property, opportunities, or ideas. When I look into the future and consider that I might lose something, I am anticipating the possibility of loss. Get this notion that *anxiety = anticipatory loss* in your mind and you are well on the way to curing your anxiety and ultimately preventing it.

Anticipatory loss is not the same thing as fear. Fear is that primal unconscious instinct that says you are in danger. Anticipatory loss is the natural understanding that everything, including our own lives, are transient. *We will lose everything in the future.* When I anticipate losing something, perhaps like someone's approval, I am not naturally afraid. I am just considering such a loss and the natural feeling would be sad: "If George doesn't like my idea at work, it would be disappointing to me." Fear comes when the brain interprets this *potential* loss as *immediate danger*. "If George doesn't like my idea at work, I will be a terrible person unworthy to work with him (shame based on fear of disapproval)." Implicit in understanding anticipatory loss is the notion that *we will be sad if this loss occurs*. If you can replace anxiety with anticipatory loss, you will be free of anxiety and all that goes with it, like anger, avoidance, and addiction. But when you do begin to replace anxiety with anticipating loss, you begin to feel *anticipatory sadness*.

Anticipatory Sadness

Sadness is the natural emotion that comes from experiencing loss of any kind. We have big losses in life and small losses, but each of these losses naturally leads to feeling an appropriate amount of sadness. Anticipatory sadness is the feeling you have when you truly look into the future and consider that you might lose something. Instead of being afraid of this potential loss and becoming anxious, you will feel sadness at this potential loss. This can feel very weird because if you feel this anticipatory sadness, you might actually start to tear up. Crying about something that hasn't actually happened but might happen—how weird is that? How can that be helpful? It can be helpful because this anticipatory sadness helps you experience love. What does that mean? When you are sad about something, you are sad singularly because you have lost something that you love. Maybe this is a job, a win at a sporting event, an idea that looks good to you, or a person, any of which you might lose. This is not an easy concept to understand because we men have not been taught the intrinsic necessity of feeling sad and the accompanying experience of love that is always underneath sadness. If a guy can look at some future loss, like a job, and allow himself to feel sad, he will be looking at something he loves, his job. The anticipatory sadness that he feels at this potential loss is not depression, and it is not anxiety or fear. It is normal sadness at potentially losing something that he loves.

Sadness, genuine sadness, cures fear and prevents fear. Sadness is not about doing anything, or even saying anything. It is just the normal, human reaction to a loss. Learn to look into the future and consider some kind of loss you might have while working to keep your mind in control of your brain's tendency to churn up fear. Do this and you will find the love implicit in this anticipatory sadness. You will see that you love something. You will see that you love a lot of things, whether ideas or people. You will discover that this love doesn't have to turn into fear and anxiety. Feel anticipatory sadness, and you will find the love underneath this process. Who taught you this central ingredient of life? Probably no one. You must learn it now: you love things, you lose things, you feel sad, then you finish feeling sad, and as a result of this process you become more aware of how much you love. You become a better person. You become a ballsy man. Then, a truly godly thing begins to happen in you: you find the essence of hope.

Hope

Face potential loss, whatever form it takes, and you will find sadness. Feel that sadness; it will end and you will recognize the love that is under the feeling of anticipatory sadness. Then, you will find something equally love-based: hope, which is *anticipatory joy*. If you look into the future and see some potential loss, you feel anticipatory sadness. If you look into the future and see some potential love, you will feel anticipatory joy, which is hope. If José can consider that he might lose his job and the money that goes with it, he just might also find some hope that he will find the right job and all that goes with it. *Hope is not certainty* that he will have a good job, and *anticipatory sadness is not certainty* that he will lose his job, but both the hope and the sadness are born of his desire to do well in life, both born of love. This feeling of anticipatory joy is not based on what *will* happen, nor is it based on what *might* happen. It is based on the fact that you love things. The more you exercise your mind to the concept of anticipatory sadness and joy, the easier it will be for you because you will not experience anxiety.

After I had a heart attack several years ago, I found myself thinking about the possibility of dying from another heart attack. I worked diligently on how sad it would be for me to die. I would not be able to finish this book. I would not be able to serve men in my therapy office. I would not be able to hug my wife. I allowed myself to feel this anticipatory sadness and it ended. In its place I found the anticipatory joy that I just might live, finish this book, see people in my office, hug my wife, continue to play basketball, read books, travel more of the world, and continue to watch my daughter Jenny mature and enjoy her life. Allowing myself to feel anticipatory sadness was hard work and I didn't want to do it. Deb and I are long-time *Star Trek* fans. On any given day we hope to "live long and prosper," as Vulcans say to each other, or, as the Klingons say to each other, "This is a good day to die." Deb and I often say one of these things to one another because we believe, indeed, it is a good day to die because we have lived a good life, but we also hope to live long and prosper. This is simply a part of looking into the future with a reasonable knowledge of having something you love and the certainty of ultimately losing what you love but without anxiety. Looking into the future with both anticipatory joy and anticipatory sadness is hard work. It takes balls, which means that you have to be honest with yourself and allow yourself to feel these love-based emotions of joy and sadness, usually in about equal measures.

Consider what you are afraid of losing. This could be an idea, a person, a piece of property, or anything else. Consider that you could lose something small, like an opportunity to be with a friend for breakfast. Note how you feel. You feel a small amount of sadness. Now, dare to consider that you could lose something large, like losing a good friend to cancer. If you can honestly consider these potential losses, you will notice that you actually start to feel sad right now. You are feeling sad in this *present* moment about something that you could lose in the *future*. Why do you feel sadness just thinking about this loss? You feel sad because you have allowed yourself the freedom of leaving the present moment of time and going into the future. When you go into the future and consider losing something that you love, you actually experience the sorrow that you would have if you lost the thing that you loved. In allowing yourself to feel this anticipatory sorrow that comes with a possible loss in the future, you actually feel sad in this present moment. When you think about it, this is no different than remembering something you have already lost and love it even though it is gone. Get ahold of this concept and you will begin to eradicate fear from your soul, which is always fear of loss, and replace it with love. Granted, finding and feeling the emotion of sadness is not easy, and it is not pleasant, but the more you do it, the more you will be reducing fear in your life. The program is to replace fear with sadness, odd as that sounds, and it takes balls to do it.

We men can cure anxiety and prevent anxiety by looking at the future with hope in our hearts, a hope that might lead to sadness, a hope that might lead to joy. It is possible to eradicate fear from a man's life if he is able to recognize current losses as well as anticipate losses that might come and allow the natural emotion of sadness to come as he feels this love. Clint and most of the men who come into my office live in fear of some kind, always of losing something that they love. It is the fear of loss that paralyzes us men. Anxiety slowly kills you. Sadness slowly heals you. Hope quickly enlivens you.

Conquering Anxiety

Consider this way of conquering anxiety:

- You find yourself thinking about some potential loss.
- Your mind moves toward worrying about this loss.
- You feel a certain queasiness in your stomach or a tightness in your chest.
- You remind yourself that you could lose something in the future and allow yourself to consider this loss.
- You feel a bit sad about this potential loss.
- You allow yourself a moment or two to feel this anticipatory sadness.
- You feel "emotional." You allow this to happen.
- Your sadness seems to wane. You note that you don't have the queasiness in your stomach.
- You feel an odd sense of joy that seems to come for no reason.
- You realize that this anticipatory joy is part of your hope for the future.
- You realize that this is a "love problem." You recognize that love is about having and losing.
- You feel empowered by this love.
- You might want to tell a special friend about this love.

Feeling sad is the most important tool in getting rid of fear. Certainly, we do not dismiss the recommendations for treating anxiety by "calming ourselves down" in some way, perhaps by meditation, yoga or by just thinking about more pleasant things. While any of these can be helpful ways of reducing the symptoms of anxiety, they do not deal with the underlying fear of loss and the love that lies under potential loss. Fear will not end by itself. *You* have to end it. You can do it but you have to have balls to engage sadness.

I experience this feeling of anticipatory loss on a daily basis. As I sit in my office waiting for a scheduled patient to show up, I anticipate that he might not show, which then gives me the thought that I had the wrong time or he had the wrong time. Regardless of whether he or I has been wrong in our timing, I do not yet know why he is not here for his appointment. I could launch into worrying about whether I made some mistake, he no longer wants to see me, or, God forbid, he has had some accident on the way to my office. Rather than going down this path of worry (anxiety), I simply allow myself to consider that I am anticipating some kind of loss.

This allows me to feel the potential loss without worrying about it, but this anticipating some kind of loss leads me to feeling a small amount of sadness. In this case I don't know whether it is my problem, his problem, or no problem whatsoever, but rather simply a loss of this hour where I might have been useful to this individual.

Over the recent days I have helped men admit to feeling helpless: a guy whose wife threatened divorce, a guy who lost his job, a guy who is facing heart bypass surgery, a guy who lost money on the stock market, an adolescent boy who fears that he will get an F in his math class that would prevent him from playing football, and many others. In fact, much of my work with men is to help them face their losses. Even harder and more important, men need to face possible losses with anticipatory loss like the man who could die in surgery or the young fellow who might not play football. Whether a real loss with sadness or potential loss with anticipatory sadness, there is always a feeling of helplessness that goes along with loss. We certainly don't want to feel sad and helpless, but *feeling helpless at times is a central ingredient of having balls*. It takes balls to allow yourself to feel the helplessness that is implicit in feeling sad. I am not suggesting that men need to feel helpless all the time or feel helpless in life at large, much less feel helpless in their work or their relationships. Rather, that a ballsy man respects the sadness that always comes with loss, whether that loss is in the past, the present, or the future. Having balls to feel sad and helpless is not about being a wimp. It is not complaining. It is about facing the reality of present losses and future losses and courageously facing these real or possible losses with honor. *Fear doesn't end but sadness ends.*

Sadness Ends. Fear Does Not.

The really cool thing about feeling sad is that sadness ends. It doesn't matter what you have lost, how profound the loss was, or how devastating the loss was. If you can allow your soul to have the time to feel sad, your sadness will end. What's even more wonderful about feeling sad is that you will be a better person when you have fully grieved over the loss you had. You will learn that whatever you love, you will ultimately lose. This is not something wrong with the world, and it is not the Buddhist belief that "life is suffering." Yes, life *has* its many times of suffering, but life is not *just* suffering. Life is loving, losing, grieving, and loving again. We wrote about this extensively in *The Positive Power of Sadness*, which you might find helpful. We lost our older daughter unexpectedly a few years ago, which was certainly the greatest loss either of us had ever experienced in life, but interestingly, this terrible loss came on the heels of our having published our book on sadness and having worked diligently with our own losses and the losses of the countless people we have seen in our offices. Certainly, the loss of our daughter Krissie surpasses any other loss, but grieving her has led to our actually loving her more, even in her absence, and loving other people more in the present. Feeling the sadness of her loss now brings us a peaceful nostalgia instead of a gut-wrenching pain. Nostalgia is the feeling of sadness and joy as we look back at something we had. We are sad for having lost our precious daughter but also joyful as we think of the forty-five years we had together, with all the ups and downs we shared during those years.

If you feel the entirety of sadness related to a loss, this sadness will end. The fact that sadness ends does not mean that your love ends. Sadness that is found, felt, and finished gives us new energy to love more, to love deeper, and to love better. We frequently tell our clients, "Find it, face it, feel it, and finish it," which means find what you have loved, what you have lost, and then allow yourself to feel the entirety of your grief. As Deb instructs her clients, *let sadness finish with you instead of you trying to finish sadness*. It is not natural to feel fear about a potential loss. It is natural to feel anticipatory sadness together with anticipatory joy when you look into the future.

Finding, Feeling, and Finishing Sadness

Sadness comes in three forms: the past, the present, and the future. In a nutshell, the better you get at feeling sadness for losses in the present, the less inclined toward fear you will be of losses in the future. Finding feelings of sadness in the future helps a man conquer and ultimately prevent fear and anxiety. The more you find, face, and feel daily losses, the better you will be at doing the same with potential future losses. Odd as it sounds, you need the experience of loss in the present in order to truly conquer these typical lifelong fears that most men have. This means:

- You need to face and feel any kind of disapproval in your current life.
- If you are in a relationship with a woman, you need to face and feel female disapproval in the present.
- You need face the fact that other people may see you as indulging with the seemingly weak emotion of sadness.
- You need to face and feel loss of self-respect.
- You need to face and feel occasional inferiority as you compare yourself to other people.

- You need to face the small failures in your daily life.
- You need to face the fact that you forgot to do something, like paying a bill on time to avoid a penalty.
- You need to face your physical limitations and injuries that occur in a day.
- You need to fail in your first attempts to communicate your feelings.
- You need to love better. This means you have to become intimately familiar with sadness that always comes from love.

The more you allow yourself these feelings of hope, sadness, and the love behind both of these feelings, the more you will conquer anxiety. Once a man finds a way to meet this challenge of being sad in the present or anticipating sadness in the future, he can find his balls. He can be a real man. He can be a woman's man, a world's man, a godly man, and a man unto himself, not afraid of others' potential disapproval or dependent upon their approval. This is the greatest challenge for most men.

Summary

- Fear is the most basic emotion that we have. It exists to keep us *safe*.
- Your brain conjures up fear to protect you from future loss.
- Fear is the basis of all personal and interpersonal problems that men have.
- Most men's fears are of personal *failure* or of someone's *criticism*.
- Anxiety is anticipating some loss in the future.
- Men can transform anxiety into *anticipatory loss*, which will generate *anticipatory sadness*.
- We need to *finish* sadness, let it run its course.
- Sadness ends; fear does not.
- Fear and anxiety end when you feel sad about what you might lose.
- The more you replace anxiety with anticipatory sadness, the more you will find anticipatory joy. Anticipatory sadness and anticipatory joy are together the essence of hope.

CHAPTER 3

Men and Anger

I JUST FINISHED A session with a couple who present with "communication problems." More accurately, the wife presented these "problems" because she thinks the man "doesn't think there is anything wrong. He just thinks that I am always criticizing him." What we have with Jan and Jim is a very typical "presenting problem" or "presenting situation," as I prefer to call it: the woman feels that the man is always being defensive and angry, and the man feels like he's being criticized all the time. In these early hours of therapy I have just begun to help them see the all-too-frequent pattern that occurs with many couples: the woman trying to help the man by telling him either what to do or how to do something while the man backs up, having felt criticized. The woman doesn't see her suggestions as criticism as much as a way to help and gain a sense of connection. The man, feeling criticized, disconnects from his wife, sometimes by silence and other forms of avoidance but more often in anger. From Jim's standpoint, it should be much simpler: he needs to do his thing and have his wife just trust him. He thinks if this were the case, then he wouldn't get angry. He doesn't understand and is frequently "frustrated" with not knowing what she wants, much less how he can provide what she wants. Today, he admitted that he is *frightened* of hurting his wife, just like the men we discussed in the previous chapter who were *terrified* of their wives. Jim is not an angry man. He doesn't need "anger management." He needs to *prevent* anger from occurring in the first place. We will deal with the tendency that many women have to "help" the men in their lives by telling them what to do in a later chapter. In this chapter we want to discuss the problem that almost all men have: getting angry too easily, too frequently, and too loudly. Additionally, we want to look at avoiding conflict if at all possible. We examine how:

- Fear always underlies any anger.
- Hurt always underlies most fear.
- Hurt comes from something that I lost.
- Something lost is something that I loved.
- Anger can be reduced to zero.

The Massive Problem of Men Being Angry

Few men escape the grave danger of being unduly angry. Ninety-five percent of people in prison are men. Most of them are angry and have let anger get the best of them. With few exceptions, anger causes more problems than it solves. Many of the men who are incarcerated came from families or subcultures that displayed anger as a primary emotion, so it is understandable that these men would see anger as natural and necessary in life. Animals naturally display aggression in order to preserve their lives or the lives of their brood. Animal aggression is not anger, strictly understood, but a necessary display that looks threatening in order to survive. Almost all the undue anger we see in men does not help men survive so much as it scares people around them, particularly women. The mass incarceration of men is due to our culture reinforcing male aggression in the form of anger.

The tendency of men to spend time surviving is not limited to the incarcerated. Few men mature in life satisfactorily to a point when they rarely get angry, which is a goal I have with every man I see in my office. Men think that they have every reason to justify the frequency and intensity of their anger, but all of these justifications are based on what they have learned growing up as males in this culture. Men's tendency to become angry comes from several sources, which together forge a feeling of desperation that leads to anger including:

- An American culture that encourages and rewards anger for men.
- A male culture that is rife with anger.
- Fathers or father figures who were unduly angry.
- Mass media that is full of anger and violence.
- Being raised with older brothers who were angry, berating, or bullying.

- Being in school where anger is subtly encouraged in athletic engagements.
- A lack of instruction in psychology, specifically in the realm of feelings in general and emotions in particular.
- Undue avoidance of conflict together with passive anger.

Men simply don't have the privilege of having alternatives to getting angry, alternatives that could help them find more productive and honorable ways of engaging the world, like:

- A culture that rewards creativity as much as it rewards productivity.
- A culture that rewards competition where men can profit from both success and failure.
- Schools that teach valuable and practical psychology, especially about feelings and emotion.
- A brotherhood among young men where they could compete, excel, win, lose, encourage, challenge, and congratulate one another.
- A father who rarely gets angry.
- A brother or other male relative who displays candor and kindness in human relationships.
- Media and movies that display men with courage, compassion, and self-reflection. In other words, men with balls.

The essence of men coming to anger so easily, so loudly, or so violently is their failure to understand their own feelings, especially the gift of emotion that all people have. When men understand and value their feelings and the breadth of emotion that always erupts from feelings, they can govern the expression of these feelings so they can be both creative and productive. In practical terms, understanding and governing emotions means finding psychologically healthy ways of facing failure and criticism. We noted in the last chapter the deep challenges men face with failure and criticism, which are two essential ingredients of successful living. A mature man, a man with balls, must face these two challenges with the primary feelings of sadness as I have suggested rather than anger or fear. Consider the following situations where you do something wrong:

- You spill your fresh-brewed espresso on your new book.
- You failed to remember to finish a project that you took home from work until you get to work on Monday morning.

- You can't find the words to express your feelings when you are challenged in some way.
- You bought something on Facebook that didn't arrive. You realize that you have been robbed by some unknown person.
- You forget your water bottle at the gas station where you filled up with gas.
- You can't seem to remember how to add a picture to a text you want to send to a friend.

Note how you would be mad at yourself to varying degrees in all of these circumstances. Note also, the trivial nature of all these mistakes or errors. Nothing is terribly important about spilling your coffee or any of these other examples of when people get mad at themselves. Consider how you look when you yell at the world or yourself after such things. In chapter one we discussed how all emotions are love-based in some way, but the most important emotion we have is sadness. In chapter two we showed how to cure and prevent fear by experiencing anticipatory sadness. While anger is the primary emotion you might feel in the instances above, the feeling that preceded anger was sadness because you lost something. Consider mistakes you might make that are of a more serious nature. Would it feel natural to be angry at yourself in these circumstances?

- You got fired because you were late too many times.
- You sustain several thousand-dollar losses in the stock market.
- You hurt the feelings of your daughter-in-law because you made an offhanded remark at a family gathering about her appearance.
- You yell at your kid because he didn't do the dishes that he had promised to do when you left the house, only later to discover that he was quite ill.
- You caused some serious damage to your car and your garage when you forgot to put the car in park.

These mistakes or errors, all of which are understandable and forgivable, can easily lead to anger, but they should make you sad, not angry. Equally important to the mistakes and errors you make is the suffering you encounter when you are criticized by someone. Note that the following examples are ones where you were sometimes right in what you did and sometimes wrong in what you did but the result was the same: you get criticized when you . . .

- Tell your boss that the company is not being honest with a customer.
- Tell your friend that he has been rude at a party.
- Challenge your son's teacher who has publicized her political persuasion.
- Give money to a charity that your wife doesn't approve of.

Or you...

- Fail to follow through with a customer at work and lose the customer to a competitor.
- Get mad at your employee before you realize that someone else had made the mistake, not her.
- Fail to renew the insurance on your wife's car before she had an accident.
- Cheat on your taxes and get caught.

Both the times when you have been *right* with what you did or said and the times when you have been *wrong* have led to someone's criticism. Your *natural* reactions are sadness, disappointment, and/or hurt. But what is the typical reaction that most men have? Anger. It would be as easy to give a list of times when someone has offended you and you get angry at that person. In these events men have skipped right over the sadness part and then rushed right into the emotion of anger. Whether the anger is at yourself or someone else, let's look at the nature of anger in all circumstances.

What Underlies Anger?

Look at each of these situations and you will see that you have been assaulted by someone, which could be yourself or someone else. If you assault yourself, you have made an error in what you did. If you are assaulted by someone else, you made an error in their judgment. They might be right in their assessment or they might be wrong, but when you are criticized, the result is the same: you have been hurt. You might even be assaulted by Nature like when the wind blows your newspaper off the porch table. Whenever you have been assaulted, you are naturally hurt and quickly recognize the the equally natural sadness that follows hurt. When you don't feel the natural hurt and sad, you will most likely resort to fear and anger. Fearing you might be hurt again is what brings you to defensive anger. For reasons that we will continue to explore in this book most men feel so much fear that they feel compelled to get angry in order to survive. Few women understand the fact that when men make a mistake or are criticized, they are hurt first, scared second, and angry third. Unfortunately, this process from hurt to anger takes less than a second, so fast that a man who is angry doesn't even recognize the precursors to his anger.

It is understandable that women don't understand this process because all they see is the anger. They have no idea that we have been hurt, sad, and afraid. You can't blame them for being upset with you for seemingly "getting angry all the time." They don't see the hurt, the sadness, or the fear. The process that leads to anger is:

- I love something (person, place, thing, or idea).
- I am assaulted: by another person, an unavoidable circumstance, or myself.
- I am hurt.
- I feel sad and disappointed.
- I become afraid of losing more.
- I rush right into anger.

Men are so familiar with being angry that they go to what is familiar to them and *feels safe*. They don't know that they have rushed right by sadness and fear, nor do they realize the more important thing: they have loved something and have lost that something. All people see is that the man is angry.

Men have not been encouraged to know a breadth of feelings, much less how to recognize and govern their emotions. They protect themselves from further hurt, but they don't even know that they have been hurt. How do we men find a way to access these things? We mature. We grow up. We grow a pair. Consider the following scenarios where men are assaulted in some way and how they might handle these assaults to prevent anger. All of these cases involve catching the hurt and disappointment and allowing these feelings to generate sadness before fear and anger take over.

The Man Assaults Himself

Jack spills his coffee on his shirt just as he is getting out of his car. When these things have happened to him in the past, he would swear (at himself) and then carry this irritability into work. Now he has learned to realize that he has a "love problem," i.e., he loves having a good cup of joe and he loves having a crisp clean shirt to start the day. He has lost both. So, sitting in the car, he takes a moment, perhaps a minute, to allow himself to just feel sad. He thinks how important it is for him to look sharp in the office even if it isn't important for other people. He realizes that looking good is for him and that he loves looking good; it has nothing to do with what other people think of him. He feels simply sad for just this moment or two and his sadness wanes. He determines that he will go right to the restroom and do his best to get his shirt cleaned. He does his best but the stain still shows a little, perhaps not so much that anyone would know, but he knows. He feels disappointed again and allows himself to feel sad (again). Soon the sadness finishes and he goes about his day. In fact, after a bit, he actually forgets about the coffee stain and goes on with his work. Oddly, someone talks to him about how his car wouldn't start this morning, and Jack was able to just share the disappointment with his office mate, eventually telling him about the coffee-stained shirt. It turns out to be a good day. When he gets home, he immediately puts stain remover on the shirt, knowing that coffee stains don't always come out, but this possibility doesn't seem to bother him because he has felt sad twice already today, and the possibility of having ruined his shirt doesn't seem to be terribly important. Jack tells his wife about the coffee-and-shirt event, and she congratulates him for preventing anger that she has previously seen with such events.

 I (Ron) recently forgot a dinner engagement with a colleague friend. Unfortunately, I have this tendency that I acquired from my family of being tardy to things, a phenomenon that has offended many people over my lifetime. When my friend texted me and asked if I was coming, I realized I had totally forgot the date. I felt bad and apologized to my friend, and we laughed at my tendency and related it to our both being "low boundary" people, meaning people who tend to value spontaneity over punctuality. I allowed myself to feel "bad" (sad) for a while, which took maybe an hour or so. We made a date for the same time the next week. Believe it or not, I forgot again. Again, I received a text from Scott asking me whether I was coming or not. This, the second time my having been neglectful with Scott in one week's time, really took a toll on me. In fact, I had to sit down and put my head in my hands for many minutes in order to even go about the evening. I truly felt sad. I didn't sleep well. I was grieving. I allowed myself to grieve. I felt a bit better in the morning but still felt bad (sad). I just had to let it run its course. Much of the day after this mistake was spent with on-and-off feelings of sadness. When I got the initial text from Scott, I immediately rendered my apologies. After the second missed date I wrote him again and said how awful I felt. I wasn't looking for approval or even for Scott's forgiveness. I just needed to be open about how I felt. I needed to grieve openly.

A few days later we were actually together at my birthday party my wife hosted. Scott was kind to me, but he enjoyed taking part in the "roast" that my wife had planned, chiming in regarding certain "lost opportunities" and that perhaps my negligence with time was an "age" matter. We were both good. I felt quite humbled by the events of the past week, but this kind of humility is not shame or humiliation. Rather, it is recognizing one's flaws, almost all of which are unintentional. I could have been angry at myself, but that would be me trying to fix the past by punishing myself. Much better to simply feel sad and learn something about myself. How many men just get angry instead of feeling the sad?

Max backs his car out of his garage and mistakenly runs into his wife's car. Both cars are damaged, although minimally. In the past Max would have been angry with himself, or worse yet, he'd have been angry with his wife for parking in such a way that he ran into her car. He did neither. He got out of the car, surveyed the damage, and just stood looking at the two cars, feeling disappointed. No one else was around. Max knew that he had to process this "assault" before he talked to his wife about it, not because he was afraid of her disapproval but so he didn't carry any fear into a conversation with her, much less any anger or defensiveness. He knew that she also would be disappointed when she saw the damage, or so he thought. Indeed, he allowed himself to feel sad long enough that he didn't feel sad anymore. He talked to his wife, and to his surprise, she wasn't bothered. Additionally, she commented that she appreciated his gentle honesty. Interestingly, not long after this incident, Max was driving on a country road, and a deer ran into the side of his car. He reported that he felt himself go towards anger by cursing, then quickly caught himself and realized that this was another sad. He was pleased that he didn't indulge himself with undue and unnecessary anger.

Assaults from Other People

Jerry was fired from his job. He had been a successful accountant for the same firm for ten years, but he had made several mistakes in his work over the past several months, enough for the owner of the firm to justify firing him. He was given a modest severance allowance as well as a reasonable recommendation, but there was no way Jerry was able to change the decision of the owner. Jerry felt devastated. He knew that he had made a few mistakes, but he had no idea that they were sufficient evidence to justify his being fired. Jerry had had a less-than-good relationship with the owner of the firm, who tended to be a bit rigid and demanding, not particularly a people person. All this having been said, Jerry allowed himself a good deal of time to simply feel hurt and disappointed and eventually to feel the sadness that always follows these feelings. He did not indulge himself with anger that the owner was just an SOB, nor with worries about the future, like finding a new job or paying his bills. He sat in his car outside the accounting firm office for a few minutes and just allowed himself to feel sad. He came home, told his wife about his having been fired and asked that he be allowed to be alone for a while, telling her that this was a difficult time and that he needed to feel through this before they discussed what might happen in the future. He said that he just needed to be alone for a while, feel sad, and allow the sadness to run its course. He was alone for not many minutes, perhaps a half-hour or so before he came back out to the living room and talked about feeling disappointed and hurt. His wife was good enough to say nothing but how she felt sad with him.

James prided himself on being a good husband and a good father, so it came as a complete surprise that his wife informed him that she had been having an affair for some time and was unsure as to whether she wanted to stay married. This situation is what we call a *potential loss cluster*, i.e., he might lose several things, namely his wife, his family, his trust in his wife, and the possibilities of losing many more things like money, house, and contact with his children, to say nothing about losing his best friend, his wife. There is a tremendous danger for James going into a worst-case scenario worrying about all kinds of potential losses, rather than simply sticking with the feeling that he actually had only lost one thing: the trust that he had had in his wife. In a situation like this, a man (or a woman, of course) must face this potential loss cluster carefully and without trying to fix the problem but rather tackling each item in this cluster honestly and honorably. James was emotionally mature enough to be able to stay away from asking questions of his wife, berating her, or even talking to anyone about it because he had learned over the years that it was best to face a loss with honest sadness rather than worry about the future. He knew that there would be a place for examination, discussion, compromise, and possibly some kind of resolution, but most importantly, he needed to feel sad so he could get his mind in order rather than being cluttered by worry about what he was *possibly* going to lose. James heard what his wife said, avoided asking questions or saying anything, excused himself from her company, and went for a walk to clear his mind, but more accurately, he needed time to just grieve his lost trust in his wife. Talk could come later.

Assaults from Circumstances

The heart attack I had a few years ago was quite unexpected because I run three days a week, work out three days a week, and play basketball up to three times a week. Furthermore, I have eaten pretty healthily for years, aside from a sort-of sugar addiction. But all this wasn't enough for me to avoid the genetic heart disease proclivity I inherited (three grandparents, both parents, my brother at the age of fifty-nine, all dying from heart attacks). Interestingly, I was able to prevent any kind of anxiety or fear even though I was, in fact, close to dying. I was disappointed, however, at several things that occurred while I was in the hospital, like being given a standard number of medications without the doctor really considering me as an individual rather than as a heart attack patient, the fact that my wife couldn't be in the vicinity of the stenting because of some hospital policy, and what seemed to be the excessive charges for my care, like $9 for one aspirin or $500 for a five-minute consultation with the surgeon. Instead of indulging myself too much in being angry, I allowed myself to be sad for all of these things, which were all losses of one kind or another. It was sad that Deb couldn't be near me when I was in surgery; it was sad that I had to pay exorbitant medical fees, and it was sad that the doctor didn't understand me as distinct from other heart attack patients. The more I allowed myself to be sad, the more these feelings finished. I didn't need to berate the doctor, the nurses, or the hospital administration because they were doing what they thought best to do, even if it wasn't right for me. Instead of going in the direction of anger, I took a healthy look at myself, namely how I live and redoubled my effort at being healthy. Now, I can look at this incident that included many external assaults. Instead of indulging my anger, I allowed my disappointment to run its course and came up with what I could actually do for myself. I did write a letter to the hospital administration and noted my concerns. I got myself off the medications that the cardiologist assumed I should take, and I have continued to maintain an even heathier lifestyle. Allowing sadness to run its course allows us to have a clear mind so we can have a clear course of action.

Greg was assaulted by a water break in his house when he was on vacation. Unfortunately, he and his family were out of town during the water break, allowing the water to ruin pretty much everything in the house that they had just bought. To make matters worse, they had just moved into a new town to begin work on a PhD program. Furthermore, his wife delivered their (unplanned) fourth child about the time they were due to return to their home. Greg and family were in a new state, a new town, a new neighborhood, and now living in a motel. The estimated time for the restoration of their house was six months, which ended up to be nine months. There were some other complications with his doctoral program to make the bad worse. As expected, the insurance claim on the house amounted to $100,000 and counting. Greg was confronted with this cluster of assaults, none of which he had expected and none of them coming from anything but an "act of God," as such things are called in the insurance business. In my many conversations with Greg, I heard of one or more of these distressing elements, sometimes complicated by visits from their family members, none of whom really understood that Greg was just hoping to work hard on his PhD and really enjoy the process. Understandably, Greg's frustration showed in his occasional angry outbursts at one or more of his family members, but what was Greg really feeling? Disappointed, hurt, and sad, along with the feeling of helplessness that always accompanies such events. Consider how hard it would be to deal with a wife, good woman as she was, who was trying to manage an infant and three other young children, who herself was also trying to manage this almost unmanageable situation. It was not easy for Greg and his wife to get through this most challenging time of their life together, but they succeeded singularly by allowing each other to feel helpless, hurt, disappointed, and occasionally irritable. The real key was for Greg to demonstrate sadness, not anger, not "frustration," which is always sadness expressed with anger.

Shit happens, right? Sometimes due to your own assaults on yourself, sometimes coming from other people, and sometimes out of the wind. Is it normal to be angry? Yes. Is it necessary? Not usually. Is it valuable? Not usually. Of course, there are occasions when asserted anger might get the job done, such as when you need to be firm with your attorney on what action to take to get the divorce through. Can you ever get to a place when you are never angry? Probably not. Should you work towards never getting angry by allowing the more important emotion of sadness to run its course? Yes. How do you get to the place where you can prevent anger from dominating your emotional experience and then allow sadness to run its course? You mature emotionally; you grow a pair.

When you grow a pair, you have come to know yourself better, you recognize all of your feelings and know that "feelings" are pure and a deep part of you. The ballsy man can then understand and accept all emotions and work to seeing the centrality of the love-based emotions of joy and sadness and lessen the defense-based emotions of fear and anger. In the previous chapter we discussed the basic anxiety that most men feel is based on fear. The fear that we men feel is invisible to the people around us; the anger that we display is what they see. Underneath both of the emotions of fear and anger are the more basic emotions of joy and sadness. You want to prevent displaying anger? Recognize that anger is always precipitated by fear, fear is always precipitated by sadness, and that sadness is always preceded by joy. If you can be a man who displays joy when you love something and the necessary sadness that occurs when you lose something, you will have grown a pair.

Summary

- Anger is a massive problem in society and causes great harm to people.
- Men tend to come to anger too quickly and too frequently.
- Anger comes to a man because he has been assaulted: by other people, by circumstances, and by himself.
- Anger is always precipitated by fear.
- Anger is visible. Fear is not.
- Men can prevent anger by allowing themselves to feel hurt and helpless, which then migrate into sadness.
- Sadness ends; anger does not.
- A man who has prevented feeling anger has felt sadness, which will make him a more loving man.
- It takes real balls to transform anger into sadness.

SECTION II

Words, Work, and Wine

Note that the subtitle of this book is "Words, Work, Wine, and Women." It is these areas where men tend to get lost, say foolish things, do foolish things, or do nothing. We will delay most of our discussion of women to section III and focus this section on words, work, and wine, the term "wine" being used for purposes of alliteration, referring to addictions at large. When men are inadequate in their use of feeling-based words, they tend to be inadequate with work, wine, and women. We begin chapter four with an in-depth understanding of why words are such a challenge for men, noting that there are some very significant neurological elements in men's lack of an emotional vocabulary. We will see how men need to have at least a rudimentary understanding of emotional vocabulary in order to succeed in life. Chapter five is dedicated to the matter of work, which often plagues men because they are working too hard, not working hard enough, or in the wrong job or profession. We discuss the difference between a job and a profession, noting that a profession "professes" something good about the man. Chapter six is devoted to addiction ("wine"), finding that there are both chemical addictions, like alcohol and food, as well as behavioral addictions like gambling, playing, or even working. We want to set the stage for section III, "Women," by helping you men deal with words, work, and wine.

CHAPTER 4

Men and Words

OF THE FOUR "W's" that bring men challenges, words are the most crucial. Most men have difficulty with women, many have difficulty with work, some have difficulty with wine, but just about every man who comes to my office has difficulty with words. While some men can find the right words in reading, writing, and speaking, words frequently trip men up, particularly emotional words. Our focus in this book is primarily on the challenge men have in expressing their feelings through words. Some people have written about men's "deficiency" with emotional words, while other writers have talked about men's "brain dysfunction" in regards to words, and there is some literature that even suggest that men are simply "emotionally illiterate." Some authors have suggested that the word difficulty with men has to do with the cultural disadvantage men have with expressing emotions, while many authors suggest the problem is not so much with words as with men "not being in touch with their feelings." I agree with some of what these authors say about men's deficiencies with emotional words, but I heartily disagree with any format that looks at what is *wrong* with men rather than looking *at* men and trying to *understand* them, specifically the challenges they have finding appropriate feeling-based words.

Instead of finding some deficiency or dysfunction with men, I suggest that it is simply *not natural for men to talk about their feelings*. Unnatural for men to talk about their feelings? Really? Yes. Their feelings are natural, yes. Their desire to communicate their feelings is natural, yes. But I don't think it is natural for men to communicate their feelings with spoken words to the extent that women do. Men have all the feelings that women have, and they have all the emotions that all people have. Men often speak out of their feelings and very often speak with a great deal of emotion, but they often fail to communicate what they really feel when they speak. There may be men who are articulate in what they think, what they believe, or what they do, but when they try to say how they feel, they often fail in that endeavor. Many men work heartily to communicate their feelings with words, but most men would much prefer to express their feelings physically, cognitively, or actively than speak them emotionally. A man's basic nature is not verbal; it is physical.

A Man's Basic Nature is Physical

A man is primarily *physical* in the way he approaches the world. Words are a distant second. If a man is true to himself, he uses few words and more actions. It is an interesting sideline to note that research has found that men actually talk *more* than women, i.e., men use more words than women, but men often fail to talk fluently about their feelings. *To understand a man, you need to watch what he does, not what he says.* Women, who are much more fluent in emotional language, have the greatest trouble with men because of what men *say*—or don't say. Likewise, women see that what men say does not seem to coordinate with what they do. Worse yet, women often conclude that men are lying when they say something. How many women have said of the men in their lives, "I can't believe what he says"? When a woman says something like that to me, I have responded by saying, "Of course not. Men are not primarily verbal animals. You can't believe what they say. They are using words to answer questions, but these words do not reflect the reality of their lives." My frequent advice to women as I work with couples is to state, "*if you want to know what a man thinks and feels, watch what he does; don't listen to what he says (yet)."* Men can augment their physical nature with words, but usually words are a very imperfect way of communicating, especially to women.

Being "Physical"

Being physical means that a man's nature is to engage the world in some way that allows him to *touch* the world. There are many ways a man can touch the world. Touching the world can mean using a hand with a machine, a baseball, a keyboard, or steering wheel, as well as of some kind of physical contact with another person. Many men do not intrinsically understand that they engage the world primarily through physical contact. Have you ever found yourself picking up a rock and just feeling your hands around it, or fondling a baseball or a tennis racket, a hammer, or a deck of cards? Have you ever run your hands over a smooth surface or a rough surface just for the sake of the feel? Have you ever touched the books in your personal library, the tools in your garage, the towels in the bathroom, or your favorite coffee cup? If you have done any of these things, you have been connecting with something physically, and in doing so, you have been communicating your feelings, even if no one else understands why you are touching something. While most of this "touching things" is natural for men, there are times when touching something is not good for you, not good for someone else, or not good for some piece of property. More than once in the use of my meager electrical skill, I have touched a live wire just to check that it is live. Sometimes, it just seems easier to touch the wire than to turn around and get my electrical tester or turn the electrical circuit off.

Many men are not only inclined to touch physical objects; many are inclined to touch other people. Several friends that I have are seemingly compelled to hug me when they meet me, one of which simply states that he is a hugger. I always reach out my hand to greet almost any man when I meet him, whether for the first time or the second time, but if the man spontaneously reaches out to hug me, I respond in kind. Some men prefer the hand bump or the slap on the back. For some reason I have developed a very odd habit of grabbing a guy's butt . . . in church of all places. Granted, I don't do this with any intention of offense, much less sexual interest, but now this ass-grabbing seems to have engendered the favor returned in kind with more than one guy at church. This very morning I reached out to hold a man during a church prayer, and he returned the favor a half-hour later with another prayer. Neither of us commented on this touching.

Understandably, any kind of physical touch, whether it is a hug, a handshake, a slap on the back, or a butt-grab, could be offensive to the receiver of such touching. I am careful whose butt I might grab at church. I am never offended by someone's desire to hug me but I also know not to initiate a hug with a certain good friend of mine. An old friend of mine used to regularly pinch my shoulder, which I found to be quite irritating even though I know it was just his way of joking around. Many men have touched women sexually without their permission, perhaps often without much forethought or reading the environment correctly. In addition to the well-meaning hugs or other gestures of friendship that men might do with someone, many men have found it seemingly necessary to get into physical fights, often because they were unable to express their feelings verbally. I have heard many men speak of "being ready to fight" if something untoward happened to them. Perhaps, there is a natural inclination men have to defend themselves physically that comes from human survival instinct, but physical fights are almost always due to men having no capacity to express their feelings verbally and find some kind of understanding and resolution. I wonder if the mass shootings that have been occurring in the United States recently, almost all by men, have something to do with a man touching a gun. More importantly, I suspect some of these men really didn't want to shoot people but couldn't find a way to communicate their feelings.

Touch Communicates Feelings

Touching the world physically, whether of objects or people, can be a very positive way of communicating feelings. There are many ways a man can touch the world positively. The term "touch" can be enlarged to include being in the physical presence of another person, a machine, or a game. Many men find great pleasure in fishing or hunting, which are very physical engagements with the world. I have a patient who is an expert archer. He often spends many hours touching his archery equipment sometimes to clean it, wax the bowstrings, and simply to appreciate that it is functioning at top capacity or perhaps to simply recall a good shot or to hope for a better one next time out. I suspect that there are times he just touches it for the pleasure of feeling wood and iron. Expert carpenters, especially those who do finish carpentry and trim often touch their work, or even the work of someone else, often as a way of appreciating what they have done or what some other carpenter has done. Many of the successes that men have in life relate to their physical touching of something, to their physical engagement of the work they have chosen, be it carpentry or the keyboard. Men touch the work they do, they touch the play they do, and they touch the people that they relate to. If men could affirm that they are physical animals first and verbal animals second, they could be better at both ways of communicating their feelings.

A good friend of ours, Tim, has two horses and two dogs, all of whom he touches regularly. Once when Tim, Deb, and I were in Iceland, he asked us to stop the car so he could go over to a fence and touch the Icelandic horses corralled there. When he touched these horses, I could see the intrinsic joy that he felt, a joy that I do not share because I am not particularly an animal person. I could see how the horse knew that Tim touched it with honest affection and a sense of connection best expressed physically. Men need to have some sort of physical contact with the property, people, and animals in their world. When the tradesman who did the flooring in our recently remodeled kitchen came to inspect the final product, he ran his hands over the butcher block countertops even though they were done by a different tradesman. The biblical accounts of Jesus' healing people almost always included his touching them, perhaps giving him the same joy that many men find in touching.

Touch as Sexual

This need for physical contact has significant complications when men relate to women. The implication of this need is that men are singularly interested in sexual contact with women. Indeed, men seek sexual contact with women and often perceive women as sexual objects, but the much larger need men have is physical contact of some kind. It is a man's basic physical nature, rather than his sexually erotic nature, that causes many men to relate to women primarily sexually. This physical-sexual nature of men is easily misunderstood by both men and women. Many women view a man's sexual interest as some kind of flaw or "sexual addiction" and might say something like "men are only interested in one thing." They often think of men as animalistic in their apparent fixation on explicit sexuality. Men are not more sexual than women; they are more *physical*. Physicality doesn't equate with sexuality. Sexual expression is the result of emotional feelings, physical feelings, and even spiritual feelings . . . or it should be. I have heard men equate the term intimacy with sexual intimacy many times, which I find interesting, but it is not my use of the word "intimacy." I find it intimate every time I have a particularly fruitful hour with a patient, read a good history book, or discuss philosophy with someone, as well as experiencing sexual pleasure with my wife, but many men have not found ways to find intimacy apart from explicit sexual contact.

I have heard the following things from various men over the years:

- If we don't have sex, I don't feel loved.
- Intimacy *means* sex, nothing else.
- I just need to be held. The only way I can get that is to initiate sex.
- I feel wanted when I have sex with someone.
- I don't know any other way of finding intimacy.
- I cannot look at any woman without having some sexual feeling.
- I feel very awkward expressing any kind of physical affection to my wife in public because physical affection means sex.

These statements suggest that men are only interested in sex, but that is not the case. Men who make statements like this have just not had instruction and privilege to have physical affectionate contact without associating it with sex. Some time ago when I was working with a couple in my office, the woman felt quite distressed. I suggested that she move closer to her husband. I was thinking that he would put his arm around her and comfort her, but to my surprise, he actually moved away from her. I was stunned. I slowly came to realize that Peter could not fathom any kind of physical contact with a woman that did not lead to explicit sex. This is a man who had come from a family with little physical contact aside from physical fighting in the living room or private sex in the bedroom. It seems that homosexual men have more freedom to touch one another and to touch women without having immediate thoughts of consummate sex. North American cultural restrictions on visible displays of male-to-male physical contact make it difficult for heterosexual men to show too much physical display of connection or affection to other men.

The last fifty years has seen an increase of the display of physical affection from one man to another, probably initiated by the general increase in freedom of the 1960s. When I attended a freshman dance at the University of Wisconsin in 1962, I was taken by the sight of two African men holding hands as they talked together. I realized that this was no homosexual display but rather a natural expression of affection that was probably more acceptable in their African culture than it was in my American culture. Some cultures allow much more physically affectionate behavior between men. Interestingly, men are culturally allowed to show far more physical affection on sports fields than they are allowed to show in off-field encounters. How is it that men can hug each other and jump on each other after a soccer goal when they never do such things on the street? It is allowed on the soccer field because the sports culture allows such displays of physicality. I believe that if men were not constrained by a whole host of fears, they would be much more physical with one another on a day-to-day basis. They would touch one another more often, whether with a simple touch on the shoulder, a grab of the shoulder, a hand around the waste, or other form of physical affection. It is not uncommon once I begin working with a man, that it becomes an assumed gesture to end the session with a handshake, a hug or just a hand on a shoulder. This kind of routine physical contact could do the world of men a lot of good, and might reduce men's tendency to pour too much of their need for physical contact into explicit sexual approach or activity.

Physicality in Work

The high need for physicality in men is more than being physical with another human being. A man needs to be physical in his profession, which can come in different forms depending on the profession a man has. We will discuss the matter of work, profession, and balls in the next chapter. If a man is passionate about his work, that work is his profession. I know of a very happy trash collector who truly enjoys his work, values his work, and sees his work as a profession. I have seen him pick some discarded piece of furniture or toy that is lying on the street, inspect it, and otherwise touch it as he feels into the decision to take it or not. I knew another trash collector who hated his work and would never tell anyone what he did for a living because he was embarrassed about his work. One of these men was able to be successfully physical in his work while the other wasn't.

Being physical at work can take a host of different paths, from the cement worker, carpenter, or other tradesman to the mathematician, IT specialist, architect, surgeon, or artisan. A man needs to have some kind of hands-on experience with his work. As I write these words, I am immensely physical in doing this work of writing. Not only do I type on the keyboard, but I have a kind of spiritual connection to the words as they come up on the screen. It is almost a physical connection between my inner spirit and the words I type. I think poets and novelists might feel even more spiritually connected to their work. I can say with assurance that a man needs some kind of physical contact with his work to find meaning in it.

Physicality is more than sexuality, and it is more than touching. It includes the use of all five senses and possibly one's sixth sense of intuition. A man is physical when he engages the world with one of these senses. Somewhere in the advancement of our society we have lost touch with some of the very important ingredients of engaging the world with all five senses. I am sure that the trash collector I noted above who very much likes his job uses his olfactory sense more than I do when I work with patients. I primarily use my sense of hearing, which is highly related to my speaking, while Deb uses her sense of vision, also related to her speaking. We are both engaging the world physically. Men need to approach the rest of the world, namely the world made up of words and conversation by first establishing a solid sense of his physical connection to the world. Then, they can approach the whole business of emotional communication without an exclusive dependency on words. What does it mean to communicate without words?

Communicating without Words

If men would operate by their nature, they probably wouldn't use spoken words very often. More accurately, they wouldn't use spoken words when they want to communicate their feelings and passions. When men must speak, especially when they speak emotionally, they are, in a sense, using a foreign language: the language of emotional words rather than emotional actions. Instead of stumbling with trying to find words to express yourself, you might have more success with helping people understand your feelings by showing them how you feel when you do something important to you. I tell men that they might do better when trying to express their feelings to say, "Please watch me while I do this thing (hammer a nail, write a poem, play on the guitar, run a race, watch the sunset, or trim the shrubbery)."

Men often speak with such a flurry or words, half-words, curse words, and made-up words that they make no sense whatsoever when they are trying to talk feelings. Many men simply drop their heads in a kind of despair knowing that they will not communicate how they feel in words. Recall the man I mentioned in the introduction who would sometimes open his mouth, perhaps utter a few sounds but not actually say anything intelligible, assuming his audience knew what he was wanting to communicate. Unfortunately, men often think that they have communicated with words when they have not. Because men are born into a society that is very dependent on the spoken word, they learn to speak, which is certainly good for them, but they always speak with a male accent.

Men Who Talk, Men Who Don't Talk

Not all men are alike. In our previous book, *What's Your Temperament*, we discussed different personality "temperaments" that people have. We have also studied differences in personality "types" for decades and found these studies to be of great value in understanding people. When I speak of men generically, it may sound like I think men are all alike, but I am quite aware that there are different psychological styles that men have and that no two men are exactly alike. For instance, a well-researched and well-known understanding of people is to recognize that some people are internal, usually identified as *introverts*, and some people are external, usually identified as *extraverts*. Extraversion and introversion are elements of how people gain energy. Introverts value quality and privacy while extraverts value quantity and publicity. In other words, introverts tend to keep all their feelings and thoughts to themselves while extraverts seem to express their feelings rather readily. As we speak, Deb and I are in the midst of a major kitchen remodel in 111-year-old former farm house. We have a very introverted carpenter and a very extraverted plumber, both accomplished people and both intelligent, not only in their trades but also in understanding much of life. While Carl the plumber, an extrovert, talks a great deal, Isaac the carpenter, an introvert, says very little. It might seem that Carl talks about his feelings more than Isaac, but that is not actually true. Carl talks a lot, jokes a lot, laughs a lot, but rarely says anything about his deep feelings. Isaac talks much less but certainly is just as passionate about his woodworking as Carl is his plumbing. An extravert myself, I rarely say how I really feel, partly due to the fact that I am pretty good at listening but more due to the fact that I cannot easily or readily express my feelings. I know how Isaac and Carl *feel* only by watching intently their *work*, not at what they say.

Our very verbal society sees words as the center of communication. Spoken words are a wonderful means of communicating, but words are not the only means of communicating, and for men regardless of being introverted or extraverted, words are often an impediment in communication. The difficulty men have in verbally expressing their feelings is the greatest impediment to men having balls, particularly when dealing with the world of females, but also in the academic world and the world of business. If a man tries to express his feelings, it's very hard for him to put together a string of words that actually makes sense. That having been said, a man who wants to grow a pair must find a way to speak his feelings with words. It is no easy task to do so because good, accurate, communicative feeling words do not come easily to men, and when you finally say something that is feeling-based, it is likely that you will not be understood, or worse yet, be criticized for what you said. Speaking feelings is hard for all men but it is especially hard for introverts. Today, I spent an hour with a couple composed of an introverted man and his extraverted wife. Yesterday, I met with another couple both of whom are introverted. In both cases the men, one thirty-five and one eighty-five, admitted that they *never* say now they feel.

Accept the fact that you are not good at expressing your feelings with words and be prepared to apologize for not being clear and then dare to go on and say more. We'll come back to how to do this later. Making multiple attempts to express yourself emotionally can end up sounding like a word salad. You need to keep going and try again and work until you succeed. This takes balls because you can't be worried of any judgment or criticism. The difficulty of expressing feelings has a lot to do with how our brains are constructed.

The Male Brain

There are several factors that relate to a man's difficulty with expressing feelings: neurological, societal, interpersonal, and personal. The neurological factor is at the center of the problem. In about 96 percent of people, the area of the brain that creates spoken language is in the left frontal cortex, an area that is usually referred to as the "left brain" (Friederici, 2011). This same left side of the brain is also analytical and conceptual. The right frontal cortex is the primary housing for emotion and feelings, which is the best reflection of a "self" or personal existence. The connective tissue between these two halves of the brain is called the corpus callosum. Information that is collected in the right side of the brain, which can be any of the five senses, gets transferred to the left side of the brain by means of the corpus callosum, where it is analyzed and translated into words. Readers of these statements should realize that I have grossly simplified a very complex mechanism of brain functioning for the sake of highlighting the importance of the corpus callosum, particularly with men. The important fact is that everyone, male and female, first gathers information (right brain), secondly feels something (right brain), thirdly thinks about this something (left brain), and finally speaks something with words (left brain). This process occurs in a split second: you hear something, you feel something, you think about something, and then you speak something. This process happens so fast that you don't actually know that you are doing these four brain functions. You might think that you see something and then comment on what you see immediately. You are not aware of the fact that you had the right brain feeling and the left brain thinking that came between seeing something and saying something. It is very important to realize, however, that much of this understanding, musing, and feeling occurs in the right brain and then the corpus callosum transfers this information to the left brain where it gets translated into words.

The reason the corpus callosum is so important in this discussion is because neurological research has discovered that the female brain has a larger and perhaps more active corpus callosum (Goldman, 2017). This fact suggests that information transfers faster from the right side to the left side of the brain in females than it does in males. More importantly, information transfers back and forth across this connective tissue faster for females than it does for males. In simple terms this means that *a woman can feel something and translate that feeling into words faster than a man can.* Furthermore, a woman can feel something (using her right brain), then think about it or analyze it (using her left brain), then feel again (right brain), analyze the information again (left brain), and then speak (left brain) with greater speed and efficiency than a man can. Other neurological research suggests that women are able to speak and listen simultaneously, a phenomenon that seems to be due to their larger corpus callosum.

When instructing women to hold back while waiting for men to speak their feelings, Deb illustrates this brain difference by describing women having access through what she calls a revolving door. Women can walk into the door of thoughts or feelings and move right through to the expression of those thoughts and feelings without ever pausing, as well as going on to the next thought and feeling without missing a beat. Men, on the other hand, are more like a hinged door: they have a thought or feeling, they approach the door, put their hand on the knob, open the door, walk through the door to gather the words for their thoughts and feelings and then have to turn around, open the door from that side, walk through, shut the door behind them, and then speak. By the time they have done this, for sake of illustration, women have made multiple rotations through their revolving door and have left men in the dust of their words. Again, a woman can have feelings, think about these feelings, speak these feelings, and hear feelings in a split second. Men can't do this. This revolving door metaphor may explain why women so often finish statements or fill in words for men, perhaps even knowing what the man is about to say or wants to say. Unfortunately, this finishing of a man's statements, adding to his statement, or correcting his statements feels like an *interruption* to a man who might really be working to find words to express his feelings.

Some authors have unfortunately suggested that this *superiority* of women suggests that men are somehow *inferior* in brain functioning. The fact that females can feel, think, and speak more quickly than males do, indeed, gives females a certain brain superiority in conversation, but does not make them superior in all aspects of communication. To be superior in a certain kind of functioning does not make me a superior person, and it doesn't make me better than someone else. Rather, any kind of superior function is a "gift," if we dare use that term, something to be treasured and used, but not abused in its use.

Women's giftedness in accessing and expressing feelings has huge ramifications in regards to male-to-female relationships. This phenomenon is one of the central components of the difficulty men and women have in conversation with women. Interestingly, as previously noted, women do not speak *more*; their words are just more efficient and more articulate, especially in matters that have any kind of emotional content. Unfortunately, the speed of expression is misinterpreted as having more feelings or deeper feelings. Men have the same amount of feelings as women do. Women are just better at putting their feelings into words.

Women, for the most part, do not know that they are superior in the expression of feelings and erroneously think that men can feel, think, and speak about feelings as swiftly and efficiently as they can. Regretfully, this verbal superiority of women, particularly in the realm of speaking feelings, has led some women to believe that men are "hiding their feelings," "repressing their feelings," or "not being in touch with their feelings." True, men fail to express their feelings in words as easily as women do, but men are quite aware of their feelings. They just are unskilled with putting these feelings into words and unfamiliar with the need to do so. When men do express their feelings in words, they speak in a curious way.

Men Talk in Cycles

Before I discuss the verbal cycling that men do, let's see how women talk about their feelings. Women talk about feelings in a direct way, which means that they speak directly about what they feel and use the word *feel* frequently. They also use a number of other feeling-based words, particularly the provocative word *hurt*. When a woman expresses herself about something that has an emotional impact on her, she is likely to say exactly what the feeling was and elaborate on the feeling. If a woman is emotionally hurt, she will say that she is hurt. If she is angry or afraid, she will use the terms anger and fear or some cognates of those emotional words. There are some dangers with women expressing their feelings directly and fluently, but for the most part women "tell it like it is" when they feel something. Women who have not learned about the differences between men and women expressing feelings, can be quite overwhelming to any man trying to listen to them when they are speaking their feelings.

Men do not tell it like it is, at least when they are talking about their feelings. They would much rather talk *around* their feelings than talk *about* them. They talk in what I call *cycles*. Cycling in talk is not the same as talking in circles, although many women think that the men in their lives talk in circles, meaning that they don't get to the point quickly. You have to listen very carefully to a man when he speaks in order to know what he really feels. His feelings are entwined in his words but rarely are men direct in talking about what they feel. If a man is talking about something concrete, or an idea, a theory, a plan, or even some form of play, he can be quite direct and to the point, but when it comes to feelings, men are anything but direct. They talk in cycles. Let me explain. Imagine a man feels something that is important to him, and he wants to communicate this feeling.

- He has a feeling, but he doesn't have the words to express this feeling.
- He knows what he feels but isn't sure how to put this feeling into words. Perhaps he has a very intense feeling but doesn't have words at his disposal that could communicate the intensity of this feeling.
- Nevertheless, he wants to communicate this feeling, so he begins to speak.
- He says something that is marginally in the arena of his feelings but not too close.
- If he gets too close to his feelings, he knows immediately that he has said something that vaguely reflects what he feels, but he is also aware that his words have missed most of the mark.
- He halts in his expression of feeling for a moment to collect himself. He recalls what he has said and is not satisfied with it.
- He goes silent for a moment, but he can't stay silent too long because he will lose the stage and any hope of communicating his feelings, so, he jabbers on for a moment.
- He might say something that is quite tangential to his real feeling, but keeps talking to keep his inertia going.
- Quite often a man might mumble or grunt or vocalize something that is nonverbal. When he is vocalizing without making sense, he is trying to find words that adequately communicate his feelings.

This is the end of the first step in a man's cycling when trying to verbally express a feeling: mumbling, back-stepping, rephrasing, and repeating himself. The man may be very passionate about what he is saying, but it is unlikely that he can adequately express his passion. Andrew is a deeply passionate man, deeply loving, reasonably intelligent, and very physical, especially demonstrated in his history of success in athletics and his propensity towards sex. One time when he was in men's group therapy, he said something like:

> I don't know. I just don't know. I feel . . . I feel . . . deeply about Samantha. No, that isn't right. Yes, it is right. I do feel deeply, but I feel all kinds of things. I just can't seem to say what I feel. Like, well, like . . . I feel a lot of feelings but they don't make sense. Maybe I love her. I think I love her. Yes, certainly I love her. But I don't know if I *love* her. I used to love her. But recently, I don't seem to have the . . . I don't know . . . the love maybe . . . that I used to have. I'm not saying this very well. I just can't put words

to these feelings. I should just shut up and let someone else talk.
I feel confused and lost.

What is Andrew trying to say? His feelings. But he doesn't have a set of words that does any kind of adequacy to his feelings. Indeed, he may have mixed feelings, or perhaps feelings that seem contradictory, yet he certainly feels quite deeply. He just can't find a package of words that does justice to his feelings. He is not alone.

My friend Frank is deeply passionate about his daughter's volleyball progress. He loves his daughter, Robin, and is hopeful that she can be successful in her chosen sport. It may be true that Robin is not as passionate about her volleyball career as her father is. Frank wants to express this feeling of passion, so he says something like, "Robin needs to practice more to get good at setting. She'll never be a hitter because she's too small." This kind of statement certainly sounds like some kind of criticism to most people who would hear this statement, but what Frank is feeling very deeply and trying to say is that he loves his daughter, hopes she succeeds, and fears that she will be disappointed and hurt in her volleyball career. He might very well be quite overwhelmed by his love for her and his passion for her success in life. But what he has said does not do justice to this love and passion. In fact, it probably communicates that he is criticizing and correcting Robin more than loving her and encouraging her. In fact, Robin says that he is *always* critical of her.

When Frank's wife is listening, she also interprets Frank as criticizing their daughter. She doesn't see that Frank is doing his best to love his daughter, build her self-esteem, and help her succeed in life. In this situation Frank could easily feel insecure about what he feels and what he said. If his wife says something corrective to Frank, it is likely that he will feel hurt, then transfer this hurt into anger or avoidance. After Frank has spoken what he thinks is an encouraging and loving statement, he will know immediately that his statement did not sit well with his daughter and his wife. What does he do then? He will go silent and sulk, or he will get angry and yell. He will retreat from the conversation and may leave the room. He is in the very difficult position of having great love for his daughter, having great desire for her success in life, and having great disappointment that his family did not hear what he *felt*. They heard what he *said*.

If the first stage of a man's cycling with expressing feelings is saying something, the second stage of cycling is a kind of retreat because he realizes that he hasn't adequately communicated his feelings. Realizing that he has bumbled his attempt of communicating how he feels, he retreats into conversation that is tangential to his feelings and may actually be the opposite of his feelings. Frank might then say something like, "Robin can do whatever she likes. Maybe she doesn't like volleyball. Volleyball isn't the most important thing in the world, anyway." If he says something like this, he has contradicted himself, and actually moved away from his true feelings of love, joy, and hope. For most men, however, there isn't much of a vocabulary for such feelings.

If Frank were exact and articulate about his feelings about his daughter, he would say something like, "I love Robin with a love that is deeper than I can imagine. She is the light of my life. Sometimes, she is more important than the rest of my family. In fact, if I were honest, I would probably say that she is my favorite child, and sometimes more important than my wife. I love her so much that I wish nothing less than the sky for her, complete success, and great joy. I see her as having great potential in volleyball. I think she could be great at the sport, and if she worked at it, she could experience this greatness, which would ultimately bring her great joy." No man in all history has said such things, unless he has slowly and painfully learned to do so. But Frank doesn't have this package of words in his vocabulary, much less the wisdom to say it. He doesn't have the balls to speak his feelings and then accept the unavoidable misunderstanding that his words have implied. He is in a tough spot: he has spoken his feelings but not communicated his feelings. He still feels love and hope for his daughter, but he now knows that he has miscommunicated his love. If he has a pair, he would apologize for his having hurt his daughter, and probably also his wife. Men cycle in their expression of feelings all the time, whether in intimate conversations like Frank is trying to have with Robin, with profound matters of life and death, or of trivial day-to-day feelings like sports.

Cycling in male conversation about deep personal feelings can continue unabated for several minutes as the man tries, often vainly, to find the correct words to express his feelings. This cycling can be very frustrating to him as well as to his listeners because much of what he says doesn't make rational sense, and his words often communicate something entirely different from what he feels. In an ideal situation the man is aware of his cycling, has control of the cycling, allows himself to cycle knowing that if he can only continue speaking, he will eventually arrive at what he wants to say. Unfortunately, his frustration gets to him and he gives up, or his listener becomes frustrated and interrupts the cycling process. In either case the man is left with a large amount of feeling that has not been expressed and the listener is left confused or irritated by his verbal cycling without evident meaning.

After my heart event I had many feelings, hope and uncertainty among them. I also had many emotions, certainly joy (because I was alive) and sadness (for having had some difficult experiences). I understand the business of feelings pretty well, and I am also blessed with a wife who understands feelings, understands male cycling in feelings, and understands me in particular. I went through many cycles while I migrated through these feelings, some of which I expressed to Deb and a select number of friends, but I kept most of my feelings to myself, especially sadness and fear. I suspect most men who have had major medical difficulties have done the same.

This whole experience provided me with opportunities to hear how men felt about my having had a heart attack. I received many well wishes, prayers, and encouraging words from men but never did any man express his real feelings about the fact that I almost died. A chiropractor friend of mine laughingly said to me, "If you ever try to die again, I'm going to adjust the hell out of you." Other men have spoken tangentially, teasingly, and off-handedly about the heart attack, sometimes telling stories of other people they know who have had such events in their lives. I know that all these men loved me in this situation, but no man ever said that directly. I just felt it. A woman might not understand how men "love" in this cycling, tangential, teasing way.

One of the more interesting encounters I had after the heart event came just a couple days ago from a neighbor who called me up just after a snowstorm that we had. The conversation went something like this:

George: So, how're ya' doin'?

Ron: I'm good, George. How're you?

George: I thought you might need some help with the snow.

Ron: Well, thanks, George, but I pretty much got it. Deb did most of the heavy lifting on the sidewalk, and I used the lawn tractor with a snow blade to clean off the driveway.

George: Well, I just want to be neighborly. Thought you might need some help. I saw Deb out there on the sidewalk, but I didn't see you.

Ron: Ya. She did all the sidewalk in the front of the house.

George: Well, you let me know if you need any help. Just trying to be neighborly.

Ron: Thanks a lot, George.

George and Ron: (engaged in a bit more conversation about the snow, the new year coming, and a bit of sports.)

This is a good example of how men talk about their feelings. Both George and I talked tangentially about our feelings and engaged in verbal cycling. If we had been more direct in our expression of feelings, the conversation would have been more like this:

> *George*: Hey, Ron. I am very concerned about you since Deb told me about the heart attack. I love you, man, let me help you with the snow. You've been so kind to me over the years, especially when my son died last summer. I just felt compelled to return the favor. No, that isn't right. I'm not returning the favor. I care for you and I want you to live. You know that many men die of heart attacks shoveling snow. Ron, you're important to me and I don't want to lose you as a friend.

> *Ron*: I love you too, George. And my simple gesture with the tragedy in your life last summer was only because I love you and felt bad for you. I felt compelled to be with you and do anything that I could do to help you through that difficult time of life. As for your willingness to plow snow, George, I appreciate it deeply. In fact, I will remember this kind gesture of calling me up and asking if I needed help with the shoveling. It's more than the snow. It's a love thing. I know you love me and it means a great deal to me.

I have known George for twenty-five years, but I have never told him that I love him, nor has he said anything like that to me. We know that we love each other. We have loved each other when we have been doing some kind of house project, when we visited about the Packers, or talked about politics. We don't particularly need to express love with words. But I know his calling me up was a gesture motivated by his feelings of love for me. This is an example of how men express their feelings. George would gladly express his feelings of love for me by coming over and shoveling snow and might actually feel pretty good about it, but he would never express his feelings of love in words.

Men don't need feeling words all the time, but it is occasionally very rewarding to hear men say something explicit about how they feel, which we will discuss later when we make practical suggestions as to how men can more effectively express their feelings in words.

Summary

- Words are an essential element in communication for all people.
- Words are not the basic way men engage the world.
- Men prefer to communicate in some kind of action.

- Men need to communicate themselves in action effectively.
- The male brain is different from the female brain in regards to the use of words, particularly emotional words.
- Men tend to talk in "cycles" when they communicate emotions.
- Men need to learn how to communicate with words, especially when they express their feelings.

CHAPTER 5

Men and Work

A MAN CANNOT TRULY succeed in life without succeeding in work. Men can do without alcohol, they can do without women, and they can even do without words for the most part, but men cannot do without work. Work is more important than wine, words, or women. For wine, words, and women to function adequately in a man's life, he has to have work that is successful, but what is success in work? More importantly, what is "work"? If I had it my way, I would have men work first, talk second, relate to women third, and drink fourth. But this is not how it usually happens. In this chapter we will be discussing how a man can find work, how he can enjoy work, how he can succeed at work... and then most importantly, make his work enhance his relationships with words, women, and wine.

Work, Job, Profession, and Life's Work

We began to deal with the business of profession in chapter four, where we dealt with words. Recall that I use the term "profession" in a very broad way, distinguishing profession from job. A job is something that a man does to make money. A job is generally something that you *do* out of necessity. A profession is something you *create* out of passion. It is ideal to have a job that is also your profession, but creating such a scenario in life is difficult. Too often, men get caught in looking for a job, not understanding the need to have a profession. A profession is not found outside of oneself. It is found inside of oneself. I believe there is a living profession inside every man. So much emphasis is on making money, having status, and creating security that men often fail to find work that reflects their inner selves and end up settling for a job. If a man seeks work primarily for money, status, or security rather than following his passion, he will not be happy in his work.

Note that the word *profession* has within it the word *profess*. This is the key to finding one's profession: *to profess*. When a man is professing during his work, he is not just working. He is alive, productive, creative, and purposeful in his work. It is much more than a job that he goes to. It is much more than something he does. The man's profession is what he gives to the world. It is his best offer to the world. A man needs to profess to *find* his life's work, profess *in* his work, and profess *about* his work.

Ideally, a young man has opportunity to talk about what he might like to do in life, dream about it, read about it, and watch other people doing some kind of work that seems meaningful and right for him. Children naturally imagine, dream, think, and sometimes talk about their musings. They often talk about what they want to do and what they want to become. Childhood dreams and fantasies often hold the key to what a child might really want to do in life. You might be able to simply watch a boy play, how he plays, what he plays with, and with whom he plays, and if you watch carefully, you might even see his possible profession.

When I was about seven, I wanted to fly to the moon. Stimulated to such thinking by my scientific brother, I set about to build a spaceship in the backyard. To her credit my mother encouraged me in this endeavor. My spaceship was composed entirely of scrap wood hammered together in some fashion. I am sure that my parents watched with amusement as I went about building my spaceship. I even recruited my second-grade teacher, Miss Current (teachers didn't have first names in the fifties), who agreed to co-pilot my spaceship. I remember working on this ship for many days and nights, but I don't remember what happened to my spaceship. Evidently, I finished what I needed to do and went on to other fantasies. The opportunity I had to explore, i.e., *profess* my interest in becoming an astronaut allowed me to engage in the thinking, dreaming, and doing part of this fantasy. I finished my spaceship because I was encouraged to do so. While I still would love to travel in space someday, I have no regrets about moving beyond this early fantasy, this early professing, because the very act of fantasizing gave me the balls to *think* more deeply and *dream* broadly about what I might want to *do* for a profession.

Dreaming to Doing

Some people are dreamers and some are doers. Ideally, a man finds a way to dream first and do second, but that's not how it usually works. Rather, men tend go with their natural tendency to dream *or* to do. I am a doer by nature, while Deb is a dreamer by nature. Both of us have matured beyond simple doing or simple dreaming. The mistakes I have made in my life have almost universally occurred by having "done" too quickly without enough dreaming to make the doing work right. The good news for me, however, is that America in general and school specifically are both oriented towards doing. As I continue to mature in life I see the necessity of dreaming, imagining, considering, or musing before I jump right into some project. People who are dreamers generally have a harder time in much of American society, especially school, and often in work. We wrote extensively about doers and dreamers in our book *What's Your Temperament*.

I have been working with an eighteen-year-old man who came into my office with his mother's handprint on his back. She was very frustrated with him because he wasn't progressing in school as she thought he should. Furthermore, he was smoking a bit of pot, spending what his mother thought was an inordinate amount of time engaging in sexual activity with his girlfriend, and he didn't seem to have any kind of understanding that he would soon need to do something in life. Kevin had talked quite a bit about taking his own life, albeit in a rather philosophical way. Mom wondered if he was truly suicidal or just talking about it. I met with him a couple of times and recognized immediately that Kevin was ideational, imaginary, creative, visual, and musical. In a nutshell, he was very "right-brained." Unfortunately, typical school does not reward right- brained activities like music, art, ideas, and creativity as much as it does the left-brained activities of reading, writing, and math. I determined that his "suicidal thoughts" were the best way he could communicate that he didn't seem to fit into the world. He didn't fit into the academic world. He didn't fit into the typical male world of sports. He didn't fit into the geek world. He did fit into the music world, but he hadn't worked hard enough to see whether music could be his profession.

Kevin and I spent a fair amount of time trying to find out what his profession might be by looking at what his passions were. At the beginning of our third session together he told me that he had found out what he wanted to be. He wanted to be a film editor. He declared that he wanted to go to a media school to learn to make movies after he graduated from high school. I thought the idea was a good one, but I knew that there would be some important hurdles he would need to jump in order to be successful in that profession. I just listened to him talk about his dream and encouraged it. A couple of days later I got a desperate phone call from him. He had found out that his 1.73 GPA in high school would keep him from getting into media school. When I had a chance to see him face to face, we began to look seriously at how he might be able to jump this hurdle, but it meant a lot more work than he was willing to do. Kevin and I have a long way to go.

Kevin is just at the stage of dreaming about his profession. I don't know at this point whether he will continue in his current interest to go into film-making, return to his passion of music, or work in a local convenience store. Perhaps filmmaking is more of a fantasy than a passion-based dream. At this point in his life Kevin isn't mature enough yet to know what he should do in life, much less how he can get there. Regardless, his possible fantasy of being a filmmaker deserves to be professed so that he can come to clarity about the whole matter of work that is so central for a man. Before we can find his profession he will most certainly have to have some kind of hands-on experience in the world of work. He will have to *do* something. This will not be easy for Kevin because he is much the dreamer and not much the doer. My hope is that I can help him through the necessary dreaming stage and talking stage so that we can find a way for him to actually do something. I wish that North America had more apprenticeships and fewer universities for people like Kevin who would probably do much better learning a profession by watching and doing than by reading and writing.

While it is hard for dreamers to find a way to actually do something in life, it is equally problematic for doers to find their profession. I know of a man who is studying to be an accountant "because they make a lot of money." Another man has a job that he hates, despite the fact that the company really likes his work. Yet another man who is a trained nurse makes nearly $300,000 per year promoting pharmaceuticals. America in general and school specifically don't help us men find a way to dream first, do second, and then find ways to adapt to the world in some kind of meaningful profession.

Doing something is very important for a man on his path to find his profession. If a man can experience some of the activities of a profession that seem exciting and stimulating, he will quickly discover whether this is a good profession for him. This experimenting, practicing, or trying out is what helps a man discover whether his "dream" is just a fantasy or if it is the stimulation towards a passion-based profession. If a man has a true understanding of what it will take to be a film editor, he will be much more likely to go through the hoops necessary to enter that profession. My building a spaceship helped me move beyond that early fantasy of becoming an astronaut. My older daughter was convinced that she wanted to be a jet pilot, a desire inflamed after watching Tom Cruise in the 1980s movie *Top*

Gun. She talked about being a jet pilot, and it seemed that such was going to be her destiny. So, Deb and I bought her a flying lesson to help her see what it was really like. She took a bit of ground school with some other students, and then had her first in-flight lesson. That was her last flight lesson. She was scared to death, especially when the instructor turned the controls over to her when she was several hundred feet in the air. No more dreams of jet flying for her. That was the last time I heard her wanting to fly jets, although I heard many more professional aspirations over the years, including being an actor, a drummer, and a professional ice skater. Deb and I did our best to help her through these, but this is no easy task for anyone, much less for a man who is a dreamer by nature.

This physical kind of professing, as I call it, needs to take the form of actually doing some of the work involved in the profession. I have had many people interested in doing psychotherapy, many of whom I have trained and supervised in my office. The essence of training in psychotherapy is to be a patient in psychotherapy first, then to participate with a competent therapist second, and then try one's hand at sitting with a patient with some supervision. Young psychotherapist-wannabes think that most people choose to see a therapist wanting to discover who they are and where they are in life. Interns learn fairly quickly that much of the work in a psychology office is dealing with people who want no more than to complain about their partners, ex-partners, bosses, mothers, or children. It takes many months, and sometimes years, for people to realize that dealing successfully with life is looking at oneself first and then at the external factors with a deeper self-understanding. I have had more than one intern decide against going into psychotherapy after realizing that it takes a good deal of patience to become a good therapist. It means listening to the likes of Kevin being seriously depressed when he can't pass math one day, hearing him overjoyed to have found his profession the next day, and being unsure of what to do the third day.

Professing by doing is ideally done in adolescence, and perhaps even a bit in childhood. It's too bad that we don't have more on-the-job learning in the form of an apprenticeship so that adolescents could really see what a certain profession is like before they spend five or more years training to do it. My father had a true musical gift of playing the piano, so much so that a professor in college said that he could be a concert pianist if he worked on it. Unfortunately, his mother wanted him to be a doctor. His mother also wanted one of his brothers to be a lawyer and another to be a pastor. Both of my uncles ended up in prison while in their professions because neither of them really wanted to be what Grandma Johnson wanted them to be. My dad forfeited his music to attend medical school but dropped out after he fainted in his first surgery class. My dad did continue to play the piano brilliantly for his own pleasure but found his profession through chemistry for the bulk of his adult career. Boys need to dream, to think, and then to do something that is driven by their passion, but few boys have this opportunity to try things out and discover the difference between a fantasy and a passion-based dream.

Most men don't find their life's work because they have not had hands-on experience in a profession that interests them. Too often, a man gets a job before he thinks much about finding a profession. It takes time and *work* for a man to find his profession. Many men have had more than one job before they find their profession and their life's work. I worked at a hot dog stand, worked in a hardware store, detasseled corn, moved furniture, and sold vacuum cleaners door-to-door before I entered my first profession, which was ministry. This first profession led me to my current profession. It is rare that a man finds his profession early enough in his life to truly enjoy it for the duration of his life.

We attended a concert last week and were simply blown away with the passionate skill of the pianist. This young man began engaging his musical passion when he was four years old and according to the bio in the program, never questioned where it would lead him. Some men know that they will become a doctor or lab tech from early ages. Deb knew she would go into therapy when she was thirteen years old. I didn't know that until I was twenty-four. Most men don't have this clear direction. They need the opportunity to have an idea, like an exciting interest in spaceship building, painting, or movie editing to come to realize that they are just stepping stones to what will become their passion-based profession. Unfortunately men who have multiple jobs are too often seen as irresponsible, or lacking "direction." Remember José whom we discussed in chapter two, who was afraid to leave his current job because of how it might look on his resume. José needs the balls to risk the disapproval of quitting another job so he can continue his passage towards his passion-based profession or to stay with it as a means towards an end. It is possible for a man to dislike his job but stay with it while he finds a way to discover and enter his profession. Sometimes, a man just needs to make money so that he can get on with his profession.

Making Money

Making money is absolutely necessary for a man, but there are huge dangers in working primarily to make money: having too much money and not having enough money. As we have noted, a man needs to work to serve the world in some way. If a man is doing something that is intrinsically valuable to him, it will be valuable to the world. If he is happy and content in his work, he will have enough money, status, and security in life. Men who have found themselves in jobs that they don't like but where they make a lot of money have a hard time seeing what work really should be for a man. Men who never seem to have enough money often live in dreams of having some perfect job that makes millions of dollars but can't seem to work at a less than perfect job to pay their bills while working towards entering their profession.

I recall one summer day when the young man who worked on our lawn tractor came to repair a broken belt and with great joy professed that we would need to find another repairman because he had just been accepted for an apprenticeship as a heavy equipment operator, something he had dreamed of since he was a little boy playing with his dump trucks in the backyard. Good for this young man! He spent several years doing small maintenance jobs while pursuing his passion. I have mentioned that I have been training a couple of budding therapists who have had "good jobs" for twenty-five years but neither being satisfied in their work. Now at about age fifty they have taken the plunge to do what they have come to love after having sat in my office as patients off and on for several years. They have been courageous in these difficult choices. Too bad no one encouraged them to seek and find their dreams earlier in their lives. Better late than never.

I just started seeing a forty-year-old who came to my office because of a lifelong depression. While bright, capable, and a man of integrity, he has not found a way to be himself, profess himself, and succeed in the world of work. He opened an acupuncture practice just before COVID began, did well for a while but then floundered. He had previously done a variety of jobs, usually semi-professional, before the acupuncture venture. Then he found himself in the position of making a great deal of money by being an IT consultant. He works for himself contracting with various companies, which leads to his working seventy or eighty hours a week. He tolerates his work and admits that he has not attended to his children, his wife, or anything else in his life. He was born and raised in semi-poverty and determined never to be poor himself. Now, he is not poor, quite the opposite, but he is very unhappy. He recently told me that his high income has not cured his unhappiness and he would "rather die than go on like this." We are slowly dealing with the suffering he had in childhood and the ways he compensated, including his drive for money.

From Doing to Talking

A man needs to talk to about his work with someone who actually cares about him and is interested in learning more about him. Miss Current's willingness to be my spaceship co-pilot encouraged me in the early professing of myself. If someone truly cares about a man, that person will be interested in the man's profession and life's work. Communicating oneself about one's work, however, is no easy task. It means much more than saying what you did, how many clients you saw, or what kind of trash you picked up during the day. Talking about your profession and your day's work means how you *felt* and what you *thought* as much as what you *did*. It will include successes and failures. It will include things you like and things you don't like. Talking about your profession will be a reflection of who you are as a man.

A couple I have been seeing for some time is composed of a successful accountant and a successful independent contractor. The wife reports that she has no hesitancy to talk to her husband about her work as an accountant, "So why is he so quiet about his work? Why won't he share with me about his day?" The man is not particularly good about talking about his work. The man wonders why his wife might be interested in his buying, building, refurbishing, and selling houses. "Why would she be interested? It's just about hammers and nails," he said once. I tried to explain that his work, his profession, wasn't about hammers and nails so much as it was about how he saw a possible project, looked at how he might make a house a better house, and what joy that brought to him. It's still too easy for him to answer his wife's question, "How was work?" with "Fine."

Learning to talk about one's work is very difficult for most men. First, it is hard for men to talk about anything that is emotionally significant to them. We studied this phenomenon earlier. A man has to be lucky enough, privileged enough, and encouraged enough to find his life's work. Then, he has to work hard enough to engage in his life's work. Talking about his work is another whole level of development. I believe that if men were first able to find and do their life's work and learn how to communicate about it, they would engender real interest from their spouses, families, and friends. There is nothing more interesting to me than hearing about a man's work when he is passionate about it. Recently, I met a scientist by chance who was working on re-myelinating nerves in the human body. This is very close to me because my older daughter suffered from multiple sclerosis. If we could re-myelinate nerves, we could cure MS. I talked to this man for not more than five minutes, but these minutes were very interesting to me partly because of my personal interest in his field of science but also because of his passion for his work.

Most men naturally profess about their work by doing, not by talking, because it is generally easier for men to demonstrate their life's work than to talk about it. How would my good neighbor Lonnie talk about his work of roofing and siding to someone and communicate the meaning that his work has for him? I have had the unique opportunity of working with Lonnie on several projects reconstructing some of our hundred-year-old farmhouse. When I watched Lonnie work on the roof, as I have also watched him work on windows and tree-trimming on our property, I see Lonnie professing his life's work. It is a beautiful thing to see. I see his pride in good work, his efficiency, his knowledge, and his kinesthetic intelligence demonstrated in these various projects. It is a work of art. Several times over the years Lonnie has stepped back for a moment and commented about how good the trees look now that they have been trimmed, how good the roof looks, or how good the windows fit into the house. He is not looking for a compliment. He is appreciating his work. He is talking about his work. He is professing himself.

Another man I know was a lifelong painter, not a canvas artist, mind you, but a painter of houses. He often talked with pride about "going to the wall," which meant his painting walls in a new house. I don't think there is any real difference between Lonnie's artistry in roofing and Jeremy's "going to the wall". Both Lonnie and Jeremy are good examples of men who, by their nature, are "doers" but more importantly, are able to profess themselves by speaking about their work. For many men there needs to be a balance of professing by talking and professing by doing. It is wonderful when a man can verbally communicate about his work, but talking about work is not natural for most men. The therapists I am training learn by watching me first and then by experimenting the trade of therapy by speaking to me after a session. They absolutely must speak of their experiences for the experience to lead them on towards their own profession. They need to talk about their work.

While watching and doing is basically a man's way of learning and communicating, we men need to add to that physical communication by talking about our work, especially with the important women in our lives. A man will not be truly successful in his communication with women until he learns to talk about his work. If he has the chance to demonstrate his work, all the better but most men don't have this opportunity. If a man is dissatisfied with his work because he has a job rather than a profession, it behooves a man to talk to the woman in his life about his dilemma. But this asks the woman to silently listen rather than suggesting what he should do.

If a woman can stand back and see what a man has done in his work, augmented by what he says about his work, she will have a much better chance at achieving a connection that can serve both the man and the woman. For the most part, our society is not set up for this opportunity because most men "go to" work rather than work in the presence of the women in their lives. A woman might be able to observe firsthand how a man works as a baker, preaches a sermon in church, or repairs a roof, but how can a woman see a man profess his work if he is working as a CIA operative or working in a sterile chemical laboratory? If it is impossible for a woman to see a man at his work, it is largely the responsibility of the man to translate his visual-physical communication into verbal communication. You can't expect a woman to really understand your work, whether it is pleasant or unpleasant, by saying nothing about what you do at work, just complaining about your work, or coming home after work to immediately grab a beer and watch ESPN.

I had a brief conversation with the garbage collector man whom I mentioned earlier, the man who loves his work despite the apparently distasteful nature of his profession. I caught him for a moment just before Thanksgiving and gave him a small tip. This satisfied trash collector took off his glove, reached out his hand to me for a handshake, and then continued to talk to me about how it was wonderful to collect trash in our small town compared to a couple of other small towns not ten miles away. We met in those moments. There we were, a psychologist and a trash collector, having an intimate conversation standing over my recyclables. I hope he has a wife or a companion who can understand him the way I did in those moments. When a woman actually understands a man, particularly about his work, she will foster the communication that will lead to connection. When man and woman are connected, this connection serves both the man and the woman. She feels a security based on a deeper understanding of the man in her life. Seeing a man doing his life's work is the best way to see the man. Hearing about his work, which hopefully is also his life's passion, is even better. If a woman has the opportunity to see the man's work and hear about the man's work, she then has the unique opportunity and responsibility to encourage him and challenge him in his life's work.

My wife and I have the tremendous opportunity of plying the same trade, although we actually operate quite differently with the people we see in our offices. Furthermore, Deb sees mostly women, while I see mostly men. Because we do essentially the same work, we have opportunity to talk about our work, our patients, our successes, our failures, our questions, and our possible answers. This is something we do most nights. Deb has been my best encourager and my best critic for the work I do. Her encouragement has set the stage for her challenge to my work. I could not hear her suggestions and challenges if I had not heard her encouragement for many years previously, encouragement based on understanding me. If women understood the men in their lives, overall communication and mutual appreciation would dramatically improve. There would be fewer divorces. There would be less unfaithfulness. There would be less need to engage in behaviors that tend to become addictive. The essence of a man talking about his work is in the value that he sees in it.

The Value of Life's Work

When a man's profession is at the center of his life, all the other elements of life should naturally flow from his work. Work is not more important than family, play, love, or other responsibilities that he has in life. Rather, work and profession need to be established in a man's life so that he can do the other essential things in life. If he is satisfied in work, he will have a sense of personal grounding, personal confidence, and personal value. The problem for most men, and ultimately for their relationships, is that work never becomes the center of their lives from which they can gain the personal grounding and confidence necessary to live beyond work.

When a man values his work, he values himself. If he values himself, he will value other people, he will value humankind in general, and he will value the world. Valuing oneself is not selfish. From a theistic point of view, self-value is recognition that God has created you as a good being. From a non-theistic point of view, self-value is a recognition of the goodness of all human beings and the natural value of the world. However valuable, productive, creative, or meaningful work might be, a man has to be aware of things that dissuade him from his work.

Challenges to His Work

This feeling of personal value in his work needs to be very solid because there will be many distracters to his work and potential challenges to the value of his work. If a man has found his life's work and enjoys his life's work, he will be both admired and envied. Usually, this envy is an appreciation for him and his good fortune to be doing what he is passionate about. This kind of envy is good because it may lead others to seek out their own passionate work. Jealously, unlike envy, is always due to someone's sense of inferiority. Whether a man feels someone's appreciation of his work or one's jealousy of his work, he shouldn't base his profession and his professing on what other people think of him or his work. If a man can hear both appreciation and criticism of his work, he can profit from both knowing what is so cogently said in *Desiderata*: "Always there will be greater and lesser persons than yourself." If you are solid in your profession, you will be able to discern both the truth and the error in someone else's perspective of what you do and even occasionally find a careful way to dismiss criticism that is toxic or otherwise damaging. The key here is for the man to value himself first, his work second, and all else third so he can always improve in all aspects of his life, particularly his relationships.

Genuine self-value and genuine self-love always lead to value and love for others. The feeling of personal value that comes from a man doing his life's work ultimately leads to value for other people. *Doing* one's life's work is initially about the man himself. *Continuing* in one's life's work becomes increasingly about the benefit it brings other people. The value that a man's profession and life's work brings to others is not more important than the value it brings him; rather, it is the natural result of bringing value to oneself.

From Self to Work to People

Any profession or work of passion can provide a stepping stone from self-value to value of others and humankind in general. It is just as valuable to the world to be a good therapist as it is to be a good trash collector, art dealer, or store manager if one's purpose is to profess himself and serve people. Everyone who does their work with their soul is helping others. As I write, Deb just texted me from the Jeep dealer who is working on her car's failed brakes. Those mechanics are certainly in the helping profession. We had hoped to take her Jeep up north today but the verdict was "it is not safe to drive!" Obviously, they have served humankind in diagnosing and repairing failed brakes. Once a man has succeeded in life, there are other important things to do in life. He then needs to get beyond success in work into success in life at large, success being defined as doing something that is good for you and good for the world. When that happens, a man has the liberty to move laterally. He might even continue to serve the world by changing professions.

Finishing Life's Work

Life's work is not necessarily for a lifetime. Life's work means that the man gives himself to his profession until the work becomes the center of his life. Then, as we have just discussed, a man moves from this work center to a broader interest and concern for other people and other aspects of a life. If a man truly finds his life's work, prepares himself for it, enters it, and succeeds in it, he may find that he actually *finishes* his life's work and then has the privilege to go on to other things that are equally satisfying. Finishing life's work means that he has achieved, produced, or created enough in his profession to feel the joy that work is meant to bring to a man. The keynote of being finished in a particular profession is feeling a sense of accomplishment and perhaps a certain decreasing interest in the profession. Lanny, an eighty-three-year-old man, was very satisfied in his profession as an astrophysics professor. He particularly liked mentoring PhD students in their work. Now, he is working to find what it means to have had this wonderful professional experience and find a different meaning in life. He has found a new passion in helping high school physics students understand the subject.

Finishing could mean that the doctor has finished doctoring and no longer feels a passion in the profession, or the carpenter has built enough houses or kitchen cabinets to fulfill him in this profession. Finishing a profession doesn't necessarily mean leaving the profession entirely, but it means that other things in life become more important. When a man finishes his profession, or begins to feel that finishing, he needs to look beyond what he has done. Many men actually finish a profession but do not recognize and accept this finishing phenomenon. Finishing a profession does not mean that a man sits around all day reading magazines or plays golf all the time. It means that the man needs to transition from one life's work to a different life's work. This transition out of one's initial life's work can be painful because of the work a man has put into it, but if a man can accept the sadness that comes with moving into a different pattern of life, his sadness and pain will end, so that he is left with nostalgia about his former work. I am trying to help Lanny find, feel, and finish the sadness of having completed his former profession while he is learning to mentor high school students. It takes balls to make this transition, but it is ultimately valuable to the man and probably to the people around him. In order to transition from one profession to another, a man needs to be grounded in his first profession.

Remember, *it is not the profession that grounds the man. It is the man who grounds himself through the profession.* Perhaps Jim can develop his lifelong desire to paint seascapes, Mark might be able to start running marathons to raise money for the local shelter, Bill might be able to work part time in a daycare because of his passion for young children, or Sam might be able to learn how to repair old clocks. I know of a man who has been successful in his career of money management but now in his retirement has taken up restoring old Volkswagens. Other men have found that they are able to profess themselves in some kind of volunteer work. I regularly see a couple of older men volunteering in thrift stores seemingly quite happily. I have no doubt that should I ask, they would report that having been successful in other professions, they have found new ways of serving the world. Unfortunately, many men are not happy in their work.

When a Man Is Not Happy in His Work

Most men are not passionate in their life's work and as a result are not happy in their work. There is no simple answer to this problem and I don't suggest one. I believe there is a way for every man to find his profession, enjoy his profession, and ultimately finish his profession, but it takes hard work, and it takes balls. It takes balls to admit that one is not happy in his work, it takes balls to believe that it is possible to find his profession, and it takes balls to do something about it. Let's start with the admitting part of this sequence.

If a man is not happy in his work, he has to admit it to himself. As simple as this is to say, it is hard for men to do. I just talked to a man who was mandated to come to my office because of his routine tardiness. As he talked, it became obvious that he was deficient in all four W's (women, wine, words, and work). Asked if he liked his work, he said, "It's a job." It is a job he has had for a year or two and it (barely) pays the bills, allowing Nick to live "paycheck to paycheck." Needless to say, this job has been unrewarding for him. As I listened to Nick's story, I learned that he never liked school (hence another W: words, i.e., reading and writing), that he had been unsuccessfully married twice (another W: women). The reason he came to see me, namely his tardiness issue, was probably the least of his worries. I learned pretty quickly that he had a problem with the fourth "W": wine. He got drunk pretty much every night, evidently to cope with disliking his work. It would be good if I could help Nick through all of these W's, perhaps starting with words and the probable shaming he had in school because he never liked reading and writing. Then I would hope to deal a bit with the women part of his life but that will wait until he can "profess himself" at work. I might also need to see if his apparent unhappiness at work is really about work or whether it is about how he sees life.

Admitting that a job is a dead end is an emotionally difficult thing to do because it involves facing the sadness of being stuck and not experiencing one's passion. Many men who are dissatisfied with their work have a very gloomy view of the future, namely feeling hopeless. Instead of facing the feeling of hopelessness and finding a way to be hopeful, most men look to money, family, bills, children, and other obligations as the reason for staying in a less than desired job. Admitting to a feeling is hard for all men, but admitting it to someone else is twice as hard. When men do say something about a job they don't like, they tend to complain: complain about the boss, complain about the coworkers, or complain about the money they are making.

If a man can find a way through all the cultural resistance and his own reticence of admitting to feeling sad, he will have to find a way through the even more difficult task of feeling afraid. When a man allows himself to admit that he is in the wrong job, he will most *naturally* feel sad, but he might be more aware of the feeling of fear associated with being out of work. Recall from chapters two and three that the prevention of both fear and anger is in the ability to feel sad first, that followed by some action. A man might be afraid that he will never find something that suits his nature, and afraid of the even deeper failure of being entirely out of work. Owning up to feeling dissatisfied at work naturally leads to an initial understanding of what he loves in life, which then leads to what he can do in life that is meaningful. If he can reach that point, he has reached into the *love* portion of his make-up. Something almost magical happens when a man finds this sadness in his work and rides it to its conclusion: he finds a very important part of himself—the desire to serve the world. He finds that he is a man, like all men, who loves much.

Once a man can admit to feeling unhappy at work, feel the sadness that comes along with being unhappy, and know that he has some kind of love inside of him that wants to show itself in work, he is ready for the second task: find ways to believe in himself, believe that he can find his profession, and somehow serve the world in this profession. When he finishes feeling sad about being in the wrong job, he will have found the joy of *wanting* to be in the right job and ultimately find his life's work. He might just find a part of his soul. *Belief in oneself is not manufactured; it is found.* This belief that I can do my life's work is intrinsic to every man, but you probably can't do this soul-searching alone. You need a good partner and probably a good therapist to assist you in the process of finding your core self and believing in yourself.

Facing Shame in Finding Your Profession

Very few men have had the opportunity I had in my family of origin to be encouraged to build spaceships out of wood in the backyard or change my college major several times and my career once before I found my profession. Most men have been discouraged from such projects, criticized, or shamed to such a degree that they have a very thick wall protecting them from the world around them, a wall that prevents them from finding the love that is resident in their own souls and ultimately their life's work. So many men have said to me in my office, "I had all these dreams but didn't know how to make them real." How many boys have been chided, discouraged, or shamed when they have espoused grand hopes, like becoming a brain surgeon, exploring the Arctic, or being a famous actor when they grew up? When parents hear such unrealistic dreams, they could serve their sons by listening and encouraging rather than saying such things are impossible.

How many highschoolers have been chided because they *don't know what they want* to do after graduation but are pressed into "just choosing" a career path? How many have gone to college because someone told them that they should go, only to drop out because college didn't seem right for them? How thwarting could it have been if I had been shamed for not "following through" on science, math, history, or theology? And yet all of these elements have helped me in my profession. How many men have been set back because a change in direction was considered irresponsible or fickle? If you have been raised in such an environment of shame, coercion, or disregard, you will likely still retain the potential shame of looking stupid for doing something that your core self actually wanted to do. If a man is to find a core belief about himself, he will need to go into these damaging childhood experiences, feel all the sad feelings accompanying these experiences and *finish* these griefs. It is not a pretty picture for most men, and it is downright scary for most men because no one has ever told them to look for their life's work, much less their souls. There is no way a man can find his life's work without going through this process of grieving while simultaneously challenging the fear of doing something stupid. A man won't be in *his* profession until he finishes the grief associated with being separated from his basic sense of self, the love associated with it, and the profession associated with this love. If you are a man who is not happy in your work, admit it to yourself, talk to the right person or persons about it, and find the love-based passion you have inside of you. You might need to overcome the shame that you suffered from your family, school, friends, or church to be able to find this passion. Then you will be able to think clearly.

Thinking Clearly

We've talked about feelings, passion, and a man's core self. Now we come to the next step in the process of a man finding his profession: he has to think clearly so he can engage his core self in the real world of work. A man looking to find his life's work needs to identify what he likes and what is important to him. At the end of every intake interview I conduct with a man, I ask him, "What is important to you?" Almost every man answers with something like, "family, children, and friends." These are admirable values for a person, but when I hear them, I am usually concerned about the absence of value in work. Sometimes, these are real values because the man, indeed, is a true family man and his family *is his profession*. But for most men they have not really asked themselves what is important to them aside from family, so they don't know how to answer the question.

Finding a way out of unsatisfactory work requires that a man look deep and wide for what is important to him, which might be as simple as taking note of what he engages in his spare time. If a man takes stock of what takes up his time, he can find something of more depth that drives him in life. You might find that you really could enjoy tweaking recipes in the kitchen, restoring old cars, or helping teenagers approach the challenge of work and profession. The beginning of finding one's true value system and ultimately his true core lies in the things that are pleasurable and meaningful to him.

Once a man has found a few things that are important to him, and perhaps a few passions that lie beneath these surface things, it is necessary to do some psychological work to discover how these interests represent something deeper in the man.

Proceeding into Your Profession

You need to think about what you might want to do, but thinking and musing is not sufficient. Doing something about your work, whether taking a course, working a part-time job, shadowing a professional, or otherwise moving forward are all means of proceeding into your profession. You probably won't be able to figure out what your profession should be without a few bumps and bruises along this path. You might start in one course and shift to another. You might even start studying and working in a profession only to discover that you need to take a bit of a left turn to find what is right for you. There are other therapeutic tools that can be used to help you get to your core self and core values, like meditation and yoga, spiritual or religious practices, and many good books to read. But it is not enough to read, meditate, and discuss your ideas. You have to do something.

To find a practical procedure for finding one's life's work and profession, a man has to feel, think, discuss, and then *do something*. Men tend to either get lost in the abstract psychological aspects or move too quickly into the concrete feeling and thinking. Men who are abstract by nature often think of everything to do but never do anything, while men who are more concrete by nature jump right into some job without knowing why. This process of finding, listening, and understanding your inner self is abstract by nature, but it is not good enough to remain in the abstraction of feelings and possibilities. Once he has found his inner core, he needs to do something concretely, which means being practical and active.

Moving back into the concrete means looking at three areas of life: possible professions, academic requirements, and personal resources. When a man begins to look beyond his job, he needs to first set aside the apparent requirements of the professions like academic degrees or technical training. He first needs to look at the actual activities that his possible profession might require. If he is curious about nursing, he needs to look at what nurses do in the various subspecialties of nursing. If he is interested in exploring what it means to be a pilot, he needs to see what pilots really do. This scouting out what is involved in being a professional takes time, and it can be very encouraging as well as discouraging. Many men are quite fascinated with the idea of entering a helping profession, like nursing, therapy, or ministry but become discouraged when they see what it really entails to be a such a professional.

After he has a bit of an idea about what it means to be working in a certain profession, he needs to examine what it takes to become that professional. This is a dig-in-and-research period for a man. Before you even apply for some advanced education, consider whether you have sufficient passion to study things and do things that you may not necessarily like in order to get to the place where you want to be. Looking at some kind of advanced training can be very disconcerting to someone who might not like reading or is older than the typical person entering the profession. This is where a man needs to courageously examine himself and the world of work.

Concretizing one's profession involves doing many things, which might be applying for a different job, returning to school, looking into alternative training, shadowing someone in a profession, or taking a job that is preprofessional but related to one's core self and core values. This will usually mean some kind of academic or hands-on training. All of this takes time: time to feel, time to think, time to talk, and time to do something practical.

Summary

- It is essential that a man find satisfaction in his work.
- A job is something that makes money.
- A profession is something where the man "professes" himself.

- You need to dream of a profession and find a way to do it.
- Dreaming alone is insufficient to find your life's work.
- You need to learn to talk about your day's work. It is good for you, and it is good for those around you.
- There are always challenges in work: finding the right profession, becoming confident and successful in the profession, and dealing with people-related challenges at work.
- Being unhappy at work will bleed into your unhappiness in all areas of your life and will lead to anger, avoidance, and addiction.
- You may "finish" a profession and then find another profession.

CHAPTER 6

Men and Wine (Addictions)

I HAVE TITLED THIS chapter "Men and Wine." I use the term "wine" generically and for alliterative purposes, referring to an addiction of any kind, including alcohol but not exclusive to alcohol. Importantly, any addiction brings a person a measure of happiness, pleasure, or satisfaction. Happy. Pleasurable. Satisfied. All of these experiences are parts of joy. We all want these things in life. Life needs to have these positive ingredients on a regular basis, and we should do all we can to have our lives filled with as much joy as possible.

If I could suggest a program that would give people happiness, pleasure, and satisfaction all the time, I would most certainly do it, but I am not able to suggest such a program. We have written this book to help men find joy in their lives and share joy with the other people in their lives. We discussed in chapter one that joy is one of the fruits of love, which most certainly is at the heart of what it means to be human. The more we love, the more we find joy in our lives and the more we bring joy to the people in our lives. We also noted, however, that love unavoidably causes sadness in our lives. An emotionally mature man knows that if he loves something, he will have joy but he also knows that he will feel sad when he loses this thing that he loves.

It is central to life that we come to grips with this fact because there is a danger of thinking that life is primarily centered around joy rather than the more mature understanding that joy is but half of what it means to love. When we fail to recognize the sadness aspect of love, we can fall prey to thinking that we don't have to ever be sad in life. Addictions occur singularly because we have not accepted the central ingredient of life that we need to love and be loved, but in so doing, we will feel both joy and sorrow.

I live in the state of Wisconsin, the home for countless breweries. The professional baseball team is the Milwaukee *Brewers*. Wisconsin is known not only as the cheese state but also the beer and brats state. The University of Wisconsin at Madison is ingloriously known as the party school of the Midwest. In a recent study, 80 percent of university students use alcohol to some degree, 65 percent of male UW students, and 45 percent of female students admitted to having had at least one blackout from abuse of alcohol (LaLiberte, 2002). To say Wisconsin is a beer state is an understatement.

Given that I live and work in Wisconsin, most of the men who come to see me have drunk a lot of alcohol and may have some kind of alcohol problem. It is remarkable what men report as their drinking patterns. When I asked one young man about the drinking pattern of his family, he responded by saying that he "came from a typical Wisconsin family," which meant that his family members regularly drank to excess. Another man said that he had given up getting "stupid drunk," and now only "gets drunk." Yet another man reported to me that he had reduced his daily beer intake to a twelve-pack every night... down from a twenty-four-pack. A man I saw today was glad to say that he was drinking *only* twenty-four ounces of whiskey a day, down from his usual thirty-six ounces. I recently had a patient go to prison for his ninth drunk driving offense, offenses that stretched for about twenty-five years. Few of these men realize that they have drinking problems. Not long ago a man told me that he drank "maybe six beers" every night, had a hit of marijuana in the morning, "a couple of hits" of marijuana in the evening, all in addition to his smoking about two packs of cigarettes every day. Then he spontaneously added that he "doesn't have an addiction problem."

I was raised in a partying family. I remember my family having parties from my earliest years of childhood. I recall one Halloween party my parents had for their friends where everyone came in costume. My dad greeted them at the front door by rising out of a coffin in a Frankenstein mask as they came up the front steps. I remember so much fun happening at the party, including the screams when the guests were greeted by my dad. When I grew up, parties became a thing that we always did, whether birthday, Halloween, or some other excuse. These parties always consisted of lots of decorations, lots of games, lots of food, and lots of drink. But the drink was never alcohol. I can't say for sure that there wasn't a small imbibing here and there when my parents had their adult parties, but there was never any visible alcohol and certainly no abuse of alcohol. In my teenage years we lived on a lake, which made for great water parties replete with swimming, waterskiing, water volleyball, and other such fun. We did so much waterskiing that we needed to try "waterskiing" with objects other than traditional waterskis. We tried out old logs and anything that would float. Once we tried to ride on an upside-down table and even a ladder. None of these things really did very well, but we had fun trying. Having fun with these kinds of things was what I considered to be a party, whether it was playing on the water with friends or sharing table games and food with a host of people in the house. A "party" in my family simply meant having fun—no alcohol needed.

In college I was a member of a fraternity but I never drank. I saw drunkenness for the first time in my life and it didn't make sense to me. I was well into my twenties, and early into my profession, before I realized that for most people the term "partying" meant getting drunk. In my mind partying continues to mean having a bunch of people together, having some kind of playful fun. It doesn't mean getting drunk. It saddens me that seemingly most people don't know how to party without excessive use of alcohol. Most adults haven't ever had what I consider to be a real party since they were kids.

An important treatment for people who are addicted to any substance or behavior is to see the origins of these addictions. Just yesterday I saw a college student whose younger brother had tried drinking for the first time over the school break. Vodka shots were the name of the game. The younger brother fell unconscious and could not be awakened. Fortunately, emergency responders were able to revive him. This older brother said that once his brother had been revived, he simply slapped him on the back and said that he would give him drinking lessons! In this chapter we want to discuss "wine" (addictive) problems of various sorts and suggest ways that we men, and perhaps women, can prevent the dangers that all addictions have for people. I offer my understanding of addictions, admittedly not as a specialist, but rather as a person who has seen addictions seriously damage many men's lives. Indeed, alcohol abuse is the most visible addiction, but alcohol actually falls into one of two categories of addictions called chemical addictions. There are also behavioral addictions.

How Does Something Become Addictive?

Addiction is any behavior that regularly interrupts the natural flow of life on some kind of consistent basis. Whether the addiction is chemical, like alcohol or drugs, or behavioral, like gambling or hoarding, the behavior that is involved in the addiction has come to adversely affect the person's life. A man's addiction to alcohol, for instance, is not so much about the amount of alcohol that he consumes but how his consumption of alcohol interrupts his life. How does something come to be an interruption of life? Why doesn't a man just stop drinking or stop gambling when he sees that these behaviors have such negative consequences? This is not an easy question to answer, but if we examine the course of how something becomes an addiction, it will begin to make sense why some people lose control over their lives.

Addictions Start with Pleasure

There is certainly nothing wrong with pleasure and the seeking of pleasure. People naturally find ways of enjoying life starting from very early childhood. The brain (apart from the mind) has only two basic functions: safety and pleasure. As we noted at the start of this chapter, we all need to seek pleasure in our lives and enjoy these moments as much as possible. Unfortunately, pleasure-seeking can lead to an addiction. No one ever seeks to become addicted to anything. Rather, people fall into addictive patterns because the behavior gives them pleasure, very often some kind of immediate pleasure. If something is pleasurable, it is only natural to do more of this activity to extend or enhance this pleasure. Very often, however, a pleasurable activity can become less pleasurable over time. When this happens, there is a danger of doing more of the activity to get the same amount of pleasure. This can be the start of an addiction, namely doing more of something in order to have the same amount of pleasure. We will shortly discuss how the brain gets involved in this process. When some activity that was initially pleasurable becomes less pleasurable, the reasonable thing to do would be to do less of that activity, but this is not what happens with an addiction.

It is pleasurable for most people to engage in some kind of game-playing, whatever their choice of gaming is rigorous chess, frivolous Monopoly, video gaming, or playing basketball. Once a man has found some pleasure in some activity, he will naturally do this activity more often. There is nothing wrong in this. I enjoy many things in life, like swimming, playing basketball, working Sudoku puzzles, reading, and writing. Deb and I have developed a habit of playing Chinese checkers when we're at the cabin, but interestingly, nowhere else. Chinese checkers is part of our cabin play. I enjoy taking a few minutes away from writing this very book to play a bit of frivolous card-based video games. All of these activities are forms of play that allow me to take a few minutes away from the responsibilities of life. Play is absolutely necessary in life. *Play is any activity, physical, mental, or relational, that has no ultimate meaning but serves as a way of getting away from more challenging aspects of life.*

Activities that are playful are essentially healthy for you. It can become a habit to engage in this pleasurable activity, whether that is some kind of recreation that you do regularly in life or just a quick game of solitaire. People who play chess initially found pleasure in the game, then they learned strategies and moves that enhanced their pleasure by winning games. Good chess players have developed an advantageous habit of watching, thinking, evaluating, and eventually moving their chess pieces effectively. Likewise, people who find it enjoyable to run might eventually develop a good habit of running three or four times a week. People who enjoy working might find it pleasurable to rise early in the morning and/or work late into the night. Other people read, sit out in the sun, or go birding because they have found the habit of doing these things pleasurable and ultimately profitable. The operative word is *pleasurable*. We have habits that we have learned because they have become enjoyable for us to do. No problem yet. Nothing wrong with good habits that are pleasurable.

When something becomes addictive, however, that which has been fun, a temporary distraction that *enhances life*, increasingly becomes a way to *avoid life*. There is a big difference between a short-lived distraction from the challenges of life and a way to avoid these challenges. An addiction can encroach on a man's life without his ever knowing that it has happened. An activity that has been fun and valuable now has become harmful to a man because the brain gets involved.

When the Brain Is Involved in Pleasure

It is important to know that any pleasure that we feel for whatever reason has caused a chemical change in our brains, namely the secretion of endorphins, sometimes called pleasure hormones. Nothing wrong with having endorphins flowing in our blood system. We wouldn't enjoy anything if we didn't have endorphins. We can churn up endorphins by just *thinking* about something we want to do or plan to do, and this thinking will then lead to the brain secreting endorphins into our bloodstreams. But here is where things get complicated, and the complication is a brain function. Your brain has two basic operations: safety and pleasure. We discussed the safety function of the brain when we discussed fear and anxiety in chapter two. Your brain works to keep you safe when it gets the message from your mind that there is some danger. Likewise, your brain works to maximize your pleasure in life. Think of it this way. Your *mind* operates this wonderful machine we call a brain just like I am operating the computer in front of me. My computer knows when I have made a spelling error and tells me. Likewise, the brain tells you when you are in an unsafe or dangerous place, like when you hear a loud siren that tells you that the ambulance behind you needs to get by you in a hurry. That's the safety part of the brain, and thank goodness that the brain takes care of you when there is danger. Recall from chapter two that the brain does not have a concept of time, so there is a danger of your brain working overtime to keep you vigilant when you think of some potential danger in the future, a vigilance that easily turns into anxiety.

Similarly, the pleasure-enhancing nature of the brain can encourage you into pleasurable activities that are unnecessary and inappropriate. In its pleasure-enhancing mode, the brain simply wants you to be happy. During your life you have had various activities that have been pleasurable. When you engaged in this activity, whether it was chemical, like drinking, or behavioral like playing Ping-Pong, you churned up the "happy hormones." Your brain remembers these events and will cause you to think of something pleasurable when you are not feeling happy. So, for instance, your brain will remember the pleasure associated with drinking or playing Ping-Pong and get you thinking of these things. Then your mind takes over and decides whether, how, and when to do this happy-producing thing. The positive aspect of this pleasure-enhancing element of your brain is that you can develop a very good habit that is pleasurable. It might be very good for you to have a drink as a way of getting away from all the work you've been doing on the house, and it could also be a good habit to regularly play Ping-Pong with a friend. Unfortunately, your brain doesn't know that some things that are pleasurable and habitual can be harmful, if they are engaged to a fault, and ultimately addictive.

The pleasure-seeking nature of the brain can easily turn a good habit into an addiction without ever knowing that it is doing anything wrong. And, as we have already noted, the difficulty that we have in this mind-brain engagement is that the "stupid" brain doesn't know the future, or the past for that matter. Your brain only knows the present, so if you're unhappy for some reason, your brain will work to find ways to make you happy *right now*. The pleasure-seeking part of the brain does not see the consequences of drinking to a fault or even playing Ping-Pong to a fault, perhaps so much so that your whole life might be ruined. Your brain has no idea that drinking to an excess can, in some circumstances, cause death, whether your own because of a dangerous level of alcohol in your system or someone else's when you kill someone on the road. Even pleasurable things like playing Ping-Pong can become addictive. I have known of many men who play softball six nights a week . . . often followed by drinking with the boys. These same men come home to an unhappy and lonely family and plop down in front of the TV without realizing that they have played "to a fault."

With the danger of making this discussion too complicated or neuropsychology too simple, allow me to discuss an important distinction I learned not long ago from a prominent neuropsychologist (Berridge, 2016). Dr. Berridge and his colleagues discovered that there are two related operations in the brain, one that we might call "chemical" and one that we might call "electrical." In simple terms, these two operations have to do with wanting (chemical) something and doing (electrical) something. In short, the brain stirs up "happy" endorphins when you *want to do something* pleasurable or plan to do something. The "electrical" operation that occurs when you actually do something does not give you the immediate pleasure that endorphins do, but the pleasure is more long-lasting.

Have you ever looked forward to doing something but then found yourself disappointed when you actually got to do this thing? You might look forward to buying a new car or a candy bar, but having bought these things, you realize having these things wasn't nearly as fun as thinking about having them. Have you ever been a bit disappointed that the vacation, party, or game was not as pleasurable as the looking forward to it? If so, you have experienced the difference between *wanting* and *experiencing*. The wanting was chemical and the experiencing was electrical. Recently, I had been looking forward to meeting an old friend but was disappointed when the meeting wasn't as pleasurable as I thought it would be. In neurological terms, the endorphins churned up pleasure in looking forward to meeting Greg, but the actually meeting of him didn't stir up the electricity of my brain. In a way, the brain gives you a "kick" when you anticipate some future pleasure, but that kick may not transfer into the reality of doing what you hoped would be fun. Addictions seemingly have more to do with the wanting than of the experiencing, i.e., more with the chemical than the electrical operations of the brain.

Simply put, it is more pleasurable to look forward to some addictive behavior than actually doing it. People who are addicted to smoking will tell you that they feel good (endorphins are churning up) when they *start to think* about smoking much more than *actually* smoking. The brain doesn't distinguish between looking forward to smoking and actually smoking because it sees the future and the present both in the present. Smokers often detest the smell of cigarettes on their breath or on their clothes and often find little pleasure in the actual smoking process. Ever watch a smoker take a cigarette pack out of his pocket and pound it on his hand, then perhaps take a cigarette out of the pack and perhaps hold it in his hand for a few minutes before finally lighting it? He is enjoying the *wanting* to smoke more than the having the *experience* of smoking. In this case the man is driven by the pleasure-enhancing endorphins of wanting more than the electrical element of pleasure. Initially, it is the wanting something that drives a person to become addicted much more than the actual engaging the addictive behavior. I know of a man who is addicted to cannabis who finds himself thinking (wanting) to drive out of state where cannabis is legal, but if he finally drives the two hours to get his fix, he doesn't really enjoy smoking pot.

Wanting gets out of hand when it begins to drive you to do something that takes your energy away from the rest of your life. It can be wonderful to look forward to playing golf or reading a book, but if the looking forward to these activities encompasses too much time, it takes you away from the rest of your day and life. You have moved from simple pleasure through a habit of finding pleasure, to being addicted to that pleasurable activity. Retaining habits of pleasure without becoming addicted to something requires a deep and ongoing self-awareness. A helpful way to approach self-awareness is to realize the interaction between the mind and the brain: the mind thinks, feels, plans, and engages the world; the brain protects you and seeks pleasure. If you plan to play golf this afternoon, your brain will churn up endorphins as you look ahead to this pleasurable activity. If, however, you think, feel, and plan so much about playing golf that you don't get your work done and end up checking on the weather every five minutes hoping for sunshine, you are facing the edges of an addiction because your brain has taken over your mind. An addiction can rightly be seen as a brain disorder, not a thinking disorder, a feeling disorder, or an interpersonal disorder. Golf, or more accurately, thinking about playing golf, has become the center of your day or perhaps eventually the center of your life. In so doing, your brain has become so focused on golf that other elements of your life have been sacrificed. You can't blame your brain for doing its job; you can, however, challenge your brain with your mind. Before we examine how you can get your mind in control of your brain, let's look at the different forms of addictions: chemical and behavioral.

Chemical Addictions

Alcohol Addiction

By far the most visible chemical addiction is the excessive use of alcohol. The professional people who deal with alcoholism do not distinguish problem drinking from alcoholism. The common definition of alcoholism used by alcohol and other drug abuse (AODA) counselors is this: if alcohol causes a problem in a man's life or the lives of his family, *he is alcoholic*. This definition puts a lot of men in the category of alcoholism. To say the least, alcohol abuse, and the consequences of such abuse, is a major problem in North America, if not in the entire world. Even so, I rarely, if ever, use the term "alcoholic" to describe someone, even if alcohol use and abuse has caused the person a great deal of difficulty. I engage in "treatment" of chemical abuse, primarily alcohol abuse in almost every man I see in my office, but I approach these people as individuals who have found a way to cope with life by using chemicals. "Coping with life" includes facing all the challenges of work, play, and relationships, not just the excessive use of chemicals.

Once a man has an excessive use of alcohol in his life, it is hard for him to see the danger of this excess. Furthermore, when men drink too much, alcohol has actually become more important to him than anything else in his life. Most men who abuse alcohol continue to do so until well into their seventies and then slow down their drinking only because of serious physical problems. By that time, many men have already lost wives, property, and jobs while continuing to abuse alcohol. Men cannot connect the losses their drinking has caused because of the powerful effect that endorphins have on them. I know a man who went to prison for his seventh DUI. He had abused alcohol every night after work, drove drunk on his snowmobile, and got drunk with every poker game he played and on every fishing outing. It didn't occur to him that he could fish, hunt, or play poker without drinking. Furthermore, his friends were always drinking with these activities, so it seemed normal to him to drink this much.

If you take alcohol out of the picture of these fun activities, many men think the fun activities are no longer fun. In fact, take alcohol out, and life itself seems dull and boring. For many men alcohol has been such a basic ingredient of play that life without alcohol seems almost not worth living. People who have not engaged in the regular and abusive use of alcohol have a hard time understanding why alcoholic men feel so deprived when they are asked to have fun without alcohol. Alcohol and activity are so closely intertwined that they seemingly cannot be experienced separately. It just wouldn't be fun to go snowmobiling if you couldn't look forward to the next bar stop. What would a football playoff be if there is not beer in hand? And all those hours waiting in the tree stand for the perfect buck to pass would be nearly impossible to endure without a twelve-pack. Fishing, hunting, playing poker, or watching a football game can be fun with alcohol, but it can also be fun without alcohol. If you were initiated to such fun things with alcohol, you might tend to associate fun with the activity *and* alcohol, not the activity alone. The pleasure that alcohol can immediately bring to men comes in various forms, including the guy who has a three-martini lunch every day and the fellow who sneaks a drink at his desk.

I have one patient, presently unemployed even though he has been very successful in his profession, who is quite lonely in his life and has never had a life partner. His partner in life has been wine. He drinks wine nightly, blacks out nightly, and then arouses sometime in the middle of the night to watch TV and then fall asleep. Another man whom I saw recently came under a mandate from work to visit with a counselor because his employer noticed alcohol on his breath. He was immediately sent for a test of alcohol content in his blood, which he failed. Sadly, his wife of fifteen years had just died, perhaps the only intimate person he had ever had in his life. He found some solace in drinking his sorrows away the night before he went to work. Another patient got himself in serious legal trouble because of a one-time incident of inebriation at a professional conference where he was the primary speaker. This man is most certainly not alcoholic in any sense of the term, but on this one occasion, he did abuse alcohol with very dire results. Another patient who has been in a stable but unsatisfactory marriage for twenty years finds it necessary to drink wine to excess from time to time when he has to have contact with his ex-wife. Whether the choice of alcohol consumption is hard liquor, beer, wine, or some combination of these, the problem is in the abuse, not the use. Note that in all of these cases men are coping with something in life, whether it is their loneliness, significant loss of partner, or trying to be a funnier person at the bar. Alcohol becomes abusive when it replaces real life with a chemically-based life. I think alcohol can enhance life when it is used appropriately and responsibly, and many people have found a way to move from alcohol abuse to appropriate alcohol use.

It's Not Just Alcohol

While there are many other forms of chemical abuse, I focus on alcohol because it is the most visible form of chemical addiction that I see in my office. Most men find at least one other form of addiction that accompanies alcohol abuse. Many times, alcohol abuse is accompanied by smoking or the use of illegal drugs or prescription drugs, sometimes in conjunction with some form of behavioral addiction. The fellow I noted above who drinks regularly every day and then smokes pot twice a day is not an outlier. One man that I see weighs over three hundred pounds, smokes two packs a day, and got himself in some significant trouble because of a singular incident of excessive drinking.

I have been seeing a heroin-addicted man, unfortunately quite unsuccessfully. While bright and very capable, he seemingly cannot find his way out of heroin use. The other day he came into my office admitting that he had "fallen off the wagon" again, leading to an arrest for possession of drug paraphernalia and was awaiting trial for his offense. Remarkably, he was under the influence while he was in my office but talked about "never using (heroin) again" when he left. When I left the office a few hours later, I saw two police cars in the parking lot where he had been found to be asleep at the wheel of his parked car. Sadly, once again, he was arrested. I can only imagine what it is like to be addicted to such a dangerous chemical. All of these drugs, legal or illegal are potentially addictive, which is defined as interrupting the normal flow of life.

Behavioral Addictions

It's fun to do things. Things like swimming, reading, gardening, or just hanging out. Not all people like swimming, reading, gardening, or even just hanging out. Deb loves gardening a lot, perhaps more than any other activity she has. I love reading and writing, perhaps more than any other activity. You have different things that you enjoy, perhaps working out, enjoying a sunset, or really enjoying sex. All of these activities, and hundreds more, are pleasurable, perhaps more to one person than to another. People need to enjoy life, play, relax, or do whatever makes them happy. We cannot emphasize enough that we want to encourage you to do what makes you happy, what is fun, what is pleasurable, and what is satisfying. Behavioral addictions do not take away pleasure; they reduce pleasure.

Behavioral addictions are exactly what the term suggests: something in one's behavior that becomes addictive. Keep in mind the basic definition of an addiction: something that was initially pleasurable that has interrupted the natural flow of life, which means work, play, physical health, and relationships. Any behavior can become addictive, even behaviors that are essential to life like eating and sleeping. An addiction starts out as something that is initially *enjoyable* and perhaps valuable, then migrates into a *habit* that can also be enjoyable and valuable, and sometimes gravitates into an *addiction*. The most important way of understanding, controlling, and eventually eliminating any form of addition is to view the addiction as something that was initially good for you then slowly begins to decrease your quality of life. Anything that is basically enjoyable and pleasurable can become addictive. In this section we will discuss eating, sleeping, working, playing, property management, screen time, and sexual activity. Note that all of these things can be life-enhancing, and some of them are necessary in life, like eating and sleeping.

Body-Based Addictions

Like all addictions, body-based addictions are very brain-based. To understand body-based addictions is to remember that your brain is interested in keeping you alive first and maximizing your pleasure second. The three basic body operations that the brain does in order to keep a person safe are breathing, sleeping, and eating. Then there are some body operations that the brain orchestrates to maximize your pleasure by secreting endorphins when you engage in pleasurable activities. These include things like resting, meditation, observing nature, yoga, play, exercise, eating, and work. You can see that all of these activities are essentially pleasurable for you.

The hardest addictions to conquer have to do with basic body safety, namely eating and sleeping. You can do without play, work, and even relationships, perhaps not easily, but you cannot do without breathing, sleeping, and eating. You have to eat and you have to sleep. Eating addictions are the hardest ones to overcome because eating has both neurological elements of safety and pleasure. Addictions in eating are of two forms: eating too much and eating too little. Anorexia, insufficient eating, is notoriously hard to conquer, and overeating is just as hard. A person who has become addicted to overeating has a brain that concludes something like, "I have to gain weight to prepare for the famine that might come." The brain thinks, "More is better, so I need to eat more" (brain seeking safety). Anorexia is quite different. The brain of an anorexic thinks something like, "If I eat very little, I will be at my desired weight and I will be liked, by myself and by other people" (brain seeking pleasure).

In addition to the necessary element of eating, the other essential activity for you to survive in life is sleeping. While sleeping is not often considered addictive, in some cases it certainly can be. Sleeping disturbances are rampant among people, which essentially leads people to sleeping too much or not sleeping enough. Both sleeping too much and failing to sleep enough result from the brain's primary function, safety. People who don't sleep enough usually say something like, "I can't get my brain to stop thinking" (addicted to thought). This is the essence of anxiety. What has happened in these circumstances is that the brain is "hearing" some danger in your life and continues to be active with your mind to figure out this potential problem. As a result, the brain keeps you awake to figure things out. When you are overwhelmed by circumstances in life, you can feel depressed. When you are depressed, your brain says that you need to sleep more to avoid the stress of life. Not sleeping enough is insomnia, while sleeping too much is hypersomnia. People who suffer from this malady have brains that see sleeping as safer than being awake.

There are other body-based addictions aside from sleeping and eating, all of which have either pleasure-seeking or safety-providing mechanisms. Body maintenance and bodybuilding are certainly good things for most people, but when a man spends four hours a day, seven days a week in the gym, he may be addicted to bodybuilding. Other physical addictions can be playing softball six days a week or running seven days a week. My trainer suggests that it is best to work out or run about four times a week, taking the weekend off to be "a normal person." There are some interesting compulsions that some people have including hair-pulling, skin-picking, and the like that bring the feelings of pleasure and safety to the people who are caught in these addictions. Even the seemingly helpful exercises of yoga and meditation can be addictive when the brain determines that the excessive use of these activities is necessary for a safe life or necessary for a pleasurable life. Your body needs a certain amount of physical exercise, generally the more the better, but there is a danger of the brain getting the message that *excessive* exercise is both pleasurable and necessary in life. What is so interesting about these body-based addictions is that they erupt from a good habit to a bad one. You can see that any good thing done "to a fault" is problematic, even relationships.

Relationship Addictions

Relationship addictions come in the forms of sexual activity and other intimate connections. I use the term "sexual addiction" with reservation because the American Psychological Association (APA) does not actually have such a diagnosis. It is not clear why some people fall into sexual activity that is harmful to themselves and to others. Sexual activity is not limited to what one does physically. It can include thoughts and feelings. In fact, there are a lot more sexual thoughts and feelings that can be addictive than physical sexual activity. Whether thought, feeling, or activity, sexual matters can dominate a man's life and become addictive. There is no specific sexual activity that is intrinsically wrong if it is not harmful to someone. Rather than examining sexual behavior itself, we find it valuable to see how certain sexual behavior can first do psychological damage to a man and secondarily to the people in his life.

Almost without exception, men who have some form of sexual addiction feel ashamed of their proclivity. They are afraid of being caught, judged, and shamed for their sexual behavior. The central ingredient in shame is fear of disapproval, and it is shame that causes men to hide their sexual activity, whether this activity is something that they do or just something that they imagine doing. Consider how difficult it would be for you, as a man, to tell someone, perhaps your spouse, partner, or good friend, about some sexual activity that you are ashamed of. It is remarkable how men can so easily feel ashamed of their sexual thoughts. Feeling ashamed of your sexual thoughts always leads to hiding these thoughts from everyone. Hiding thoughts can lead to hiding behavior. Hiding and the shame that causes hiding work directly against a man being ballsy in life. The really sad thing about hiding sexual thoughts is that sex itself is perfectly good and godly. Sex in all its forms can bring us great joy and bring our partners great joy. Why should we be so ashamed of what we feel when it comes to sex? The probable answer to that question has to do with the American culture that tends to see sex as dirty, sinful, or just wrong. Unfortunately, when men begin to hide their thoughts and sexual behavior, they can easily fall into some kind of compulsive sexual activity that becomes addictive.

I once had a patient who worked eight hours a day, slept eight hours a day, and masturbated eight hours a day using pornography. Nothing physically or psychologically wrong with masturbation, but eight hours a day of masturbation interrupts life's normal flow. In fact, this particular man had no friends and no meaningful activities aside from pornography and work. While this is an extreme case, a good deal of research in sexual behavior suggests that masturbation and the use of pornography almost universally causes men shame although men often say, "I know there is nothing wrong with masturbation." Excessive or compulsive masturbation can lead to other forms of sexual addiction. Boys who are introduced to masturbation early in life often fail to develop a sense of good sexuality and tend to become sexually addicted in one or more ways. Simply stated, masturbation, specifically the fantasy that usually accompanies masturbation, does not have to do with reality. When a man engages in something unreal, there appears to be a tendency to feel ashamed of that activity. Furthermore, as we have discussed, the brain gets involved in anything that is pleasurable and can lead a man to fall into an addictive pattern of masturbation because the brain knows nothing about reality and relationships. The brain does not have an understanding of mature sexuality and certainly doesn't have a moral compass.

While masturbation, often with the use of pornography, tends to be the primary sexual addictive behavior, there are other forms of sexual activity that can be just as addictive, namely promiscuity, forced abstinence, or alternate forms of sexual activity. I won't examine the recently popular polyamorous view of sexual life, leaving that discussion to people more skilled in sexual study, but my uninformed opinion is that such activity is not substantially different from promiscuity. My concern is not the singular affair that someone might have but the experience of promiscuity that drives a man to more and more sexual flings and partners. A former friend confided in me that he had been with as many as twenty-five women over a period of about fifteen years of marriage. Another man admitted that he had "never been faithful to any woman." One man reported that he was embarrassed because he had been sexual with only twenty-five women. Intimacy includes body, mind, and heart connections, something that is not possible with promiscuity.

Relationships are not singularly sexual, and there are many other forms of relationship problems that are essentially addictive in nature. Many people are unable to survive any time alone. They just need to have some person in their lives. You might think that this is a typical female phenomenon, but there are many men who are addicted to having to have a relationship. A man I knew some time ago who had been rampantly promiscuous, allegedly because he was dissatisfied in his marriage, said, "I just have to be with some woman to be happy in life." He could not consider being single, even for a week or a year, if he chose to divorce his wife. While it is wonderful to be in a relationship with someone you love, many men fall into relationships because of their inability to be alone. The key in the feeling of having to be with someone is the lack of a man being able to stand on his own two feet before engaging in a relationship with someone. Too often, men marry or otherwise couple with someone, too quickly finding it intolerable to be alone. Many men try to cure a deep-seated inability to be alone and find meaning in life with finding a woman to cure this loneliness. A woman can help a man find his balls or work against his being ballsy, but she cannot cure a man's lack of self.

Sexual activity is certainly a form of pleasure, but it might also be considered to be a form of play. There are many other forms of play that can be addictive.

Play Addictions

Such a wonderful thing play is: an activity that takes us away from the rigors of life so we can return to real life refreshed. We don't need less play in life. We need more play, but this play needs to be refreshing and restorative, not a way to avoid the rest of life. I use the term "play" to refer to any activity that is pleasurable without any particular benefit of production. Play is one of the essentials of life in addition to work and relationships. Many people have little or no play in their lives because they work too much, spend too much time with their relationships, or have fallen into a depressive mode of life where nothing is interesting or valuable. Ideally, play temporarily takes us away from the other important things in life, like work and relationships, and allows us to engage in an activity that has no ultimate value to society in general or other people specifically and then being refreshed, we return to those other important things. Play can be physical, cognitive, or social. As a result, play can be good for body, soul, and relationships. Video gaming can increase one's visual-motor and visual-spatial abilities. Chess can be good for memory and other strategic functions. Basketball can be good for one's physical coordination and social engagement. On the basketball court I cooperate with my teammates and we together compete with our opponents. This is part of play. Gardening can be creative and nurturing as play. Painting on canvas can be as playful as driving to the lake for a picnic. In its essence and its purpose play is good for us. But like anything else, this very valuable portion of life can become addictive.

It is really sad that so many components of play like sex, engaging in a delicious meal, or enjoying a glass of wine can become addictive. Even working to finish a project or assignment can be enjoyable at first but can slip into an artificial form of perfection. Addictions are all artificial relationships, be they with a person, an activity, or a substance. Many people have an artificial relationship with their computer screens.

Screen Addictions

Screen addictions have become increasingly prevalent in the world at large. They include television, computers, video gaming, and cell phones. In many cases screen time is harmless, whether scouring the internet for some new information, reviewing "likes" on one's Facebook account, vicariously enjoying players seen on TV, texting someone on the cell phone, and of course video gaming. Many men love to have the giant TV screen and sometimes their own "theaters" at home. Certainly, this is fun for people and not intrinsically addictive. I don't want to take away good fun things from men's lives, and while none of these screen time activities is intrinsically bad for men, any of them can come to dominate a man's life. When this happens, he has lost his balls to the screen. I hear from many men that they can't resist watching the playbacks or the scores and engage in fantasy football. That they can't avoid checking to see if they have received a return text or that they just have to check the phone for any connection, be it email, text or otherwise. As a result of these activities, they can't stay attentive to their work, much less to the enhancement of any real relationship they have.

Among all of these potentially addictive screen time activities, the constant use of texting seems most deleterious to much of life. It is simply easier to text than it is to talk; it is easier to text than to listen to someone else talk; it is easier to use texting lingo than to work at finding the right words to express your feelings. You can have a sense of a relationship when you are having technology-based engagement with someone, but texting can lead to an avoidance of writing an email, making a live phone call, taking a few minutes to visit someone, or God forbid, writing a letter. Texting and other forms of technology are now a part of our civilization, and such technology has enhanced the lives of many people. I am grateful I can easily text my daughter and wish her a good day. It is so easy, so convenient, and it is genuine. The trouble is when these engagements become too convenient, too easy, and a replacement for the rest of a relationship, like seeing someone face-to-face, real discussion that requires give-and-take, play, and work. When screen-based contact becomes the primary means of communication, it has become addictive. Have you noticed that when you are having a back-and-forth texting exchange with someone, it becomes harder to stop? This is evidence of one of the defining elements of addiction: an inability to stop the activity.

The same thing happens when men become involved in sexual screening. There is an immediate pleasure that drives him to seek more. I hear of men who "just have to" connect with someone. Consequently they are on their devices all the time, giving them an artificial sense of connection. One man texted his girlfriend so many times every day that she broke up with him after he got angry that she didn't respond within a few minutes. He noted that he saw she had received his texts and had opened them but didn't respond. His felt sense of immediate need to connect got the best of him and he lost whatever genuine level of connection he might have had with her. Some men have to have face time with the women in their lives, while others spend an inordinate amount of screen time between pornography, random sexual phone encounters, and real-person conversation. The ramifications of these artificial sexual connections are large with men, and they usually result in deep pockets of shame. This begins a vicious cycle for men: I engage in this artificial (temporary) connection. It gives me immediate pleasure. I feel shame. I can't tell anyone. I feel disconnected. I go back to the artificial relationship to feel connected again. The danger with these so-called relationships is that they can easily be discarded just as quickly as they are discovered, something that you can't do with people you actually see. What lacks in all of these artificial relationships a sense of concern or commitment to a real-life relationship. All of this excessive internet use and cell phone use is evidence of a man without balls, namely a man who does not have a sense of self and the complexity of what it means to love a real person and receive love from a real person.

In some ways, I think the screen relationships are some of the worst and most dangerous addictions for men. Not only can screen time replace a real-life relationship with an artificial one, screen-time addictions can lead you to other forms of addictions, like gambling.

Gambling Addictions

Gambling at large is a serious addiction. I understand that a good deal of gambling is now done on some kind of screen, much more than with casinos and lotto. Perhaps what makes gambling so addictive to some people is the excitement of possibly winning while pushing buttons and watching the screen simultaneously. This furiously fast, short-lived thrill is an important part of understanding gambling at large. Many forms of play that can become addictive have more to do with finding short-lived thrill than sustained pleasure. Recall how endorphins create short-lived pleasure and can lead to addiction. Gambling is one of the easiest illustrations of how the brain and mind are out of coordination. The instant pleasure of the sounds and sights of gambling doesn't give the mind enough time to slow the brain down before it wants more pleasure. I heard a research psychologist tell of a man who was deeply in debt, to the tune of nearly a million dollars, largely because of his gambling habit. Interestingly, this same man borrowed some more thousands, gambled more, and found himself nearly a million dollars ahead, only to then continue to gamble and find himself back in severe debt within a few hours. His brain got the message that he should gamble to feel good, and his brain won over his mind.

Work Addictions

There are many men who really enjoy work more than anything else in their lives. I admit to being one of those people. There is nothing wrong with enjoying work more than the rest of life. When work has encroached on a man's life and has had adverse effects on play and relationships, he has worked too much. I have known many men who have worked their profession for eighty hours a week, and many more who have worked their primary job for forty hours and then two other jobs for an additional forty hours. Some of them may really need to work that much to make ends meet. It is not so much the quantity of work that makes a person a workaholic, no more than it is in the absolute amount of alcohol that makes a man alcoholic.

It is the encroachment on the rest of life. The addicted worker is working *all the time* at the expense of all the other important elements of life. I just did an intake evaluation on a couple who came to me because they each had worked so well and so much that they had lost touch of each other. The man admitted to working 70 hours a week regularly but then, because he was so spent from work, he came home and went to the garage to "work" with his hobbies. Excessive work can also adversely affect a man's physical health. My inclination to work too much most certainly was part of the cause of my heart attack and the delay of an early recovery because I went back to work a week after the incident.

Aside from men who are addicted to work, there are men who are addicted to *avoiding* work. When a man has not found the intrinsic joy of working and the accomplishment of such work, he will see work as a necessary evil rather than an essential ingredient of life. The damage that occurs when a man has found a way to avoid working is huge, mostly to his own self-esteem but also to his personal mental health, his physical health, and the health of his relationships. Men who are addicted to *not working* amuse themselves with thinking about finding the perfect job by scouring the internet for jobs or pretending to apply for jobs by rewriting their resumes to perfection. I see a man who has been largely unemployed for two years and when he was working, he wasn't really productive at work. He is not the only man I have seen fired for the lack of production. These men are dreaming instead of working, and they convince themselves that they are "working to find work" when in fact they are working to avoid work.

A third kind of work addiction is actually not working at all. This can be quite devastating to a man because so much of a man's real self-esteem comes from his finding his profession and plying his trade. I saw a man who proudly told me that his wife, child, and he were all on disability and had a "stable income" from this source. But he wasn't happy and was addicted both chemically (alcohol) and behaviorally (gambling). What is the origin of addictions? We know the brain gets involved, but is there another element underlying addictions?

The Issue Underlying Addictions

Uncover an addiction, find a depression. Uncover a depression, find sadness. Uncover sadness, find a loss. Uncover a loss, find love. This is the paradigm Deb and I have used for years to help people deal with the difficulties they have had in life. The process, as we see it, is based on love, namely something or someone that I love. If I lose something that I love, I will first be simply sad. Then, if I don't allow myself to finish the sadness with normal grief, I will become depressed, which is the result of being unwilling or unable to grieve. Addiction often results from such a loss and the failure to grieve. We have written more specifically about this process in other books, so I won't elaborate on it here, but rather suggest that under all addictions is the "love problem" we mentioned in earlier chapters. Remember, this love problem is losing something that I love and then replacing it with some behavior that becomes addictive. If you uncover any addiction, you will ultimately find the real person. If you find the person, you will find his (or her) gifts and abilities and true joy of loving something. You will also find a person with intrinsic self-confidence. But this task is impossible for someone to do from the outside. You have to have a skilled therapist (or friend, mentor, minister, or teacher) to help you find the love that always underlies addiction. Addiction develops as a means of covering a loss of some kind. This loss has usually not been adequately faced, felt, and finished. The facing, feeling, and finishing of a loss is something we discussed in chapter two. This is the essential psychological basis of an addiction. Do this facing, feeling, and finishing of loss, and you will be much better able to manage the brain's part in addiction.

One of the reasons it is so hard to give up an addiction is that it uncovers a depression, perhaps a depression that the man has been hiding for many years. It is a tough sell to addicted men to suggest that if they give up on their addiction, they will first find a great amount of sadness. The good news is that a man can find something of tremendous value if he can conquer the addiction and weather the storm of finishing great sadness. When a man finds this great love that he has, he can then find creative and productive ways of giving this love to the world.

Let's have as much fun as we can, as much play as we can, as much work as we can, and as much pleasure as we can. If we truly trust ourselves with fun, play, and pleasure, we will enjoy many of the aspects of our lives and find ways to adjust to the challenges of life.

Summary

- Addictions are initiated by finding some kind of pleasure.
- Pleasure-seeking can lead to habits, which can lead to addictions.
- Addictions are brain-based. Your brain seeks to help you find pleasure or safety.

- Addictions are psychological. They are the result of a failure to face the loving process and the losing process.
- Chemical addictions include alcohol, other drugs, and food.
- Behavioral addictions include body-based pleasures, relationships, play, work, and sex.
- Preventing and curing addictions rely heavily on a man being able to talk about his addiction inclination.

SECTION III

The Big W: Women

IN THIS SECTION WE will discuss what seems to be the most challenging thing in men's lives: women. We have discussed the necessity of a man having a good grasp of words, being confident in his work, and being able to stay away from "wine" (addictions) in the previous section, all of which have strong implications for how a man can be ballsy with women. Remember, "ballsy" means being honest in all ways: namely with words, work, and wine, but most importantly with women, which is a man's greatest challenge. In order to be ballsy with women, a man has to have mastered words, work, and wine. Too many men bring their insecurities with these first three elements into relationships with women. Sadly, women make judgments about who a man is, how he feels, and what he does when they see men fail in these first three "W's." But there is more to the business of how to successfully relate to women than words, work, and wine.

In the following chapters we will look at three things: (1) significant differences between men and women, (2) how to deal with female disapproval, and (3) finding the right woman. We have all heard some pop-psychology about how men think this way and women think that way, but little of this is of much value to us men when we are trying to understand how a woman actually thinks, how she feels, and how she communicates. Many of the differences we see between men and women are cultural, many of these differences are neurological, and many are unique to the person. All of these differences cause huge communication problems between men and women, which ultimately lead to men being afraid of female disapproval. Men have to get over being afraid of potential disapproval of the women in their lives, which is no easy task. Finally, we dare to suggest ways to find the "right woman," knowing that there is no perfect woman just as there is no perfect man. The idea of finding the right woman starts with being the right man, which means feeling confident with yourself and willing to admit to your mistakes. We will look at how a woman can be "right" because she has a sense of self and a life apart from a man. We will learn that there are ways to study women and understand what they think and value, but ultimately, we need to trust our feelings, not necessarily our emotions or our thoughts.

CHAPTER 7

Men and Women: Different Creatures

WHILE WORDS ARE THE most formidable obstacle that men encounter in life, women are the most challenging. Few men understand how to relate to women, especially in the realm of feelings. In order to really grasp how men are so challenged by women, we need to first paint a clear picture of what is the basic nature of men, and then, what is the nature of women. Much has been written on the subject of gender differences, including a wide range of research, theory, and opinions. There is great diversity among the opinions rendered on this important subject, including suggestions by some authors and theorists that gender differences in communication are largely socially induced, while others suggest that these differences are more biological or neurological in origin. Further complicating this discussion is the increasing theorizing coming from the LGBTQ quarter. I defer a broader discussion of gender matters to writers who are more fluent and experienced in this area. This discussion erupts from my own experience of being a man, having a practice devoted to seeing men, reading as much on the subject as is possible, and looking for practical ways to help men and women communicate. I offer the information in this chapter with the understanding that I have much to learn in helping men and women communicate.

The Nature of Men

Over the past twenty-five years there have been a number of volumes published on the nature of manhood, some of which are worth reading. These volumes have focused somewhat on similarities with women and differences from women, but most of these books have focused on men's alleged *problems*. Instead of talking about men's so-called problems, I prefer to talk about basic manhood and the difference between the basic nature of men and the basic nature of women. Allow me to first summarize some ingredients that I believe are central to most men.

Physicality

We have discussed the physical nature of men, contrasting it with the verbal nature of women previously. If a man is to be confident in his relationship to a woman, he needs to be confident in his physicality. A man needs to know that being physical in the world is central to his existence. Many men are delayed in this awareness due to the highly verbal nature of our advanced culture.

Most males engage females unprepared to deal with the words that dominate such relationships. Unfortunately, what happens to many men is that their physical encounters with the world take a back seat to verbal encounters with the world. How good would it be if a man could enter a relationship with some kind of physical engagement rather than a verbal engagement? To engage the world with *physical confidence* a man must first be aware of his physical encounter with the world and value it. His verbal encounter with the world comes second. It is important for a man to physically *feel* his encounters with the world: the water he showers under, the pavement he walks on, the car he drives, and the physical tools he works with. Just being aware of these physical connections keep a man aware and appreciative of his physical nature. If he feels confident in his physical engagement of the world, he can then engage the nonphysical world including things emotional, things verbal, things interpersonal, and things spiritual.

As we have noted, it is important for a man to engage the nonphysical world with words and appropriate emotion to avoid the danger of being inarticulate, contradictory, or even abusive in his language. If a man hasn't developed some ability to express his feelings in words, there is a danger that he will revert to singularly expressing feelings with physical action. The emotionally immature man too easily can engage his physicality as a means of defense rather than an expression of his feelings. The physical fights men have with one another and the physical abuse they inflict are based on men *not being physically grounded* and hence not confident to engage the nonphysical world of emotions and appropriate words. Good physical confidence helps men approach the matter of words and women without feeling

MEN AND WOMEN: DIFFERENT CREATURES

insecure about themselves. Some of the men I know have found different ways of grounding themselves in their physicality:

- A seventy-five-year-old man who values waterskiing so much that when he injured his foot waterskiing, he spent six months with a trainer specifically designed to get him back on his skis. One summer he skied one hundred times.
- A man who works as a roofer offering bids for some of the most challenging historic roofs in Madison.
- A man who is a trainer and spends upwards of twenty hours of training every week.
- A man who works so hard when playing basketball that he frequently re-injures his ankle every few years.
- A man who is not so much an avid reader but has an immense library where he often simply picks out a book, feels it, pages through it, and replaces it in his library.
- A man who physically inspects every dish served in the restaurant.
- A man who cuts, splits, and stacks wood for his wood-burning stove.
- A man who walks four miles every day.
- A man who plays golf every day in the summer.
- A man whose primary activity now that he is retired is to restore old Volkswagen cars and buses.

Very often, a man's physicality can lead to his profession as it did with the roofer and the chef, but many men are not so lucky. In chapter five we discussed how a man's work and/or his profession is central to his nature. Recall that I use the term "profession" to include any activity, whether creative or productive, that reflects a man's passion in life. Importantly, there are many different forms of being physically grounded. You don't have to be a tradesman or an athlete to be physical. You just need to know that as a man you engage the world with your body first and words second. Grounded in being a physical being, a man can move forward in life with the other elements that are central to mature manhood, one of which is being a father.

Paternity

Being a father is important to all men, whether they have children or not. I use the term paternity to mean a way that men establish and maintain relationships with other people. This relationship could be between a man and another man, a man and an adult female, a man and a group of people, and of course, a man and children. Paternity is more than a biological condition. It is a way of relating to other people. To *father* someone is to bring to that person a sense of *origin* and in that feeling of origin, a feeling of security and safety. Fathering brings to the fathered person a feeling that she or he exists. This fatherhood business is physical, emotional, and spiritual. A man's love brings a sense of connection that grounds the other person to humanity at large.

Regretfully, many biological fathers are not relational fathers, meaning that many fathers don't engage their children relationally. There has been a distinct improvement in fathering over the last thirty or forty years. Yet, there is an absence of good fathering in many quarters in America, largely due to the fact that many of us men have not had particularly good role models for what it means to be a good father. Good fathering comes from a deep spiritual nature that exists in all men who are mature enough to lend it. It is possible for a man who is not a biological father to be a good father figure. You can be a good father to anyone in your life if you understand that you have a gift and an obligation to father the world. I have had many opportunities to be fatherly to the countless men I see as I sit with them through their traumas and disappointment. One of my current clients addresses me as "Uncle Ron" because he feels a kinship with me. Similarly, clergymen, doctors, teachers, and coaches can provide fathering as a part of their work, but you can be a father to your employees or coworkers if you get a grasp of what it means to be fatherly.

Many cultural rituals bring this sense of origin and belonging to children as they enter adulthood. Passage of rites and other rituals are often instituted by men. Some primitive cultures initiate a boy into the adult world with some kind of physical ritual. Most religions have some kind of ritual that suggests origin and belonging. Baptism in the Christian community is a symbol of origin ("You are children of God"), and communion also symbolizes this connectedness to people of a similar faith. Bar mitzvahs are a means of helping Jewish boys join the community of men, as are similar traditions and rituals in other religions. In all three Abrahamic religions God is generally considered to be male and fatherly. Regardless of whether God exists or is actually male, God is generally conceived as a being that exhibits fatherhood, among other characteristics.

Fathering is not limited to one person engaging in the process. Fathering can be done by a group of men or by a community at large. We see something of this when men find brotherhood in sports, the military, pool halls, and other social groups. I had a "pledge father" in my college fraternity who guided me into the process of becoming at active brother in the fraternity. It is noteworthy that paternity and fathering are not even the exclusive right or privilege of men. Women can also be fatherly to children and other adults and engage in successful fathering, but this is outside the purview of our current discussion and beyond my level of expertise.

I had a pretty good biological father who, despite some very grievous mistakes, taught me many valuable lessons in life, not the least of which was respect for women. I learned to do my share in doing dishes after a meal, expressing gratitude toward my mother, the value of work, and the value of honesty. He also initiated me into understanding spirituality, socialization, play, and good table manners. I count several of my therapists who served the fathering role for me, as well as a few teachers, uncles, grandparents, pastors, and coaches. Not many men have been so fortunate. Sadly, in my practice I hear of very few good biological fathers. If we can learn what to do and what not to do from the father figures in our lives, we will be better at rendering fathering to our children and others in our lives. Physicality and paternity can propel us men into great things.

Propulsion

Propulsion is the way a man *engages* the world. A man needs to truly *enter* the world. He can't stand by and wait for the world to engage him. He needs to make some kind of impact on the world that includes his physicality, his profession, and his paternity. A man who propels himself into the world knows that he has something to give to the world. He also knows that the world has something to give him, but his confidence is based more on what he has to give than on what he has to get. A man knows that his engagement with the world is essential for him and for the world. Engagement is essential to give meaning and purpose for him. It is essential for the world because he has something very special to give the world . . . something that no one else has.

What is this "something special" that a man has to give to the world? Asking this question reminds me of a conversation I once had with a friend, Chris, who was very bright, very experienced in various aspects of life but was not very well directed and productive in life at the time of this conversation. I told Chris that he had something very important to give to the world. Chris' response was immediate and animated: "What is it?" he asked, evidently believing that I knew what his special something was. I remember that Chris almost danced as he contemplated the fact that he had something to give the world. In that moment Chris felt that he had something very special to give to the world, even though he had no idea of what that might be. It was quite a remarkable moment to watch this man feel his sense of purpose in the world, even though he didn't yet know the details of his contribution. He just felt it. I hadn't created this feeling; I had just brought it to his mind. I am glad to report that Chris did eventually find several ways to engage the world and give to the world some of his specialness before he died.

Engagement in the world can be profound and large, or it can be simple and small. A man's engagement can be in one arena one year and in another the next year. Several professional actors have become politicians, one of them a US senator, one of them a governor, and one a president here in the United States, as well as a former actor who is now the heroic president of Ukraine. Many lawyers do not continue to practice law, as such. They migrate into various aspects of business or politics that require knowledge of law. Many carpenters end up as contractors or in real estate management after beginning as tradesmen. Many people remain in their chosen profession by continuing to *propel* themselves into ever newer aspects of their professions. Propulsion and engagement with the world are not easy. The key to success in life for a man is to engage. Engagement, simply put, is putting to use one's passions and abilities. One good thing that has come out of the pandemic starting in 2020 is that many people, forced to be at home, rediscovered their passions and as a result, have begun to redirect themselves into passionate professions. Putting your energy into engagement with the world will bring you great joy and bring joy to others. Additionally, engaging the world will also bring you face to face with mistakes and failures.

Failure

We men just have to get used to failure. Engagement in any part of life requires many trials and many errors. Failing in life is an absolute necessity for a man to find his balls. *The fear of failure that most men have comes from not having had enough failures in life*. When a man has tried enough and failed enough, three important things happen: (1) he becomes *familiar* with failure and loss, (2) he *learns* from failure, but most importantly, (3) he becomes *unafraid* of failure. The stories of inventors and initiators in the world are replete with failures. I understand that Thomas Edison had more than three thousand failures before he succeeded in creating the electric light bulb. Alexander Graham Bell had a similar number of false starts and failures. Each of these men said something like, "I did not have three thousand failures. I just *learned* three thousand ways that the light bulb (or telephone) *didn't* work." A study completed some years ago noted that most business CEOs had been fired from at least one job, and many from several jobs. We have had several presidents in the US who lost their first elections, or even second elections (Jefferson, Jackson, Lincoln, Cleveland, Johnson, Nixon, and Reagan), but then they eventually succeeded in getting elected, some with distinction.

I have been fired three times in my work life. I failed as a vacuum cleaner salesman. I failed twice in my professional career. I failed in my singular attempt at political office (local school board). I failed my first attempt at a master's degree final examination. I failed my professional licensure test twice before barely passing it the third time. I failed in my first marriage. In high school I had some modest athletic successes but ultimately failed at football, basketball, and hockey and was only mediocre in volleyball and tennis. I failed at my first hundred attempts at getting published, and wrote five books before I actually published one.

There is a central ingredient necessary for a man (or anyone) to cope with failure and loss: grieving. Recall that we discussed the centrality of sadness and grieving in chapter one. While it is necessary to learn from mistakes, errors, and failures, it is even more essential to allow oneself to feel sad when these failures occur. A man copes with the loss that one feels in failures and mistakes by feeling sad. I felt sad every time I was fired and every time that I failed something. When I took my licensure test for the third time, I thought I might not be able to take it a fourth time if I failed. It took me hours, days, and sometimes weeks to cope with other losses. The key to ultimate success in any profession, or any aspect of life is to face loss, feel loss, and finish loss. This means that the man has to admit that he feels sad then actually feel the sadness and allow the sadness to run its course. Often, a man needs to find someone with whom he can honestly share his failure and sadness. Most men haven't learned to be sad, much less to be sad until the sadness finishes. Equally important, most men do not know how to speak about their sadness to others. More often than not they find some way out of the sadness by avoiding feelings altogether, becoming angry, or engaging in some addictive behavior. These escapes from facing failure, loss, and sadness are particularly evident in men's dealing with women. Before we deal with how men might be more manly and courageous in their dealings with females, we need to examine what it is that men encounter when they become deeply involved with women.

The Nature of Women

It is beyond the scope of this work to adequately examine the basic nature of femaleness, much less the differences among women and the nuances that different women bring to the table. Instead of providing a full examination of things feminine, we want to focus on certain elements that tend to be typical of women in their dealings with men that are relevant to our study of men. The following is a list of those elements. Please note that this list is not meant to represent all that is female, nor is it intended to even suggest that these are the most important aspects of femaleness. We cannot speak as to how this list fits all cultures. Rather, these are the elements that are central for a woman when she engages the world in general and men in particular. The basic elements include: (1) spiritual, (2) life-giving, (3) intuitive, and ultimately (4) verbal. Note that we place the most challenging element that is basic to femaleness at the end of the list. This is no accident, but rather its placement as last on the list is to suggest that the preceding three elements create a foundation for women's superiority with words, especially emotional words. You will note that our interest in writing this section is to help men understand and appreciate women, particularly the gifts that they have. Only tangentially do we suggest that women can profit from this discussion.

Spiritual

It is challenging to talk about things that are spiritual, but it is very necessary. However neurological factors, personality factors, and family of origin factors are part of us, we must face the necessity of talking about spirituality, ubiquitous though this term is. All humans are spiritual, but not all humans are religious or even believe in God. Women are not more spiritual than men, but they tend to have an easier access to their spiritual experience and use of the term in their conversation. It can sometimes seem to a man that a woman can find something spiritual in just about everything. Women have what appears to be a special appreciation of the spiritual basis for all things and all activities. It may be that women more naturally retain this appreciation while they continue in their daily activities. This ability might keep them more grounded in all activities, like interpersonal relationships, work, and play. More relevant to our discussion, however, is the ability that women have to appreciate the spiritual nature underlying every activity and experience that other people have. It is in this recognition that a woman can appreciate the spiritual basis for another person's activity and assist in helping that other person keep grounded while in the activity.

It is just as essential that a man gain a depth of understanding and appreciation for his own spirituality and how this part of his humanity connects him to other people, the world, and the universe, but I don't think that things spiritual are in the forefront of most men's minds. Many men do not make the conscious connection of their spirituality and their activities as easily as women. A man's inclination towards activity and production does not often give time and space for him to attend to the spiritual nature of work and other physical activity. It is as if men do what they do so they can get something done and do not give credence to the spiritual drive behind the activity. This lack of awareness of a spiritual drive behind a man's productivity is probably rooted in certain cultural experiences that militate against a man's coming to grips with his own spirituality. If a man is truly self-aware, he can play football, re-roof his house, play a flute, or write a book, being aware of the physical, emotional, and the spiritual nature of all of these activities. Perhaps the largest difference between men and women in regards to spirituality is that women are more inclined to *speak* of their felt sense of spiritual connection to many things.

If a man understood that the woman in his life might just have a better vocabulary for spirituality, he might be able to accept the spiritual nature of his life more readily. Ideally, a woman could bring to a man this appreciation of the spiritual nature of all things and all activities. A woman can help a man become aware that these activities are not separate from people, the rest of the world, or the rest of the universe; they are connections to people, the world, and the universe. Women need to be solidly aware of their own spirituality and what it means, all the while being able to allow a man to experience and express his spirituality in his own manner and in his own vocabulary.

Life-giving

The life-giving nature of women is central to her nature. It is present whether the woman is single or partnered, old or young, gay or straight. The life-giving nature of females is not limited to their having giving birth to children because this life-giving nature of women is more than a physical condition. While never having given physical birth to children, Deb has been mother to our two girls and has been life-giving to countless women whom she has served in her office. This central ingredient of femaleness is enlivening. I like the Old English term even better: *quickening*. Women bring to any relationship this life-giving, enlivening, quickening element. It is obvious that they bring it to their children, first in gestation, next in birth, and then in early nurturing of children. However, the life-giving nature of women is more than a physical act, and it is more than something they give to children. They give it to all the people in their intimate lives. And they can bring it to the men in their lives. What a truly wonderful thing women bring to men: life itself.

Just what does this mean that women bring life itself to men? Are we men not alive before we engage women? Certainly. Are we not capable of living alone and being successful in life? Certainly. The life-giving nature of women is not literal, like something that keeps men alive like mouth-to-mouth resuscitation. The "life" that a woman provides men is different from the air that keeps men alive. It is the stuff of meaning, purpose, and direction that is central to manhood. I believe that a woman can, when she is at her best, bring the best out of a man... and make him really *alive* in life. Feminine enlivening is a *spiritual* phenomenon, but I'm not sure that many men know that women have this gift.

This life-giving ability that women have is paradoxical for men. First, most men don't realize that the primary women in their lives can bring life to them. Secondly, men really need the life that women can bring them. Few men are truly successful and happy in life without life-giving women in their lives. Thirdly, men have a kind of resistance to this enlivening essence of women: they don't always want it. Perhaps men are aware of the *essential* nature of feminine life-giving to their success and then resist it, or even resent it. It is not easy for men to admit that they really *need* the enlivening spirit that women bring to their lives. Men are of two minds in regards to the life-giving nature of the women in their lives: they want it and they resist it. I just spent an hour with a couple where the woman desperately wants to give life to her husband and hasn't been able to find a way to enliven him. The man, like so many men, is self-made, self-assuring, and self-critical, which has made him very successful in his profession, but he has never been enlivened beyond work. I hope I can help this couple engage this process of enlivening because experiencing this aliveness together sustains and enhances a man-woman relationship.

Motherly

Simply stated, most women are naturally inclined to mother the people in their lives, just as men are naturally inclined to father people. The motherly nature of women falls together with their life-giving nature but is also different from this enlivening that women do. Mothering is *protecting, nurturing, and comforting*. It is most obvious with children. Women also bring their mothering ability and quality to their relationships with men. They want to protect them, nurture them, and comfort them. Men need these things just as every human being needs these things.

Men need protection. They need protection from the many dangers in the world. They need protection from dangerous people and dangerous situations. They need protection at work and at play. And they need protection from themselves sometimes. Far more accidents occur with men than with women. Over 95 percent of incarcerated individuals are men, often coming from the dangerous activities they have engaged in (Federal Bureau of Prisons, 2022). Men die earlier than women somewhat due to their lack of personal care in how they eat, work, and play. Women see the dangers that are in men's lives and can be of immense help in protecting men from these dangers, whether from circumstances, other people, or themselves. Unfortunately, men don't appreciate women's desire to protect them . . . even though they need it.

Complicating this already difficult scenario where a woman sees dangers in the man's life and seeks to protect him is the fact that women do not always see the whole picture of a man's life. They see the dangers, but they don't always see the profit of some dangerous activities. Furthermore, in their desire to "mother" the man by protecting him, they can conclude that some things are dangerous that are not really dangerous to the man. A man needs to engage in some things that are dangerous in order to feel confident and capable. This doesn't mean that a man needs to jump off a building to see if he can fly, but rather he needs to jump right into something that may be a failure or lead to someone's disapproval. Too often, women *project* their own fears onto a man, which means that they wouldn't want to do something that the man wants to do. This *projection* of their feelings, predominantly of fear, onto the man can be very bad for the man. A man can have a reaction against a woman's protecting nature, so much so that he will act even more dangerously in his life in order to disregard her protection and enhance his self-reliance. It is a delicate balance that is a woman's lot with the man in her life: she will see dangers more than he will, but she may not have the drive that he has to succeed against all odds. A man needs to balance his need to propel and fail with the value a woman can bring him in facing unnecessary danger. Few men know how to do this balance.

The second element of mothering beyond providing safety is nurturing. Nurturing is perhaps what we most often think of with "mothering," but it can be problematic for men. The beautiful and natural tendency for women to nurture men is something that men do need to survive in life and succeed in life, but how it is rendered and how it is received is the challenge. However godly it is for a woman to nurture the men in their lives, it is also dangerous. The first danger is that men become unduly dependent on the women in their lives and fail to develop ways and means of taking care of their own physical needs. While the world is now much more egalitarian in house and home chores, many men still depend on women to maintain their basic lives like when and what they eat, what they wear, or keeping track of appointments and other chores. The other danger is that men become resentful of women who nag them about what they consume, what they wear, or how they spend their time. It takes a mature woman to truly care for a man without intruding or indulging. When a woman tries too hard to nurture a man, it is up to the man to know that her motherliness is good for him or perhaps not so good for him. This may come as simply as saying "no, thank you" to an extra helping of food at dinner when the man is not really hungry, a decline of a hug when the man wants to be left alone, or more profoundly, a decline of nurturing when the man needs to stretch the limits of his domain in life.

The third element of good mothering, beyond protection and nurturance, is comforting. Men absolutely need to be comforted, and one of the best ways a man can be comforted is by the woman in his life. If a man is ballsy enough to be honest with his needs, comfort from the woman in his life might be the best, perhaps the only thing, that will assuage his wound. On occasion when I am moved to tears for some reason, Deb will simply put her hand on me. This form of comfort is all I need. Properly and appropriately rendered, the comfort of a loving woman can restore a man to his best. This having been said, there is also the danger of rendering comfort when comfort is not needed, when it is rejected, or when it is indulgent. Hard as it is for a woman to accept a man's resistance to comfort, it is sometimes necessary for him to do that very thing, i.e., push away her attempt to comfort him. There are times when a man must simply face the trials of his life on his own, blundering through some project becoming withered in the process. When a woman interrupts this process, she runs the risk of impeding his projecting forward into life, as we discussed earlier.

Verbal

We have already discussed the important neurological differences between males and females, differences that make feeling-based conversation very difficult between them. As we have noted, women process information faster than men. More importantly, women process emotional information much faster than men. In simple terms, they recognize feelings faster, think faster, and verbalize faster than men when they are dealing with matters that have an emotional element to them.

This verbal nature of women, like their life-giving nature, is paradoxical for men. On the positive side of this phenomenon, men profit from women's superiority with words, particularly emotional words. Men depend on women to carry the load when it comes to expressing emotionally laden words. Men depend on women to know how women feel, how men feel, and how everybody feels. This often makes women the caretaker of the emotional elements of relationships, or more accurately, she speaks of these elements. Men need to recognize and verbalize their own feelings but do it in their own way. Too often, women say something like, "Why can't you just say what you feel?" when they are frustrated with a man's inability to speak his feelings. If you hear this from the woman in your life, simply say, "Give me a moment, please, and I will do my best to say how I feel, but this is not easy for me."

While I want men to know their feelings, value their feelings, and speak their feelings, we men generally feel inferior to women when it comes to emotional words. We men defer to women in this realm . . . and pay an awful price, the price of failing to mature in emotional awareness, emotional expression, and reception of emotion. Too often men let women speak for them: to their children, to their friends, and even to other men in their lives. Eventually, a man will resent a woman telling him how he feels . . . even if she is right. Men need the emotional-verbal ability that women bring to the table but more importantly they need to learn to speak their feelings by themselves.

We have discussed some of what it means to be a man and some of what it means to be a woman. It is important for us men to understand our nature and the nature of the women in our lives. These different natures are gifts that can enhance our daily lives and our relationships. While there are dangers in all gifts, more importantly, there are great possibilities with the effective use of these gifts. The more we see these positive aspects of one another, the better we will be able to appreciate the gifts that can enhance each other.

Summary

- Men and women are very much alike in many ways.
- Men and women are also quite different in many important ways.

- Men have the ingredients of physicality, paternity, and propulsion as basic aspects of life.
- Men need to be able to face failure and criticism without fear or anger.
- Women have the ingredients of spirituality, life-giving, motherliness, and being primarily verbal.
- It is important for men and women to understand their similarities and their differences because both men and women have different gifts.
- Understanding the differences can enhance communication and decrease misunderstanding and conflict.

CHAPTER 8

Men's Fear of Women's Disapproval

HAVE YOU EVER SAID that you "got in trouble" with the woman in your life? Have you ever been in the proverbial doghouse for something that you said or did? Have you ever been afraid of coming home late because of what you're "going to get" when you get home? Have you ever conjured up some kind of excuse because you forgot your anniversary? Have you ever worried what your wife was going to say when you bought that new video game or table saw or booked that golf tournament with your buddies over your anniversary weekend? If you have ever thought these things, felt these things, or did these things, you are in the vast majority of men who are afraid of women's disapproval. Did you ever ask yourself, "Why am I so afraid of what the woman in my life is going to say to me?"

We have just examined some gender differences that have significant effects on how men and women feel, how they express their feelings, and how they hear feelings. In our study we have suggested that there are basic differences and qualities between men and women. We have suggested that these natural differences are "gifts" that often cause relational difficulties, especially with communication. While making occasional suggestions for women, our task has been distinctly on how men can find their balls and be ballsy with confidence and humility. In this chapter we want to tackle one of the predominant phenomena that occurs with most men: the fear of female disapproval. We believe this fear is largely related to a failure for men and women to understand that they have different gifts and abilities. Because of the fluency with which most women can express their feelings, men feel inferior in almost any emotional conversation. They just can't keep up with women in such conversations because they can't adequately access and express their feelings. Consequently, men avoid saying how they feel even more, which then migrates into saying very little at all, which finally leads to men being dishonest in some way. This unfortunate sequence of events leads to men being afraid of women and women not trusting men. Sadly, men then feel that the women in their lives are predominantly critical instead of understanding that both the man and the woman have failed to communicate.

If you are a man who is frustrated as to how to successfully relate to the woman in your life you are not alone. The mythical Adam of the biblical Genesis account said, "This woman you gave me, God; she is the problem." Most men say the same thing about the women in their lives. Adam was wrong when he blamed Eve, just as men are wrong when they blame the woman in their life for their own failure to relate to women effectively. If the woman isn't the problem in a man's life, he must be the problem, right? Wrong again. The man isn't the problem either. The *problem* is in the verbal interface between the man and woman. Men and women are, in a sense, using different languages, each of them expecting that the other person will understand what they are saying. Rarely is this the case.

Our task in this chapter is to understand the pervasiveness of men's fear of female disapproval and find ways men can overcome this fear. To resolve the problem the man has to come to grips with the differences of how men and women engage verbally, as we detailed in the last chapter, and take this as a challenge to find a way to adequately communicate with the woman in his life. This takes balls, and it is your responsibility as a man to start the process of understanding one another. We have two major goals for this chapter: 1) to help men and women understand the nature of fear of disapproval that men have and 2) to help men overcome this fear by finding ways to carefully engage the differences in how men and women communicate.

Disapproval

No one likes disapproval, and no one likes to be criticized. It doesn't matter whether the person who is seemingly criticizing you is right or wrong. It doesn't even matter whether your critic thinks he or she is criticizing you. If you feel criticized, you are criticized. If someone criticizes you, you will not like it. You will be hurt. Then, as we discussed in earlier chapters, if you're a typical man, you will race right by hurt and sadness into fear and then into anger, avoidance, or addiction. Most men are afraid of any kind of disapproval, but they are especially afraid of disapproval that comes from their female partners. They might be able to handle disapproval that comes from a parent, a sibling, a supervisor at work, a coach on the sports field, and even a good friend, but not so easily from an intimate female. Simply stated, men don't have the balls to hear female disapproval and deal with it honestly.

Women don't like disapproval any more than men do but they have experienced a lot more social disapproval than men have in their growing up years. How men and women grow up with disapproval is quite different. Women have grown up with female disapproval in the form of drama and gossip accompanied with verbal challenging, something most men have not experienced. Men have different challenges in their teenage years. They are criticized for what they do, like their performance on the athletic field, the English class, or maybe the car they drive. Rarely are men criticized for the words they use or the relationships they have. When a man is challenged by the woman in his life for the words he has used, he is in a whole new world, and he is completely unprepared to engage in a conversation about his words, much less his feelings underneath his words. Furthermore, he comes into a relationship with a woman with a completely different idea of what it means to relate intimately to someone.

Entering a Relationship with Different Experiences of Disapproval

The disapproval boys have experienced is in what they *did* or what they didn't *do*, not usually what they *said*. It is easier for men to face disapproval in school, at work, or in sports, because it is related to their *performance*, not their words. I remember feeling awful when I was teased by other boys or criticized by a teacher or a coach. I even remember being criticized for what I said in class, very often due to my extraverted nature to shoot my mouth off, but I don't remember suffering any kind of gossip or direct assault on me for my physical appearance or the clothes I wore that is common with girls. How and why we were criticized has a direct bearing on how men and women deal with criticism as adults. When they were in school, girls used their verbal expertise to vocalize their hurt, challenge the assault, and then possibly negotiate some kind of conflict resolution. Conflict resolution for boys could lead to a physical altercation or utter silence. These are very different ways of hearing criticism and handling criticism: men think of what they *did and what they can do*; women think of what they *felt and what they can say*. Men react; women talk back.

Women have had much more experience with discussions that are emotionally confrontational because of what they experienced in middle school and high school. We men might be pretty good at debate regarding facts, and some men are good at physical fighting, but most of us are woefully unprepared for discussions that are emotionally laden. Because of these profoundly different experiences in disapproval, a typical woman tends to enter a male relationship with the assumption that there will be a mutual exchange with the man that is a combination of facts and feelings. A woman can make the understandable but erroneous assumption that she can say what she doesn't like about the man, that he will be able to digest her disapproval, and that he will engage in back-and-forth statements that are emotional in form. She might even think that if she says that the man has hurt her (emotionally), the man will be understanding and apologetic for what he said or did. It is at this point where most male-female relationships fail in communication. The woman expects to engage in emotional statements and the man expects to engage in factual statements. Ideally, they do both of these things, but that rarely happens. They are speaking different languages.

With some exceptions men enter female relationships with the physical and cognitive perspective of what it means to relate to someone else, as we discussed in the last chapter. You work hard, you play hard. While there are many men who have a broader perspective of a female relationship that includes words and emotion, most men are not so skilled. Rather, when men are challenged by a woman who says that he hurt her, men look to see *what they did wrong*. He might think, for instance, that he works hard "to take care of the family," and he plays hard because "he enjoys his friends." When he hears his wife say "you are always working or playing," he can't see what he has *done wrong*. He doesn't see the emotional aspect in this interaction. He might even say something like, "I'm doing what I think is best to do for the family and for me. Why don't you do what you think is best?" He is not even aware of his emotions of joy and sorrow that occur with work and play. So, when his wife expresses her hurt, a word that is not really in his vocabulary, he is nonplussed. Then he goes into anger, avoidance, or addiction rather than engaging in a fruitful emotional conversation with his wife. Consider a possible conversation between Ben and Glenda when Ben comes home late from work:

> Glenda: "Why are you so late? What were you doing?" (These are rhetorical questions that actually mean "I don't like it that you are late." The woman does not say this directly, but the man hears her disapproval in her voice and the implications of these rhetorical questions.)
>
> Ben: "I needed to finish a project I was working on." (He feels hurt but doesn't know how to express this hurt. He also feels defensive and is ready for a fight if his "explanation" isn't sufficient.)

Glenda: "I am so hurt that you work late. You don't seem to care about the family." (Now she is in attack mode and has used the "H" word [hurt] in the midst of this attack. She assumes that he will respond to her hurt and make some kind of apology.")

Ben: "What are you talking about? I'm working hard for the family, for Christ's sake. Why else would I be working?" (Now, he is in anger mode, having run right past his hurt, let alone her hurt.)

Glenda: "All you think about is yourself. I don't know why I put up with it." (Now she is in full attack mode, with highly emotionally laden language that she has used many times to protect herself.)

Ben: "I'll see you later. I'm going downstairs." (Now he is in avoidance mode. He may go into addiction mode with drinking or playing video games.)

Glenda: "Don't let the door hit you in the ass when you leave." (She has "lost" the argument and takes her last swing at Ben.")

Obviously, I have collapsed this conversation from minutes into seconds, but the essence is the same. The man is seeing facts, and the woman is seeing feelings. She sees the facts but cares about the feelings, which is what she communicates. He sees the feelings but cares about the facts, which is what he communicates. Then they go off to their respective silos: he goes to the basement to play video games or to drink; she goes to eating or calling a friend to find some solace in her hurt.

In the above conversation Ben hears Glenda saying that *he is wrong in working* so much. He doesn't hear that *she is hurt*. When confronted with the "H" word from a woman, he might say something like "what do you mean you are hurt? Tell me something concrete, something real!" In fact, the woman is telling the man something real, but the reality is emotional and abstract. He is looking for something concrete that he did wrong. Glenda is hoping that when she tells Ben that she is hurt, this comment will lead to a conversation about her feelings and maybe his feelings. Ben doesn't see it that way. He feels criticized. He is not aware that he is hurt as much as she is hurt but his hurt has come from what she said whereas Glenda's hurt came from what he did.

We previously have discussed how men get hurt about the same amount as women do, but they are usually not aware of having been hurt. Women see that the men in their lives are defensive and angry when they are criticized, and they don't know what to do with male defensiveness. Women do not always recognize that defensiveness is a cloak of hurt. Many women have not understood why a man simply leaves the room or otherwise runs away from an argument when she wants to talk about it. Men often leave an emotional discussion saying, "I don't want to argue." "I don't want to argue" for the man means that he doesn't know how to engage in a verbal discussion that has to do with emotions and words. For a woman this statement means, "I don't want to be close to you by sharing feelings together."

We discussed hurt and the feeling of helplessness quite a bit in chapters two and three. Here, I want to remind you that hurt is central in any relationship and that most all men get into trouble and lose their balls when they fail to communicate that they are hurt, especially to women. It is so easy for a man to be hurt with a cut and yell "ouch" or some expletive but almost impossible to admit to relational hurt with words. My very first therapist said, "Say ouch when it hurts." Most men never learn it. What might have happened if Ben had said to Glenda that he was hurt when she asked why he was late from work? It might have led to a good conversation, but it might also have deteriorated further. We men need to use the "H" word judiciously.

Expressing Hurt and Helplessness to a Woman: A Warning

It is immensely helpful in a female relationship for the man to talk about his hurt and the woman to listen, but it is immensely difficult to do. If a man is to have the balls to tell the woman in his life that he is hurt, whether or not the hurt came from her or from someone else, he will be changing the entire pattern of emotional conversation. Women are not familiar with hearing the "H" word from men, and they may not deal with it very well despite their proclivity to emotional talk. Likely, if a man talks to the woman about how she has hurt him, she could easily say something like, "Well, Buddy, you have no idea of how much you have hurt me for years," thus displaying the undue use of the "H" word in her vocabulary and the monopoly she has had using the word. A woman hearing the "H" word for the first time in their collective life might be quite overwhelmed by hearing a man's emotion and unprepared to respond favorably to it.

I have been working with Bill on and off for several years after he came to my office with the proverbial female hand in his back. In fact, the only reason he comes to my office is because his wife continues to insist on it. The most recent time I saw him, he even joked about the hand in his back and the foot in his butt, both coming from his wife. Earlier in my work with Bill I had the notion that he was capable of speaking his feelings because, despite his insufficient education, he is quite bright, analytical, and very truth-seeking. I erroneously thought that, due to his high intelligence and apparent wisdom, he could speak his feelings. Bill told me that he had been criticized by his wife for something he had done. I understand verbal criticisms as "assaults." I suggested to Bill that he tell his wife that her words hurt him, thinking that this would be a beginning way of communicating to her about his feelings. This seemed simple enough, and a way to begin to help Bill express himself and find his balls. Bill went home that day and told his wife that her words hurt him. Her response: "Oh, you poor baby. You are hurt. Well, isn't that too bad? Perhaps you should go back to Mama and cry it out." Wow. Of course, Bill was nonplussed to say the least. Here he was following the advice of his therapist, advice on how to deal with his wife's reported criticism, and when he got this assault, it made matters even worse.

I learned from this experience with Bill that a man needs much more than the right words when speaking to a woman, particularly to a woman who has been hurt by him and angry with him for years. I no longer advise men to speak about their hurt this way until they have learned enough about themselves, gained confidence in themselves, and have learned all the ingredients necessary when speaking to a woman. The task of speaking feelings of hurt and helplessness needs to be grounded in solid self-esteem, which itself is grounded in self-understanding and self-acceptance. To speak to a woman adequately and effectively, particularly about being hurt, a man has to know who he is, like who he is, and feel confident in who he is. Hurt is so central to what it means to be human that a man must have confidence in speaking about it as well as some liberty in negotiating the conversation with the woman in his life. When men get better at expressing hurt and other emotions, they will be consequently better at hearing emotional words.

Gaining Confidence in Conversation with Women

True confidence is composed primarily of the element of *truth*, so when a man expresses his feelings, his confidence is in knowing that his feelings are real and true. Confidence in speaking feelings is not assurance that what you say is perfectly said, much less being perfectly understood. The Latin origin of the word *confidence* is "with truth." From this same word we get fidelity, which means truthfulness and trustworthiness. If a man begins a conversation with a woman with confidence, i.e., knowing that what he wants to say is "with truth," his confidence is not in the *words he* says; it is not in what the woman *hears*; it is in the *experience* that he has had in feeling his emotions. This confidence allows him to have many trials and errors when he speaks his feelings. To talk to a woman about feelings, a man must be truthful to himself and feel the essence of this truth in his discussing these feelings. I hope in your reading this book, you have begun to feel what you feel, and think about what you feel, you have begun to recognize what your truth is. I hope that you see that you are a man with a passion, that you have as many feelings as anyone else, and that you are about paternity, fathering, and propulsion all in the larger understanding of those terms. If you are a man who knows his feelings, a man who is willing to face his feelings, and a man who trusts these feelings, you are prepared for communicating your feelings.

Men, I want to give you a format for how you can gain confidence in your conversations with women. Having a concept of how to talk about your feelings to a woman is much more important than having the "right words" like in Bill's dreadful experience. I'd like to suggest a metaphor for having a successful conversation with a woman. This is a platform, or what I prefer to call it, a *stage* on which you can present your feelings to the women in your lives. You need many "rehearsals" to get it right, just like any actor needs to become familiar with his script. This format is not about acting or having a memorized speech. It is a way for you to create a safe place to talk and to listen.

Staging

I have been talking all along about speaking about your hurt, which is the dominant element in your fear of a woman's disapproval. To move forward with balls in communicating your hurt is a process I call "staging." As I noted in brief earlier, I want you to consider that you need a figurative stage from which you present your feelings. We think that you will find that this "staging" will become a practical as well as perhaps (eventually) an enjoyable way to engage. There are three steps to staging: *setting the stage, keeping the stage, and exiting the stage*. It is paramount that a man learns to clearly state that *he is talking about himself*. In other words, a man should begin any effort of communicating his feelings with a preparatory statement that what he is saying is about himself. This is what I call "setting the stage."

Setting the Stage

You could begin a conversation by saying something like,

- "I've been doing a lot of thinking about myself lately that I would like to tell you." Or . . .

- "I'd like to tell you about myself. It is important that I tell you about me because I want you to understand me. I want to understand you." Or . . .
- "I want to tell you about me."
- Or any package of words that hopefully excites your listener because you want to reveal a part of yourself.

Note that I suggest that you use the term "thinking" rather than "feeling" in this initial statement. You might remember when you heard the woman say, "I want to tell you my feelings," you got prepared for being criticized. While it would seem that a man could begin a conversation with a woman by saying that he wanted to talk about his feelings, it rarely works well to say that. When a man sets the stage by stating that he is going to talk about what he "has been thinking," the listener might be more attuned to his statements. This must seem like a convoluted way of beginning to say how you feel, but it is the best way to *start* the communication process.

These kinds of statements *set the stage* for a man to confidently begin to speak his feelings. This way of talking is important because most women have never heard men really talk about their feelings. They have heard anger; they have encountered avoidance; they have seen addiction; they have felt demeaned or even threatened. When a man says that he is going to talk about his feelings, he needs to be prepared that this will come as a kind of a shock to the woman, and she will probably not be prepared for it, expecting that his feelings will be something negative about her. Be prepared for a bit of defensiveness with the woman, for instance her saying,

- "What have you done now?" Or . . .
- "Did you buy another gun for your collection?" Or . . .
- "OK. I'm ready. Let me have it." Or . . .
- "What does that mean (that you want to talk about your feelings)?"

In addition to an introductory statement, I suggest that you have a couple of statements ready to say when speaking your feelings. These statements are what I call "go-to" statements. Go-to statements are used as prompts or "cheat sheets" when it would otherwise be easy to get off track. These statements are used to steady yourself when you get lost in your feelings, thoughts, or words. They can help you fumble around a bit while you get your footing on the stage so you can continue to speak. You might say something like,

- "Excuse me. I'm not communicating." Or . . .

- "My bad here. Let me try again to tell you what's on my mind." Or . . .
- "This whole feeling thing is new to me. I'll try to clear it up."

Men need these kinds of fumbling statements ready to say because it is rare that a man adequately communicates his hurt feelings the first time he tries. A normal man is just not ready to talk about his feelings, and he is probably not very good at it. Did you hear the word that I used here for a man who isn't good at speaking feelings? *Normal.* I didn't use the terms inadequate, stupid, or wrong. As we have already noted, confidence erupts out of trial and error. You will make mistakes in what you say when you enter into the murky waters of expressing feelings. It is wise and prudent to be prepared for this. This setting the stage is not speaking perfectly or communicating. It is a big mistake that all people make in thinking that because they have *said* something, that they have *communicated*. Rarely do men adequately communicate themselves when they talk about any feeling, particularly hurt. A man can initially speak himself, fail in this initial attempt to communicate, and then say something like "I am sorry, I am not very good yet at speaking my feelings on this matter, and I will try again." However, this takes balls because you're openly admitting to your limitations.

You also need to have a few go-to statements to use when you are interrupted by the woman. Remember, she is doing what she has done since she was twelve: speaking and listening at the same time. She thinks that you can speak your feelings and hear her feelings in quick succession or simultaneously. She doesn't think that she is "interrupting." She feels that she is helping you speak your feelings. You can't speak and listen in this fashion. Consider saying something like,

- "Please let me continue." Then add, "I'm not good at this." Or . . .
- "I need a moment to think about what I'm trying to say. If I can continue to fumble around here, I might actually eventually make some sense." Or . . .
- "I have learned that you, as a woman have a much better ability to talk about feelings and listen about feelings. I need a moment to think." Or . . .
- "Sorry to look so demanding here, but I need to speak first so I can really attend to what you think."

Having these prompts at the ready will keep you grounded and in your confidence that you are a good man, that speaking your feelings is simply not your strong suit. Of course, you have a right to speak your feelings, but you can't actually say that because it will certainly sound like a criticism.

Know that this whole matter of staging is not a woman's way of having a conversation, so it will be hard for her to accommodate to the procedure. It will be even harder for you to keep the stage.

Keeping the Stage

Once the stage is set by having made an introductory self-statement that is essentially, "I want to tell you about me," and you might have used your go-to statements as needed, you need to *keep the stage*. Keeping the stage is a mix of fumbling through what it is you want to say while coping with the interruptions you will undoubtedly hear from the woman. This twofold keeping the stage is essential in the process of communicating yourself. You might feel, "Forget this. I can't do this," possibly laced with a variety of curse words. Keeping the stage is also difficult because *most people, male or female, are not very good at letting someone speak their feelings without interrupting*. Once you climb on the stage and begin to say how you feel, people will tend to jump on the stage and tell their own stories and express their own feelings or try to correct your story. Feelings expressed by one person almost always stimulate feelings in the listener. You have to be prepared for this reaction and find kind ways to keep the stage.

A man who has set the stage has said, in effect,

- "I am going to try to express my feelings. This is difficult enough for me."
- "I want to listen to you, but it would be helpful if I could speak for a minute or two before you respond to me."
- "I need a bit of time to express my feelings because I'm not particularly good at this." Or . . .
- "I'd appreciate it if you could do me the favor of hearing me out as I wander through these murky waters of feelings." Or . . .
- "I need to hear your feelings and thoughts later, but I am fumbling through this whole thing, and I need a bit of space, please."

You have to know these kinds of statements will not bode well with most women. For one thing, the woman in your life may have never heard your feelings so she will not be familiar with you taking the stage. Additionally, saying something that allows you to keep the stage sounds terribly selfish. To most people this sounds like "my feelings are more important than your feelings," or worse yet, "I am more important than you are," but keeping the stage is neither of these conditions. Rather, it is a necessity for a man to be on stage and stay there until he truly feels that he has communicated his feelings. For the moment it is all about him, and he needs the moment to be all about him. He can't be thinking of what she might think about his feelings. He needs to be thinking of his own feelings while working to find words to express these feelings.

It asks a lot of a woman to simply listen to the man's performance on the stage without interrupting. In fact, it is nearly impossible. She doesn't think she is interrupting. She thinks that she is helping when she adds something, challenges something, or asks some question. Worse yet, she thinks that she can tell you how she feels while you are telling her how you feel. Men need to climb on the stage, stay on the stage as long as they have feelings to express, and not share this stage with the woman. This will take some practice, and many trials and errors. It will eventually work, but only after the woman sees, and begins to understand, that the man needs the stage to himself if he is going to talk about his feelings. He can't talk about his feelings and hear the woman's feelings. He can't even hear her questions. He can't hear her sighs. He can barely hear her breathing. This holding the stage is shaky ground for any man and he needs to maintain confidence in his feelings, not in his words. This takes balls. When I work with couples to improve their communication of their feelings, I suggest that the listener say, "Thank you for telling me your feelings. I don't fully understand. Please tell me more." To do this, however, a person, male or female, must be aware of their feelings in order to contain them while the other person is expressing theirs. Perhaps the worst part of keeping the stage is resisting the woman's questions.

What often happens in the process of a man expressing his feelings is that he says something that doesn't make sense to the woman. Sometimes what a man says one minute is not the same thing he says the next minute, which can be very confusing to the woman who is trying to make sense of what the man is saying. But this is the way we men have to speak our feelings, i.e., knowing that words are not the best way we communicate, and when we do use words, they are approximate. Even in these circumstances it is important to avoid asking questions and avoid answering questions. Too often, a man asks if she understands what he is saying, or worse yet, if she agrees with what he is saying. You don't need the woman's approval of what you are saying. You don't even need her understanding, at least at the beginning of the process. What you need is her silence. You have no idea how hard this is for women to do, because they are not used to having a one-way conversation about feelings. What makes holding the stage even harder is the fact that when you start to express your feelings, you will be inconsistent.

If the man is truly trying to express his feelings, he can't simultaneously be cautious about what he says. He can't be consistent. Recall that we noted that feelings are not words; rather, words approximately represent feelings. The man can't readily find words that adequately reflect his feelings. He needs room to say things that seem to be true, followed by his own immediate corrections or additions. He needs to say things that he is certain of in one minute and uncertain of the next. Expressing feelings is not just a rational event; it is an emotional event that has some rational thoughts with it. Emotional events do not lend themselves very well to words of any kind. This all takes balls.

You can be successful in keeping the stage if you keep a couple things in mind:

Make simple statements. My wife always instructs her clients to "full stop" when they have said something. Full stop is the British term for what a period does at the end of a sentence. Deb works primarily with women who are often adept at constructing long and complicated sentences. She encourages them to make short full stops when they say something significant so they can gain clarity and be grounded in their own feelings. I want to help you men do the same thing. Make a statement, hopefully that is feeling-based, and give yourself a moment to think and feel about what you just said.

Make statements about yourself that don't necessarily have to do with your relationship. You might say something like,

- "I am enjoying my job."
- "I am sad about our son's failing grades."
- "I am afraid of what the doctor is going to tell me."
- "I talked to my brother today." (Perhaps a brother that has caused you great trouble in the past.)

Notice that each of these statements is feeling-based. These types of full-stop statements give you a stable place before you say more about yourself. Here is where it would be easy to lose the stage to questions or interruptions. For example, if you tell your wife that you are afraid of what the doctor might say, I can almost promise you she will attempt to interrupt you and . . .

- Attempt to assure you everything will be okay. Or . . .
- Chide you because you should have gone before now. Or . . .
- Dismiss what you say entirely. Or . . .

- Say something like, "Don't be such a baby!"

These kinds of interruptions would be where you use your "go-to" prompt, take back your stage, and say, "Please let me continue." If you are lucky, she will back up and let you go on. She can learn to do this the more you speak your feelings because she will begin to understand how men talk feelings.

Be repetitive. It is important to repeat your go-to statements. *Repetition is reinforcement.* Variation skips you around. You don't want to skip around; you want to stay on point, to stay on stage. You may have to say the exact same thing more than once. Just say something like, "I know that I have said this, but permit me to say it again just for my own peace of mind."

Use qualifiers. Typically, men fumble around while attempting to speak their feelings. I suggest that men use the terms *hurt* and *helpless*, on the one hand, and *joy* and *success* on the other, like

- "I'm really not good at this talking about feelings, you know."
- "I wish I could speak about my feelings more fluently and correctly."
- "I feel pretty helpless when I try to speak my feelings."
- "I'm just not good at being hurt and admitting that I am hurt."
- "I am glad that I sent the e-card to my mom."
- "I enjoyed teaching Johnny how to play chess."
- "I feel good with my work at the office today."
- "I am looking forward to Christmas with your family."

Count on your fingers. This suggestion is just a way to encourage you to only say two or three things, at least to begin with. Just keep count on the two or three things you want to say and stop when you are weary of speaking. Sticking to just two or three feeling-based statements will help you stay true to what it is you want to communicate. It will help you stay on track. If you have a heavy-laden agenda, you are bound to get all the more fumbled.

Appreciation. Like all good things, having the privilege of staging should be appreciated. Tell your partner that you appreciate her listening to you. Even if it is just one feeling statement that you give. Then it will be time to get off the stage.

Exiting the Stage

The last ingredient in a man's successful communication is climbing *off* the stage. Exiting the stage is like finishing a performance. You have given your best. You are tired. You are satisfied with some things you said and less satisfied with other things, but you are *finished* for now. You leave the stage by declaring that you are finished expressing your feelings. You need to say something that is declarative: (1) that you are finished talking, (2) that this is not the time to listen to the woman's response to your feelings, and (3) that you will hear her thoughts and feelings at a later time. You should say something like this:

- "I feel finished expressing my feelings."
- "I need a bit of time before we delve further into what I have said."
- "I know you would like to respond to what I have to say."
- "What I have said is far from perfect. I am not entirely satisfied with what I have said, but I ask you to give me some time to process what I have said before we talk further."
- When we talk further, I would like to hear from you, both your thoughts and your feelings.
- I suspect that my saying that I need to stop talking might be hard for you.
- I will ask you to talk further after I have collected my thoughts.

You certainly won't use these exact words but I want to communicate that this business of "exiting the stage" is a delicate time for you and for the woman. Difficult for you because you have spoken your feelings, possibly for the first time in your life; difficult for you to admit to feeling hurt and helpless; and difficult to keep the stage when you really wanted to avoid the whole thing and have a beer. This is also a delicate and difficult time for the woman. Know that having spoken your feelings (ideally) without the woman having spoken hers is not a woman's way of having a conversation. She will likely be disappointed and possibly irritated for your seeming to control the conversation. This is why it is essential that you assure her that you will return to this and hear what she has to say.

If she protests too much at this hiatus in the conversation, you might say something like this:

- "I am sorry that my putting a pause on our conversation has hurt you."

- "I am just learning how to talk about feelings. I am not yet very good at it, and I need to think about what I said."
- "I can only imagine that this seems unfair and not what you would like."
- "I think your feelings are just as important as mine."
- "I promise that I will come back to this and hear what you have to say."
- "I will get back to you as soon as I can."

Once you get familiar with this very male way of speaking feelings, you might be able to immediately listen to the woman, but this most certainly will not be the case when you are learning to talk feelings. Consider the times you have said some kind of feeling that then led to the woman speaking her feelings, which then led to some kind of argument, or irritability at best. The hiatus in the conversation that I am suggesting is necessary for you until you have your feet on the ground in speaking feelings. This procedure of setting the stage, keeping the stage, and exiting the stage is not the only way to have a feeling-based conversation, but it is best for most men, at least at the beginning of their speaking their feelings.

Many mistakes have been made by men who have expressed their feelings in some way and then stayed in the same room and heard the woman's retorts to his feelings. Men in this situation become irritated and confused and usually resort to anger and swearing or to utter silence, which is avoidance. Most men are simply not capable of a back-and-forth conversation about feelings the way women want to have a conversation. Granted, it is difficult for the woman to hear a man's feelings without expressing her own, but if you handle this right, she will be learning about your feelings, including your joys and sorrows, and ultimately know you better. If she knows you better, she just might love you better. She may even come to understand your need to retreat and muse about what you said.

When you exit the stage and retreat from the conversation, you need to take an honest inventory of how you spoke, what you spoke, and how you felt when you spoke. Then, when you are ready to return to the conversation, do it. Do it so you can keep your word and hear what she has to say. *A man who retreats must return.*

Yielding the Stage

Ultimately, and with practice, you will be able to give your wife or partner the stage when you return. If a man can listen immediately after having spoken his own feelings, there can be real benefit to the woman, the man, and the relationship. Whether a man yields the stage immediately to the woman or returns after his retreat, he will need to hear her out. Men can learn how to listen, but it takes a lot of practice. What they will likely hear from women will generally be difficult and confusing to them. It takes years of practice for a man and a woman to have a feeling-based conversation where they both speak their feelings without interrupting one another. Men and women need to go carefully and listen to one another as they talk about their feelings. The more men communicate their feelings, and the more they hear the woman's feelings, the more they will understand each other. When you understand someone more, you will unavoidably love that person more.

What to Expect When You Yield the Stage

When a man is ready to yield the stage to the woman, he needs to be prepared:

- He needs to be prepared for being understood and not understood. He needs to be prepared for challenge and criticism as well as acceptance and appreciation. He can't know exactly what to expect.

- He needs to give her the stage as he has asked that he be given the stage. He needs to listen, and listen, and listen. Listening doesn't mean that he understands, and it certainly doesn't mean that he agrees with the woman. It means that he is quiet. It means that he gives the woman a chance to speak her feelings until she is satisfied that she has expressed them adequately and completely.

- Keep in mind that the woman will perform on the stage much differently than he has performed. She will talk about her feelings much differently than he has done.

- More importantly, she will have many things to say about what he has said. She will most likely challenge much of what he has said. She will undoubtedly say that he is "wrong" about a lot of things. She will most likely be hurt herself and express that hurt as being a deeper hurt than the man has expressed. Simply put, she will not likely understand that the man has expressed his feelings as well as he could. Be prepared for her hurting you in the process of expressing her feelings and govern your tendency towards anger and avoidance.

- Be prepared for questions from the woman. This is tricky. Women will ask questions that sound legitimate, and they will want you to answer these questions. Just as we advised you to avoid answering questions when you are on stage, you should not fall prey to answering questions when she is on stage. This is particularly hard, both for you and for her.

How to Deal with Questions

The stage is a place for statements, not questions. Avoiding questions might seem very strange at first because most conversations include a number of questions. Being on stage for a man is not a conversation. It is a presentation. When you watch someone on a literal stage, whether a Shakespearian actor or a lecturer, you are there to listen. Questions that are asked when someone is on stage deter individuals from speaking when they are diligently working to express their feelings. Restricting questions will be hard on the woman. She might say that she wants clarification, an explanation, or a reason for what you said or did. This kind of questioning seems very reasonable to a woman, but you should do your best to avoid answering and clarifying what you said, much less justifying it. In these circumstances use some "go-to" statements:

- "I will clarify what I said later, right now, tell me more about how you feel."
- "I will answer your questions after I hear more from you."
- "I am sure a lot of what I said wasn't right. For now, I just want to hear more from you."
- "This sounds like an important question, but I think it is more important that I hear from you first."

This "avoiding the question-and-answer form of conversation" is hard both on the man and on the woman. If a man tries to answer a question, he will lose his thought or intention, or more importantly, he will lose the course of his feeling. It is hard on the woman because of her speed—she wants to understand *right now*. If the man gives himself enough time, enough room, and enough misfires in his emotional expression, he will eventually find the right package of words, perhaps interspersed with physical movement and physical gestures, to truly communicate his feelings. When this happens, there won't be a need for questions. The woman will understand and come to know him. And she will love him better.

Many questions are of genuine inquiry, or they are questions that seek some clarity, but they are still interruptive in the initial stages of the feeling-expressing process. Questions can be very fun to ask and to answer, especially if there is a spirit of genuine inquiry between two people where they are both seeking to find out something about one another, or seeking to learn something from one another. Questions might actually come after each person has an opportunity to express their feelings and thoughts, but this should come in a spirit of genuine inquiry, in a spirit of true interest in the other person. Take time to notice any questions you might ask and discover the statements behind them. The more you state yourself and the more you can hear someone else state himself or herself you will mature into a place of genuine questions that encourage rather than attack.

Speaking Better, Listening Better, Loving Better

I don't want to paint a bleak picture of conversation between a man and a woman. Rather, I want to paint a picture of a man having the balls to admit to himself that he is not good at expressing his feelings and then moving forward into the whole arena of feelings with continued balls, knowing that a feeling-based conversation with a woman is a challenge worth the effort. The first few times you try to express your feelings and then hear her feelings might be a total failure, but if you keep at it, you will get better at talking, and she will get better at listening. It can be wonderful. It can be loving. It can be connecting. It can be enhancing. It is difficult to get to the wonderful, the loving, and the connecting. Most people have no idea how hard it is to learn to truly communicate. They think it is easy or that it should be easy. It is nothing of the sort. I put the bulk of the work on the man to set the stage, keep the stage, leave the stage, and then yield the stage. The man has to have a good grasp of the only communication process that works for him: talking *or* listening to the woman, not talking *and* listening to her. More importantly, he has to realize that he is changing the rules of the communication game. He is changing the way men and women usually talk.

Summary

- Fear of disapproval from women is the heart of much that goes wrong in a man's relationship with a woman.
- It is not the woman's fault that men are afraid of her disapproval.
- To avoid the fear of female disapproval, a man has to be confident with words.

- Men tend enter a relationship with a woman without an understanding of what is expected of him.
- There is a central place for feelings in a female relationship, but boys are rarely taught about the importance and centrality of feelings, so they come unprepared into a relationship that has a significant emotional content.
- A man needs to learn how to *stage*, i.e., first by speaking and then by listening.
- A man needs to adequately communicate feelings of hurt and helplessness as well as the emotion of sadness that accompanies such feelings.
- A man needs to adequately communicate his joys and successes.
- It is important for a man to avoid asking questions and answering questions. Rather, he should make statements.

CHAPTER 9

Finding the Right Woman

THERE ARE MANY ASPECTS of balls that we have discussed: words, work, and wine. We have talked mostly about what it is about a man that leads him into trouble in these various aspects of life and have examined how it is important to have balls in all of these areas. We have just discussed men's fear of women's disapproval and how to find confidence in talking to women. Our focus in this book has been on the man: how he is constructed, how he acts, how he feels, and what he should do in life. Now we are going to bridge into a sensitive area, namely the difficulties that men have with women. I enter this discussion with some trepidation and concern because the focus of this book is on men having balls, not on women, and particularly not on women's "problems." I have already noted how distasteful the terms "problems" or "issues" are to me. If we see that various aspects of life are problematic and challenging, rather than problems and issues, we can look at the difficulties that we have in life and find ways to deal with them. Let me begin this discussion by noting that the present discussion is presented as a *perception* that I have of women and a perception that many men have of women. The ultimate purpose here is to understand, admire, and uplift the women in our lives by understanding what happens in relationships that are right and those that are not right.

Although the title of the chapter is "Finding the Right Woman," we will begin by identifying what it means to be the right man. The right man has balls, meaning that he is courageously honest with what he is and honestly humble with what he is not, what he is good at and what he is not good at. We follow this brief study of men with what I call "the strong woman," or "right woman," namely a woman who is self-aware enough to also be courageously honest and honestly humble. We then examine how we men often find "the wrong woman," namely the woman who has not developed herself and as a result enters a male relationship with a limited understanding of herself, which leads to a limited understanding of the man. We look at how men fail to find the right woman and as a result, fall into relationships with women who are not mature.

The Right Man

"Finding the right woman" has more to do with the man than it has to do with the woman. Being the right man with a woman requires him to express his feelings even if these words are spoken more slowly and carefully than women speak. It means having work that is satisfying, creative, and productive. It means having no significant avoidances in life in the many forms of "wine." Being the right man also means learning how to understand women and how to say yes to some and to say no to others.

If you aren't yet the right man, you certainly won't find the right woman. If she is the right woman, she won't settle for anything but a man with balls. In our discussion with many women while thinking about this book and writing it, all of them have agreed that it is hard to find a man with balls, however odd that sounds. Women say that they would be immensely happy to find a ballsy man. Sometimes, women may have a better grasp of what a ballsy man looks like than men do.

The right man is not looking for the *perfect* woman. He is looking for the *right* woman, the *good* woman, the *real* woman. He is not looking for a woman to make up for his deficiencies in life or to cater to his fantasies of what a "perfect woman" might be. He is not looking for a woman to cure his loneliness, to satisfy his hunger for intimacy, or to cure his insecurities and ailments. He is looking for a woman to *complement* him, which means add to him, not *compliment* him, which means approving of him. Approval is a delightful thing, and we all need some amount of praise and appreciation, but only when we already have a solid sense of self. A complement should only reinforce what we already experience. *Wanting* favor is natural but *seeking* favor is an attempt to make up for your undeveloped self-esteem. Approval and appreciation *add* to the good of who we already are. It does not, however, make you perfect.

If a man tries to be perfect himself, then he will have the mistaken notion that he will find a perfect woman. He may find pieces of perfection in a woman, like personal beauty, intellectual brilliance, or financial success, but these things do not make a woman perfect because there is no perfect woman. If a man allows himself to be drawn only into the visible perfection of beauty, brilliance, or money, he will not find a real woman because beauty is skin deep, brilliance is brain deep, and money is purse deep. None of these things alone makes a good woman, a real woman, or the right woman. A man needs to know implicitly and explicitly that he is imperfect and inclined to mistakes. The right man, the ballsy man, is self-aware, namely of his strengths and his limitations. He knows that the right woman needs to add to him, not fix him or always approve of him. There is always an opportunity for a man to mature. Present yourself as a man with confidence and humility, namely a man who both succeeds and fails, and you will be the right man.

The right man seeks the right woman, knowing that she can add to him, but the responsibility of maturing is his own. We all need others to participate in our lives, but this does not mean that we cannot be satisfied, happy, or successful unless we are in a relationship. It means that we recognize that we are interconnected, and we need others for completing our task of maturing in life. Completing is about adding to ourselves, not being dependent on another to be our sole source of purpose or drive. A man can be a good man alone. He can be a productive and creative man alone. He can be happy alone. Happiness must already be resident in a person to which other people add elements of life. If a man is seeking a perfect woman to cure himself, he will not succeed. Being the right man is being a man who is incomplete and knows that he is incomplete yet willing to grow. He knows that there is something that a woman can provide to add to his life even if he doesn't know what she might add. The right man knows himself, likes himself, is true to himself, expresses himself, and uses these qualities in his search of a good woman. In addition to knowing that he is imperfect he knows that he is incomplete. He does not avoid life with some kind of addiction in hopes that an addictive behavior or substance will fill his emptiness. This is a man with balls. If a man presents himself to the world in this manner, he will find the right woman. And the right woman will be attracted to him.

The Right Woman

The Right Woman Is a Strong Woman

A strong woman is a happy and satisfied woman. While she might long for a good male relationship, she doesn't *need* a man in her life. She is aware of her inner strength and relies on it even when she is lonely and hopes for a good man. Being strong is not the same as being perfect or invulnerable. Being strong means she knows her strengths, knows how to use them, and knows her limitations. She stands up for what she feels is right and is unafraid of criticism or challenge. This does not mean that she is not hurt because everyone is hurt in intimate relationships. A strong woman is aware of her hurt yet capable of keeping her feelings and thoughts to herself sometimes while speaking such things at an appropriate time.

The Right Woman is Self-Aware

A self-aware woman can do quite well alone or with friends, whether they are male or female friends. A self-aware woman is just that, *aware* of her strengths, her weaknesses, her desires, and her limits. She knows when she is happy and sad, she knows when she is self-fulfilling and when she is lonely. She doesn't cover up her limits and weaknesses with artificial self-confidence but seeks to always get better at life. A strong and self-aware woman can be honest with what she feels without demanding that someone take care of her to alleviate the insecure feelings she has. She can express her feelings of loneliness without falling into a neediness that demands someone take care of her or pacify her whims. A self-aware woman is more than someone who has read a lot of self-help psychology in order to "feel good about herself" because her self-awareness has come from good self-examination, possibly with the assistance of a good mentor or therapist.

The Right Woman Is Self-Directed

It is possible for a woman to be happy and satisfied while in a primary relationship in one of two ways: she has a male who exercises leadership with statements and follow up, or she can take the lead and find other activities and people in her life with whom she can share her thoughts and feelings. Women fall into aggressive or passive behavior when they are not self-aware and lack their own initiative to think and do what they believe is right and productive. The right woman comes into an intimate male relationship with self-confidence and understands that a successful relationship is one in which the man and woman complement each other. She is the woman that knows when things are going as they should or when they are not going as they should. She has the wisdom to look at herself first, examine her own thoughts and feelings, and then to examine the relationship and the man to discern what is needed. A self-directed woman is happy; she is purposed in life; she is able to give and receive. She can trust her own contribution in life at large as well as in the relationship.

The Right Woman Is a Leader

The right woman knows that sharing the load of leading is a good thing but does not succumb to helplessness if there is no one else to share the load. A woman who is a leader seeks to establish and utilize equality in any relationship she has, whether intimate, friendship, or professional. A mature woman seeks a union with a man where they can mutually benefit from one another. She needs other people in her life who provide a sense of completeness to her just as a man needs this same sense of completeness in his life. The right woman can lead, follow, or cooperate in a male relationship without falling into passiveness or aggressiveness. She knows that true leadership is about working together. Her leadership is built on her knowing her strengths and limitations as well as her successes and failures. She admits when she is wrong and pursues the truth when she knows that she is right. This right woman can see when she has made an error and make apologies without being defensive and avoidant. Equally, she can see the mistakes of others and give space without judgment.

The Right Woman Trusts Her Intuition

Women often sense when "something is not right" in a primary relationship, very often before men recognize such things. When this is the case, she is on the right track, but she has to guard against coming to any conclusion. When a woman experiences this kind of intuition, she is in a very opportune time but also a very dangerous time. The opportunity is for her to find a way to be true to herself and exercise that true self to the man in her life. The danger is that she could fall into the artificial security of telling the man what he should do, complaining to him about what he is not doing, or tolerating the man until he does what she thinks he should do. I think it is possible for a woman in this situation to know that the man has something, that she has something, and that they together can have something even greater without exactly knowing what these things are. The gift of intuition is communal as well as individual. This means that the woman knows that the man and she can be something great and do something great, but they both have to do their parts. The successfully intuitive woman knows what she feels even if this feeling is vague, like "something is not right here." Ideally, a woman who trusts her intuition can assist the man to exercise appropriate leadership so that they can truly co-lead in life.

Trusting intuition requires patience. It is particularly hard for a woman to be patient when she feels that something is missing. Patience for a woman isn't passivity. It doesn't mean that she waits until her husband says something. It doesn't mean that she badgers him until he eventually sees the light. It means that she feels something, knows something, and works carefully to say something. It means that she knows that there is some kind of greatness with the man, with herself, and with the two of them together. She knows something, but often she doesn't know what that something might be. She may not know how to explain this "something is not right here," much less how to solve the challenge, but she knows that things can be better.

A woman who combines self-understanding and leadership with intuition is, indeed, a very powerful and effective woman, not only in a primary relationship but also with friends, family, and work. Intuitively known, patiently mused, and carefully expressed, her intuition can offer something of profound value to a man. He will feel her solidity perhaps without knowing what he is really feeling. He will be stirred to find his own self-awareness, which always leads to self-confidence and then leads to one's own style of leadership. The mature, intuitive woman is able to know something and wait for the right time, the right place, and the right words to express her intuition. Genuine loving silence is one hallmark of personal security.

Intuition is not primarily noticing something that is wrong. In fact, the very best part of intuition is knowing when something is right. The right place to go for a vacation. The right school for the children. The right congregation of people for the family, whether that is a church, a volunteer organization, or a party. The right woman can do well by trusting herself when she sees what is right, good, or necessary. I have learned, albeit slowly, that Deb most certainly has better intuition than I do. In our earlier years it was occasionally hard for me to trust her intuition when we were trying to discover what we might do, where we might go, or when we should talk. I remember fondly and with great appreciation that it was she, much more than I, who led us to a most glorious and fruitful time in Newfoundland, Canada. I recall the moment when I pointed out an advertisement for a psychologist position in St. John's, Newfoundland. Having read this ad to her, she immediately said something like, "Apply, Ron! It's right." Within a week we were on our way to St. John's, where we truly flourished, individually, collectively, and in serving this fine community of people with a rich Irish heritage. I doubt that I would have applied for this job were it up to me exclusively, but it turned out to be the right thing to do. Now thirty years after that initial decision, we retain close contact with our Newfoundland friends and professional relationships. The right woman knows something and adds to that intuitional knowledge the wisdom of when to speak and when to wait. Deb didn't wait. I'm glad she spoke.

There Are Many Right Women

There are countless examples of women who have demonstrated qualities we have been discussing. Women like the anthropologist Margaret Mead and scientist Marie Curie were both married, but we don't know much about their marital relationships because they had such a profound influence on the scientific community. Likewise, there are many political figures, like Golda Meier, Indira Gandhi, and Margaret Thatcher who were successfully married but had equally profound effects on the political landscape. There are many successful writers and artists who have made similarly positive effects on the world with or without a marital partner. Most of the psychoanalysts that dominated the first half of the twentieth century were women: Anna Freud, Margaret Mahler, and Melanie Klein among them. We can only wonder what their intimate relationships were, but I suspect that they found a way to be true to themselves and true to the men in their lives.

The right woman knows herself, values herself, and trusts herself. She is capable of being alone and even better at fostering community with someone else. Not all women have these qualities.

The Wrong Woman

The wrong woman may simply be a woman who is wrong for a man by not being a good match. Frequently, a man and a woman are significantly different in personality factors, like temperament or personality type. Indeed, "opposites can attract," but there is a huge danger of getting intimately involved with someone who sees the world significantly differently or has a significantly different value system. Deb and I have largely the same value system, even though we have different things that we value. Our greatest challenge over our years together, however, has been in how we see the world, what psychologist Carl Jung calls the "perceptive function." There are also cultural differences, intellectual differences, and differences in family values that can make a relationship difficult. We discussed such differences in our book *What's Your Temperament?* There are many other fine books that examine personality differences that can be very valuable for people who have matured enough to profit from understanding such things.

SECTION III: THE BIG W: WOMEN

Basic Characteristics of the "Wrong Woman"

Aside from many ways of understanding the differences people might have, I want to bring to our attention a more significant element of the "wrong woman." The wrong woman is not self-aware or self-directed but rather has found a way of managing life through accommodation instead of adaptation. If I accommodate to something, I find a way to live with it, but I do not feel satisfied in life and consequently am not able to forge a mature intimate relationship. A woman who has adapted to something understands that the person in her life is unique, different, and occasionally irritating, but she has learned to accept and adapt rather than tolerate and resent. A woman who doesn't know herself might initially be very accommodating to a man and hence very attractive. Such a woman might be very sexually active, very affirming, and very kind but lacks a good sense of self. Men become attached to women who are wrong for them because they are not aware of their own feelings and because they don't have a strong self-identity. This can lead to being attracted to a woman who might end up being the wrong woman.

There are a number of significant challenging characteristics of the wrong women that need to be warning signals to men. These characteristics are largely in the realm of *low self-awareness, dependency,* and *"emptiness."* These things are not necessarily easy to see, especially at the beginning of a relationship when everyone is on their best behavior and putting their best foot forward. The primary characteristic of the wrong woman is a woman who lacks self-awareness. If she is not self-aware, she will look to her partner for absolute security and identity. A woman with low self-awareness is unable to see her strengths and enhance them. This lack of self-awareness can lead to an inability to have reasonable conflict, which then leads to undo accommodation or defensiveness.

The second characteristic of the wrong woman is dependency. Dependency is being dependent on things that are external to her rather than being dependent on herself. Such a woman feels adrift in the world if she doesn't have an external source for self-identity. Dependency can be obvious with some kind of addiction, like alcohol, hoarding, or food. The subtle external dependencies can be on parents, her children, doctors and other professionals, or her friends. A dependent woman is more likely to be watching her Facebook hoping for "likes" from everyone or is frequently talking about herself instead of exchanging ideas and opinions in conversation. Women who are dependent tend to seek out multiple authority figures for all their answers instead of thinking for themselves.

In addition to a lack of self-awareness and dependency the wrong woman has, for lack of a better description, what we call a deep hole in her soul. This is the woman who has never been loved right and has not developed a good psychological foundation for life. This hole is displayed through the dependency and lack of self-awareness we just mentioned, but it goes deeper: she has no real sense of her own self and her value. Initially a woman with this characteristic can be very attractive because she asks questions and listens intently to anyone, but she doesn't have much to say about herself, largely because she doesn't know what she really feels and what she thinks. She will tend to defer to another person, especially a man, and in so doing might say and offer agreement without awareness of her own position and opinions. The predominant factor in such a person is a deep sense of fear, which might show in anxiety, panic attacks, or agitation, especially when she feels disapproval. Importantly, such a person might be very attractive physically because she has learned to magnify her physical beauty, and she might be very attractive socially because she is seemingly so attentive to others. The empty woman, despite any external persona of confidence or engagement, will display a kind of emotional hunger in life, i.e., she is never emotionally satisfied. Without going into the clinical manifestations of this phenomenon, it is best to simply say this kind of emotional hunger in a person is due to never having been loved right. Consequently, she does not know how to give appropriate love to anyone else. She may also be a person who has historically "found love in all the wrong places." A woman with a history of several failed relationships with men she describes as abusive or controlling may be displaying her hunger and felt emptiness. She may have settled for anyone at any time without a discretion as to that other person's character. Some forms of the wrong woman are as follows:

The Complaining Woman

A person who complains isn't looking for answers or solutions because he or she is looking singularly at what they don't like, not how things could be better. The woman who falls into this habit of complaining, whether the complaints are about the men in their lives, their children, their friends, or their work mates is not a pretty picture. Her tendency to complain also has profound social consequences, namely people tolerating her, getting mad at her, or avoiding her altogether. This makes life even harder for the woman. The more she complains, the less she is heard, understood, or respected. Worse yet, the more she complains, the worse she feels about herself.

When a man is connected to a woman who is inclined to undue complaining, he usually does all the wrong things: he goes silent (avoidance), he gets angry, he finds some kind of addiction to give him a feeling of short-term happiness, or he simply lives with a constant state of anxiety because he never knows what the woman in his life is going to complain about. She ends up complaining more and more about the man as if he could somehow magically solve the neglect, abuse, or trauma in her earlier life. The man starts by tolerating her, comes to resent her, and eventually avoids her.

The Unhappy Woman

The unhappy woman is a difficult phenomenon to deal with. It is fair to say that many women have suffered greatly in their lives, long before they established an intimate male relationship. Causes of life's general unhappiness are too many for us to elaborate on here, but they include neglect, abuse, indulgence, and trauma. While basic unhappiness is usually caused by such ingredients in childhood, people who are unhappy at large have come to believe that *there is something wrong with themselves*. Instead of turning on the man and complaining about him, she turns on herself, believing that there is something wrong with her. People who think there is something wrong with them will hide from life and fall into survival mode. This is one of the hallmarks of the woman we described earlier who "has a hole" in her soul. The unhappy woman is often diagnosed as "depressed," but a diagnosis of depression is not generally helpful, largely because the underlying unhappiness is not understood or dealt with. The unhappy woman is, indeed, depressed, but much more importantly, she is simply not happy. I think "not happy" is a far more meaningful and descriptive term than depressed. This woman, similar to the complaining woman, lacks some solid sense of self. The man may have genuinely fallen in love with an unhappy woman and overlooked her deep unhappiness because of his love for her. Granting that an unhappy woman can be a very good person at heart and perhaps a person who the man really loves, men need to see the signs of a woman who is fundamentally unhappy and recognize it as a true danger to him and for their relationship.

Some men try everything to make the unhappy woman happy but rarely succeed in that endeavor. Some men fall into yelling and other forms of undue anger, thus falling into repeating the unhappy woman's abusive past. More often, however, men tend to avoid their unhappy women. This avoidance only exacerbates her sense of loneliness. A ballsy man can give a woman a sense of hope together with a feeling of truly being loved.

The Children-Focused Woman

One of the most human and most loving aspects of life is motherhood. Whether we watch the birds care for their young ones or see how whales care for their young, it is truly a remarkable thing to see motherhood. Motherhood with women is no less remarkable and central in life. I truly admire the many wonderful mothers who properly care for their children. Without despairing over motherhood at large, our intent in this section is to identify women who love and cherish their children to a fault. More importantly, women who focus unduly on their children are coping with something that is missing in their lives, often a ballsy man. Far too many relationships are held in place "for the children," a phenomenon that is not good for the man, not good for the woman, and not ultimately good for the children. A woman's undue focus on children can be an indicator of her own indulgent or neglectful childhood or a way of tolerating an unsatisfying male relationship.

A good family is not child-focused; it is love-focused together with a good measure of limiting. The child-focused woman tries to make the family stable by focusing on her children, but children do not make a family stable. Stability is based on parents, not on the children. Wonderful as it is to have children and love them, children should be an *addition* to a stable and meaningful life, ideally with two parents who have a good sense of self and a good spousal relationship that makes children feel safe in life. Children who feel the stability of parents profit greatly from the love and opportunity that parents afford them.

The child-focused woman lacks the self-awareness that we discussed as the essence of the right woman. This lack of self-awareness then leads her to focus on her children in place of having a true self-confidence and self-value. When a woman doesn't have a ballsy man in her life, she can create her own sense of safety by undue attachment with her children. Even worse, a child-focused woman can use her love for her children as a means of punishing the man in her life for failing to have balls. Undue child-focus is a kind of addiction.

The Addicted Woman

Aside from the complaining woman, the unhappy woman, and the children-focused woman, there are other categories of women who may not be the right woman, all of which are forms of accommodation. These accommodations become addictive. An addiction, whether behavioral or chemical, is a way someone has accommodated to an unhappy and unsatisfying life, first with a brief escape from life, then with a habit of escaping, and then with a compulsion towards the addiction. Women are inclined to addictions just as men are, and they can become just as dangerous as an addicted man. The child-focused woman is "addicted" to attending to her children, which is a form of behavior addiction. Women can be addicted to a myriad of other behaviors or chemicals. Some women become nonsexual while others become promiscuous; some work eighty hours at work, while others just stumble on in an unchallenging job and simply exist for happy hour; some women eat too much, while others try not to eat anything in a vain attempt to have the perfect body. Women who have fallen prey to these accommodations and addictions began the cycle without self-awareness and then vainly try to find some means of self-satisfaction with some form of addiction.

Simply put, the addicted woman is not the right woman. The child-focused woman is not the right woman. The unhappy woman is not the right woman. The complaining woman is not the right woman. Who is the right woman? The right woman is strong. The right woman is self-aware. The right woman is self-directed. The right woman is a leader. The right woman trusts her intuition. Only a man with balls will find such a woman.

Summary

- To find the right woman you have to be the right man. The right man is ballsy: honest, courageous, confident, and humble.
- The right woman is strong in herself, self-aware, self-directed, a leader in her relationships, and trusts her intuition.
- The right woman values her emotion, particularly the emotions of joy and sadness, but she is not dominated by emotion.
- The wrong woman has self-esteem troubles, is unduly dependent, and has a feeling of emptiness in her that she wants the man to fill.
- The wrong woman can be generally unhappy, unduly child-focused, addicted, or inclined to complain.

SECTION IV

Mature Manhood

GOD KNOWS, THE WORLD needs good leaders. Our nation needs good leaders. Our communities need good leaders. Our families need good leaders. Good leaders bring the best out of people. Good leaders could equally be men or women. We have dedicated this book to how men can be good leaders. We will leave the subject of how women can be at their best to other authors. We hope to help you, as a man, become such a leader. There are many values that I hold dear, many people that I love, many philosophical and theological beliefs that I study, but there is nothing that I value more than helping men be ballsy. In this section we will summarize much of what we have said about being a ballsy man, focusing primarily on emotional maturity. You may not become the next Mahatma Gandhi or Winston Churchill, but you just might become a good leader in your community, in your profession, in your family, and in your friendships. Our conception of what it means for a man to be ballsy and mature is that he exhibits characterological elements of his personality that are paradoxical:

1. Confident and humble.
2. Kind and outspoken.
3. Courageous and careful.
4. Imperfect and unafraid.
5. Inspiring.

Notice the somewhat odd combinations of characteristics that lead a man to be inspiring, e.g., "confident and humble." A mature man is both of these things, but it takes balls to get there, which means a lot of personal work. This is a short list that immediately comes to our mind when we think of a mature man. Do any of these characteristics look familiar? Of course they do because they are functionally the same characteristics we have already highlighted for a man with balls. A mature man has gone through the process of gaining his balls by fumbling through speaking his feelings and come to know how to really listen to others. A mature man is able to say something and to do something in ways that communicate and inspire through both his words and his actions. The result is those under his influence experience his confidence and are inspired to be their own best selves. We include examples of how a man can be ballsy in all aspects of his life including his family, his intimate relationships, and his work.

CHAPTER 10

The Emotionally Mature Man

Emotional Maturity

WHAT DOES IT MEAN for a man to be emotionally mature? Simply stated, it means that he is aware of his feelings, appropriately expressive of his feelings, and governing of his emotions. If a man is mature in this way, he will then be aware of other people's feelings and patient with people who do the hard task of communicating their feelings. Consider the following examples:

- Sam is *excited* about a new job possibility. He couldn't wait to go home and tell his wife the new possibility. He told her that he *felt so good* that he almost jumped out of his chair when he got the email about the job opening at work.
- Jim is *disappointed* that he didn't get the promotion that he was looking for. He came home and immediately told his wife about his disappointment.
- Frank played a great game of softball, hitting two homers and being part of a triple play. He told his parents of his success, told them that he was *proud of himself*, and that he is looking forward to more improvement in his game.
- Jack almost got into an accident on his way home from work because a driver in front of him didn't see Jack's car and pulled out just inches away from sideswiping him. He took the next exit off the interstate and sat and *felt relieved* that no one was hurt.

- Claude *felt particularly good* at having passed his calculus test because he had failed the two previous ones. He went back to his dorm *feeling happy* that he had continued to work towards his goal of passing calculus.
- Jeff was *hurt* by a good friend who betrayed his confidence. He allowed himself to just *feel sad* and let the feeling of sadness run its course. He even found a way to forgive his friend without thinking about getting even.
- Brian got word that his cholesterol numbers were much better than the last time he had blood work done. He *laughed at himself* when he considered indulging in a juicy hamburger but chose instead to take a walk before going back to work.
- Jerry lost his wedding ring when he took it off to wash his hands in a public restroom. He told his wife about it, saying that it was the most important thing that he owned and that he *felt quite sad*.
- Nick got his seven-year chip identifying his dedicated sobriety. He didn't feel the need to tell anyone but *enjoyed* the moment of recognition.
- AJ was criticized at his job for a project that he worked hard to complete. He values quality above all else and thought he had done as well as he could. He allowed himself to just *be sad* and not speak to anyone about it for a while to let the *sadness run its course*.
- Jonathan got word that his liver is functioning at 16 percent. At first, he was *scared* but then allowed himself to *feel sadness*, knowing that the future was unknown and included some difficult options.
- Laurel has been working on overcoming his lifelong tendency to get angry too easily and too loudly. He's beginning to learn to *"just be sad"* at work when one of his team members made a mistake and loses a contract.
- Craig seemingly has finally found the love of his life after many failed relationships. He *feels content, proud of himself, and immensely happy* with having learned how to more honestly share his feelings.

Notice the predominance of joy and sorrow in these vignettes. The primary evidence of emotional maturity is feeling the emotions of joy and sorrow that occur every day and minimizing the defense-based emotions of anger and fear that we discussed in chapters two and three. Emotional maturity maximizes the "love-based" emotions of joy and sadness. The emotionally mature man knows that there are joys and sorrows throughout life for everyone and that it is difficult for everyone to allow these most important emotions to be felt and finished. While allowing for joys and sorrows in life and consequently reducing anger and fear, an emotionally mature man develops other characteristics including:

- He knows what he values.
- He knows that his values have an emotional component.
- He is self-confident in what he feels.
- He realizes that his expression of feelings is imperfect.
- He recognizes his limits and stretches beyond his limits.
- He is aware of hurt from criticism and mistakes but is not afraid of it.
- He is able to discuss and debate facts without emotional explosions.
- He takes the necessary time to state himself and re-state himself.
- He listens carefully to other people's feelings.
- He initiates conversation and discussion with others.
- He takes action based on understanding one's own feelings and other people's feelings.

A man who has characteristics such as these is a man who has worked diligently on knowing what he feels, expressing what he feels, and governing what he says about his feelings. The key to this kind of emotional maturity is being self-aware. As you become more self-aware, you will notice that you have a very positive effect on the people around you: they too become more self-aware.

Self-Awareness and Self-Confidence

Self-confidence is just what that word suggests: you having confidence in *yourself*. Self-confidence has nothing to do with anyone else. You don't need someone's approval or praise to be self-confident, but you do need self-awareness. Our focus in this book has been on helping men become aware of their feelings first and carefully govern their emotion when they try to express their feelings. In order to be aware of your feelings you need to be a person who knows as much about yourself as possible. In chapter one we discussed how feelings are communicated in the four dimensions: physical, emotional, cognitive, and active. You need to know which of these four expressions of feelings is your primary means of expression. You might, for instance, know that your preferred expression of feelings is cognitive. If that is the case, you know that you like to think about your feelings and then speak your thoughts about your feelings. Likewise, you will be most interested in hearing other people think and talk about their feelings cognitively. If your primary means of expression of feelings is physical, emotional, or active, you know that you prefer to express feelings in ways that are physical, emotional, or active. This is important because knowing your own preference helps you communicate yourself better. Equally so, being familiar with these different preferences will help you know how to better listen to others.

You can also remember that most men prefer to communicate through action more than words. An action statement is something that a man does that reveals who he is and how he feels. Ideally, a man should offer some verbal explanation of what the action means to him, but if a man can demonstrate his inner self with what he does, this could be a good start towards maturity. He might communicate his feelings by doing things for other people:

- Mowing the lawn for a friend who broke his leg.
- Repairing his wife's flower cart.
- Playing basketball with his daughter.
- Playing Monopoly with his son.
- Helping his wife, kids, or friends fix their computers.
- Giving a spontaneous hug and kiss to his wife or kids.
- Helping a friend change the oil in his car.
- Taking advantage of the "parent/child exchange program" at school where your kid stays home and you go to school for a day.
- Bringing your son to your work to show him what you do.
- Making your next sexual engagement very special.

In addition to the things that a mature man might do for other people, he demonstrates leadership by what he does for himself:

- Singing a favorite song in the car, even though he can't sing very well.
- Running three times a week in order to get in better shape.
- Doing some artistic painting that he used to do but hasn't done in years.
- Learning to play the guitar.
- Working hard at his profession.

- Taking care of his body with proper diet and exercise.
- Having a good recreational life, both alone and with family members.
- Greeting people with a smile, shaking their hands, giving them a hug, or kissing people.
- Spending time alone, perhaps in the garage, perhaps reading, or just staring at the stars.
- Producing things that he is proud of, maybe a swing set for the kids, a bookshelf for his wife, a repaired computer for his daughter, maybe a book he has written.
- Giving an occasional weekend to Habit for Humanity.

We had a friend of mine lay new flooring for our remodeled kitchen. I watched in amazement how Jon was able to go about this profession with such ease and competence. I yet look at the refined corners of the kitchen floor with appreciation of Jon's work but also of Jon as he demonstrated himself in this activity. Deb even walked in and caught him singing on the job. I feel the same appreciation for the work our neighbor, Lonnie, did on our roof, which I still admire now ten years after he did the roofing (and many other projects). Lonnie and Jon didn't have to say anything about themselves; their work said enough. The examples of men demonstrating their feelings through their work are countless.

There are many areas of life of which you need to be aware that lie outside the purview of our discussion, like your physical abilities and limitations, your intellectual abilities and limitations, your philosophical orientation, and your cultural awareness. Additionally, there is the important area of psychological understanding that has to do with normal differences in personality, such as personality type and temperament. We have discussed these issues in our book *What's Your Temperament?*

Self-awareness includes knowing that feelings erupt from what we call your "inner spirit" and that this inner spirit and the feelings that erupt from it are *perfect*, however odd that sounds. Instead of using the term inner spirit, some people use terms like soul, self, core, or God. One's inner spirit is not something that is visible. More importantly, it is something that you cannot communicate adequately in words. You can *feel* your feelings, *know* your feelings, and *sense* your feelings, but you will never be able to fully communicate your feelings to anyone. The truly confident man does not despair over this fact but remembers that his feelings are perfect and that whatever words he uses to express these feelings are imperfect. How odd is it for a man to feel confident knowing that whatever he says, the words will always be imperfect? An emotionally mature man accepts this paradox. You become *confident in yourself*, not in the words you say or how they are understood by the people who hear your words.

In your confidence you recognize:

- Sometimes, you will communicate well . . .
  - and you will continue to speak well.
  - and you will be appreciated.
- Sometimes you will fail to communicate well . . .
  - and you will be disappointed in what you said.
  - and you will be corrected.
- You will stand firm when you are convinced that you are right . . .
  - and you will be appreciated.
  - and you be criticized.
  - and you will listen to both appreciations and criticisms.
  - and you will consider all that is said in response to what you said.
- You will communicate your feelings . . .
  - which will stir other people's feelings.
  - which will stir more of your own feelings.
- You will carefully end a discussion when it is appropriate to do so.
- You will be able to initiate a discussion and engage others in what they feel.

Indicators of Self-Awareness and Confidence

Stating and Stabilizing Yourself

In chapter eight we discussed "staging" as a way to initially gain confidence in talking to women. *Stating* yourself is just what it sounds like: speaking your feelings regardless to whom you are speaking. We use the term *stabilizing* to describe a second stage of communication. Although we speak of stating and stabilizing as separate elements, they are both parts of presenting yourself and clarifying yourself. Stating yourself may be more than talking. It may include you doing something that displays your action and communicates who you are. If you state that you need to wash the dishes more often, you need to do it. When you state yourself, whether in words or action, you are declaring, "This is who I am and what I can offer to you." When a man states himself, he gives the world around him something of what it means to be a human being. Stating is the foundation for interactive communication. It stimulates other people to feel, think, and speak for themselves. A mature man is willing to declare himself because he wants to be known better and he wants to know other people better. He is aware that he may not be understood, but he is not afraid of being misunderstood or criticized. Rather, he knows that he may be liked or disliked, valued or disvalued, approved of or disapproved of. He has the balls to state himself, regardless of what the results of his stating himself might be. This awareness does not make him immune to the feelings of hurt or disappointment. He has learned to *stabilize* himself.

Stabilizing is effectively dealing with the results of what a man has stated. The results of his statements might be other people's reaction, no reaction whatsoever from others, or his own reaction to what he has said. He might have to say more; he might need to listen more; he might need to clarify; he might need to hear an emotional reaction to what he said. Stabilizing does not mean he is right. It means that he has started the process of understanding between someone and himself. The mature man is aware of the reciprocity of a relationship. He is interested in being known better and knowing people better. A mature man knows his conviction and is willing to stand on it; all the while it may be debated or challenged. He does not passively listen to challenges nor impatiently listen until he can defend his statement. He doesn't make promises attempting to convince anyone of anything or demand that his way is absolute. He is exercising the confidence that comes from knowing himself, which means knowing his feelings and thoughts. He knows that if he makes an important statement in words or action, this statement will be provocative, possibly hurting people but hopefully inspiring them to also speak themselves courageously. He demonstrates stabilizing through patience and acceptance. The mature man is confident enough to really give thought to the challenges of others or to their suggestions. In fact, a mature man may come to retract or change his original statement. He is stable, and his stability gives a sense of stability to his environment. Consider the following examples of mature men stating and stabilizing:

Mack: Monica, I want to tell you something that has been on my mind for a long time.

Monica: This sounds like I've done something wrong. What did I do now?

Mack: No, my dear, it has nothing to do with you or what you did. Rather, it has a lot to do with me. I want to tell you what I've been thinking for a while because these thoughts seem important and may impact you or us in some way.

Monica: It still sounds like you're going to tell me something that I did wrong or something bad.

Mack: Not in the slightest. So let me tell you what has been on my mind a lot lately.

Monica: This is beginning to sound interesting.

Mack: Yes, I think it is very interesting, and even exciting, but know this: I am not sure where these thoughts are going and I want to keep you informed about what has been on my mind for a while. You up for hearing it?

Monica: Alright.

Mack: (*Stating*) I've been thinking of changing my career.

Monica: Why in the world would you do that? You've worked hard at your restaurant and have a good reputation, as well as making a good income.

Mack: (*Continues stating*) Allow me tell you a little more about my thoughts about the change I've been thinking about. I think that I might like to become a counselor of some sort. This would mean some kind of graduate school training and all that might follow.

Monica: That seems crazy. How are we going to afford that if you give up the restaurant? You do remember that we have a set of twins to raise and get through college?

Mack: (*Stabilizing*) I know this may come as a shock to you. I haven't worked out what I might do or even if I would do something like this. I just wanted to share my thoughts.

Monica: It still sounds crazy.

Mack: (*Continues stabilizing*) Tell me, Monica, what do you feel when I share this idea? I mean apart from it sounding crazy.

Monica: Honestly, I feel scared. We depend primarily on your income since I went to half-time to care for the twins.

Mack: (*Continues stabilizing*) I would not do anything that would harm you or the family. I am just thinking, and I am finding it increasingly important to tell you my thoughts and feelings.

Monica: That's good to hear, the part that you wouldn't do anything to harm the family, I mean. This seems like your idea is coming out of the blue and it takes me by surprise. I don't understand it.

Mack: (*Continues stabilizing*) I want to be more open and honest with you. My hope is that I can be more of a man, a better husband, and a better father by telling you more about how I feel.

Monica: Okay, that sounds good to begin with, but it also sounds like you are just thinking of yourself. It reminds me of your brother, Jim, who just quit his job and hasn't worked at finding another one.

Mack: (*Stabilizing*) (He is offended to be compared to someone who is not responsible but keeps his feelings to himself, knowing it is more about Monica's feelings than himself. Then he states himself again.) I'm really sorry for springing this on you, Monica. I agree with you about Jim, and I promise you that I won't run off and do something crazy like he did. I'm looking into what, how, and if it is possible for me to change professions. I'm sorry this scares you.

Monica: I feel better with your assurance that you're not going to do something crazy.

Mack: (*Continues stabilizing*) I assure you of that. Let me continue to think more about this for a few days, and I'll get back to you.

Monica: I look forward to it.

As a mature man Mack knows that he can only give Monica his initial thoughts. To do more would overrun her feelings. Mack knows that what he has to tell her is significant and possibly life-changing for him and his family. He is not in a rush to persuade her of anything (which demonstrates his patience), and he recognizes that what he is stating is hard for her (which demonstrates his accepting). Furthermore, Mack recognizes that when he talks to her again, he will need to state and stabilize all over again. This is not a concern for Mack, as a mature man. He knows to take his time and allow his wife to gain more confidence in his initiating this discussion. This is an element of wisdom: giving people time to catch up with your thoughts and intentions. It takes wisdom to know that if you force a conversation, you will most likely lose your audience. This is actually part of the process of stabilizing, knowing when to stop and when to keep going. Mack did not lose his stability when he was criticized by Monica's initial response that he sounded crazy or when she compared him to his irresponsible brother. Mack was confident enough to give her permission to be emotionally affected by his statements without defending himself or trying to change her. A few days later Mack resumes his process of stating and stabilizing:

Mack: (*Stating*) Monica, I'd like to talk a bit further about my ideas about possibly changing professions.

Monica: I have been holding my breath. I hope you haven't quit your job and signed up for some kind of graduate program.

Mack: (*Stabilizing*) No, nothing as dramatic as that. I told you that I am not going to run off half-cocked.

Monica: So, what are your thoughts? (If Monica responds with this statement, it means that she is less defensive, less afraid, and perhaps a bit more ready to hear what Mack is thinking and feeling.)

Mack: (*Stabilizing*) I think you know that I have been less than happy with my job for some time. It has been difficult for me to admit that I have been unhappy at work because I have done a good job establishing and maintaining the restaurant. It has been a good piece of my life. I am proud of how popular it has become and glad that our investment has paid off. The difficulty is that the work is not as meaningful for me as it once was. Since I decided to do some psychotherapy, I find myself excited with how much it has helped me. I feel excited about real thinking, real feelings, and real action that have helped me mature emotionally, spiritually, and hopefully relationally. The restaurant was exciting to start up and exciting to keep going, but the idea of helping others like I have been helped in therapy has excited me like nothing ever has. I just feel better about myself, better about you, better about us, and better about our kids. Yet I don't feel any better at work. I don't know, Monica, perhaps I don't have the stuff to be a therapist, but therapy has been so good for me that I have been thinking that I just might be able to be good at it.

Monica: I am beginning to see the picture, much better than I did when you brought it up last Thursday. Perhaps you could tell me more about what you think we could do about this major idea.

Mack: (*Stabilizing*) I have a lot of thoughts, but frankly, it is my feelings that seem dominant in this whole arena. Simply put, I don't feel excited about work now, but I do feel excited about the possibility of doing something more meaningful.

Monica: Again, how could we possibly do this thing? How could you do it, when would you do it, and can we afford to do it?

Mack: (*Stabilizing*) These are all good questions, but I don't have answers to any of them. Not yet. If you don't mind, I'd like to stick to the feelings, which means feeling, thinking, and talking to you, before we decide together if, how, and when we might do this together.

Monica: I can live with that. I feel safer now that you have stated yourself more clearly. I am looking forward to hearing more.

Mack: (*Stating*) Thank you so much for understanding. Indeed, it is up to me to do the thinking and feeling and then to keep you informed. We can eventually decide to take some kind of action, postpone any action, or not take any action.

Another example of stating and stabilizing is Gordon. Gordon is a very articulate man, well-read, intelligent and very dedicated to his work, which for the most part he enjoys. He was recently called in by his boss because he had failed to follow through on a new company policy. Gordon works for a wholesale clothing company. He has enjoyed his position for several years. Particularly, he has enjoyed servicing his accounts by maintaining relationships with his customers. He has enjoyed meeting with them regularly, perhaps having a beer or two with some of them, and visiting some of them at their retail locations, seeing how they are doing with the products his company distributes. It is this personal interaction which gives satisfaction to his work. But recently, the company has suffered a bit and evidently needs to boost sales to continue to thrive. As a result, Gordon and his colleagues need to push more sales in addition to maintaining and servicing their current accounts. They need to do some cold calling and develop new accounts. Gordon and I talked about how he needs to more effectively express himself at work so that he can continue to succeed and perhaps improve in his profession.

I suggested to Gordon that he initiate a conversation about his work with his supervisor, something like this:

Boss: Gordon, we are not entirely pleased with your work performance lately. It seems that you have avoided doing a number of things that need to be done around here, and things that I have specifically asked you to do. For instance, I have asked you to make some cold calls to potential customers, and I haven't seen you doing that much, and we haven't seen any new accounts being opened from your corner.

Gordon: (*Stating*) I know that you are right about what you are saying, Boris. I apologize for not bringing this matter to you. I am sorry that I delayed talking to you, which in turn forced you to bring this to me (courage to admit error). To be honest, I need to really evaluate if I can meet this new work requirement. The truth is, I haven't yet found a way to do what you have asked me to do and enjoy my work. I particularly enjoy maintaining and servicing my current and old accounts. I know that I need to do some cold calling, but it is difficult for me to do. It goes against my nature to be outgoing like that (*stabilizing*). It takes a lot of energy for me to talk to someone who I don't really know or someone who might not be interested in what I am selling. I hope you can give me a day or two to digest what you are asking of me.

As with Mack and Monica's theoretical conversation, this theoretical conversation between Gordon and his boss is not likely to evolve just as smoothly as I have proposed. If Gordon were truly confronted by his boss, the confrontation might be essentially critical and hence more challenging for Gordon. In most conversations between a boss who is challenging and an employee who is being challenged, things are not quite as clear, and they are not nearly as honest. Remember that being ballsy means being honest. It doesn't mean saying everything you think or feel. Furthermore, many bosses wouldn't want to give much time for this kind of response. In portraying this conversation between Gordon and his boss I am hoping to suggest that a man needs to be self-confident, self-expressive, and honest. He needs to state and stabilize himself in these qualities. I have suggested that Gordon do three things in responding to his boss: (1) admit to his failing rather than pretending that he has done what has been asked of him, (2) make a genuine if brief apology for his avoiding talking about the problem, and (3) make some kind of honest statement about what he will attempt to do. The preceding monologue might take several meetings but the content is the same: Gordon being honest with his feelings and forthright with what he says to his boss. This takes a good deal of both honesty and courage, which means that it takes balls.

Larry is a good man at heart. He doesn't like conflict. He wants to always "give the other guy a chance." His wife has a large family that always spends the major holidays together. Larry always goes because he loves his wife Nancy and loves her family. Larry told me that he was having some stomach distress when he thought about going to an upcoming Christmas holiday at his in-laws. He told me that his wife's uncle, Frank, was a challenge to be around but then added that he didn't hate Frank. He simply didn't like him. As Larry told me about Frank, it seemed that part of the challenge is that Frank seems to be a very outgoing fellow compared to Larry, who is introverted by nature. He asked me how he might deal with the party and Larry.

First of all, I admire Larry for being so courageous to admit that he has a hard time with Nancy's Uncle Frank and that he wants to demonstrate leadership and handle the Christmas holiday with kindness and confidence. Situations like this are very difficult because it involves loving but not liking. I suggested that perhaps Larry could be "balls forward" and be more honest about himself and with Uncle Frank. Such a conversation might go like this:

Larry: (*Stating*) Hello, Uncle Frank. I am glad you were able to come to the Christmas party. Nancy has told me that you haven't been well. How are you doing now?

Frank: Hey, I am great! Just great! Don't let those darn doctors ever fool you. They are always just making things worse and I won't have anything to do with that stuff. I am in charge, buddy, I am in charge!

Larry: (*Stabilizing*) (He is already beginning to feel the unease in his stomach with how strongly Frank presents himself.) I can hear your confidence (giving a lot of space to Frank to do his feelings which are hidden behind his defensiveness).

Frank: You better believe I am confident. I have always been confident. I know what is best for me!

Larry: (*Stating*) Uncle Frank, tell me more. (Containing his own feelings and desire to counter Frank.)

Frank: You should have known me when I was a young buck! There was nothing that I couldn't do!

Larry: (*Listening*) I am interested. (Here Larry is giving Frank the stage, hoping that he will begin to hear more of what is really important to Frank.)

Frank: Well, I was, I was good worker!

Larry: (*More listening*) I don't know much about the work you did, please tell me.

Frank: I worked for the post office, and I did a mighty fine job. Anyone who knew me back then would tell you that was true.

Larry: (*Stating*) You know, Frank, I believe you (giving Frank more of the stage).

Frank: Yeah, I did good. I worked hard and provided for Evelyn, God rest her soul, and our kid, Johnny.

Larry: I never met your wife, Evelyn. Nancy tells me that she was a tender soul.

Frank: (Beginning to soften now that someone is honestly interested in him and his story) Well, she was indeed, a very good and tender soul. I could tell her all the things I did, and you know what, she could see right through me all the while I was rattling on.

Larry: Sounds like she really loved you.

Frank: (Now beginning to wipe an eye) Yeah, she loved me. I miss her even now after many years. You know, Larry, you have a good wife too. My niece Nancy is just like Evelyn. You take good care of her. You do that.

Larry: (*Stating*) I appreciate that, Uncle Frank. I do love Nancy, but it doesn't hurt to be reminded.

Frank: (Slapping Frank on his back) Well, son, I knew you were a good man when Nancy first brought you into this wild family. I wasn't always sure you could endure us, you being so quiet like you are. We like to just let loose at these parties (he laughs loudly). Good to have you in the family, Larry.

Larry: (*Stabilizing*) (having given the stage and contained throughout this conversation) Uncle Frank, I must say, I really enjoyed this conversation. You ready for some of those Christmas cookies? I am, come on, let's go eat some.

Frank: Hey Nancy (shouting across the room), you sure married a good one, you did!

Larry: (*Stabilizing*) Uncle Frank! (laughing at his own pleasure in being recognized) You are embarrassing me!

Frank: Ah, it's just my way of loving you, Larry. I don't mean no harm. I just like to say things the way I see them.

In Larry's next session, he reported that although his encounter with Uncle Frank didn't go exactly as we considered, he was surprised how giving Frank the stage compared to resenting his boisterousness was a way of getting to know a part of him that he didn't realize existed. It was easier to stay with loving him even though he still didn't like how loud he was. Larry was successful in initiating a discussion but in a subtle but direct way. Encouraging discussion takes a good deal of thought, thought based on how you feel so you can speak yourself clearly, understand what others feel, which then leads to valuable discussion.

Encourage Valuable Discussion

Knowing that your own feelings can never be perfectly expressed, you realize that when other people express themselves, they encounter some of the same difficulties in communicating. Because you have gained confidence in your own feelings, you are more generous with others trying to communicate their feelings. You get to the point where you can listen, know that what is being said is approximate, and then are able to encourage your friend to continue speaking.

Let's discuss Allen and his wife, Jean. Jean wanted to purchase a new car. Allen was afraid of being a "pushover." The matured Allen could be able to engage his wife something like this:

Allen: Jean, you have mentioned wanting to get a new car. Please tell me about that desire.

Jean: I am not sure I want to do that. In times past you have gotten mean and just pissed off when I wanted to tell you things. I suspect you will do that now and just tell me that we don't need a new car.

Allen: I'll give you that much. Certainly I have been quick to jump the gun when you talk about big purchases. I am sorry for that. Please, I do want to hear about this now.

Jean: The bottom line is that my car is just too old, and I don't feel safe in it.

Allen: That sounds very important, please go on, love.

Jean: Allen, you know there are no cameras in my car. New cars have rear cameras. I can't see behind me as well as I used to. Mercy, what if I hit someone because I can't turn around enough to see if they are there?

Allen: I agree. That would be terrible.

Jean: I would rather die than hurt some innocent pedestrian.

Allen: Go on Jean. I am listening.

Jean: Like it or not, Allen, we are aging, and I don't know about you, but I want to keep driving, and I want to feel that I can do so responsibly. I really need to upgrade my car.

Allen: Jean, thank you for telling me about you. I feel a lot of love for you right now. I admire your concern for us and the welfare of others.

Jean: That is good for me to hear. I really thought you were going to just write me off on this.

Allen: I don't want to write you off. I think this deserves another discussion or two before we make any decisions. If you are willing, let's just appreciate this beginning conversation and leave it for tomorrow when we can talk again. Is that okay?

Jean: Yes! Thank you. I really don't want to rush into a big purchase, but I want to feel safe. I am not saying I have to have a new car, just a safer car. Thank you for listening to me.

Jean: One more thing if you don't mind.

Allen: Sure.

Jean: That therapy you've been doing seems to have had a good effect on you . . . and on me.

Allen: I'll tell Dr. Greg that you appreciate his work.

In this situation Allen has learned how to first trust his own feelings, and now he is able to trust hearing his wife speak about hers, even if they have different opinions on a course of action. In this case I suspect that Allen and Jean will more easily come to the best decision. Allen paved the way for Jean to talk about what was most important to her, safety, even though initially her comments were emotional and informational, namely just getting a new car. There is always much more behind someone's initial emotional expression. It takes a mature man to wade through it.

Varieties of Stating and Stabilizing

Stating by Apologizing

Apologizing comes naturally when a man is emotionally mature because he knows that his expression of his feelings, whether verbal or active, could easily offend someone, thus causing emotional hurt. The ability to apologize is a natural part of having confidence in yourself by knowing that despite your best efforts, you will make mistakes and/or misspeak your feelings. Apologizing is really about confession. The biblical Greek word for confession, *homologeo*, essentially means saying what is true. When I apologize to people, I am confessing that I know that I have hurt them. You can apologize for what you said, how you said it, or because what you said hurt someone else. You don't have to be wrong in what you said. In fact, what you said might have needed to be said. But that doesn't take away from the fact that you may have hurt someone in the process of your expressing your feelings or opinion. Recently, I wounded a woman with what I said while I was doing marital work with her husband and her. What I said to her needed to be said because it was true and important. Furthermore, no one else would be able to say what I said as therapist. She said that I had hurt her more than anyone she could think of, likely because she had come to trust me in therapy. In fact, I apologized several times "for hurting her" without the caveat that what I said was right in my eyes. She said she appreciated my apologizing to her, and by the end of the session she apologized for having hurt me in times past.

When you apologize for hurting someone, you are not necessarily suggesting that what you said was wrong but rather "confessing" that you know you have hurt the other person. This is substantially different from when you have heard people say something like, "Well, I'm sorry if this hurts you," which actually means that you are not really sorry. You can be sorry for hurting someone while at the same time believing that what you said needed to be said. This is delicate, and it takes both wisdom and balls.

Apologizing for actually having been wrong in what you said or did is a different kind of apology, and it takes balls of steel to do it. I regularly give men the assignment, often in the presence of their significant other, to *never* get angry. Then, with a wink I add, "*When* you get angry, apologize for getting angry." Doesn't this seem like a contradiction?: "*Never* get angry and *when* you get angry, apologize"? Men often laugh at my suggesting that they should never get angry, quickly followed by my suggestion that they should always apologize for when they get angry. I want them to become aware that they have actually been disappointed at something, not angry at something. This is hard enough, but my suggestion that they should apologize, to their wives or anyone else, for having been angry asks even more of men. Why do I ask men to apologize? Because I want them to develop big enough balls to admit to error and find the humility associated with a mistake, however small the mistake might have been. I am asking these men to confess that they have been wrong.

Let me tell you about Ben. I first saw Ben nearly ten years ago. When he first came to me, he was dealing with having been raised a son of an alcoholic. He spent a few sessions with me and then did not come back. Recently, he came back into my office together with his wife, Janice, to do some marital counseling. Ben is a brilliant physician who has developed a thriving alternative medical practice. He reports that he demonstrates the utmost care and patience with everyone at work, his patients as well as his staff. With Janice, however, his anger flairs in an instant. Ben came in with his wife, stating that he knew he has been unkind and wanted to find a way to be more honest with her. One example that they told me about and which prompted Ben to return to my office was described by himself as "childish" and which brought him great shame. He and Janice had been to the grocery store, and when she got to the car, realized she had neglected to purchase toilet paper. When Ben heard this, he blew up and slammed the shopping cart into his car. Now, several months into my joint work with Ben and Janice, I see significant mellowing with Ben. He is learning to express the deeper feelings of hurt, disappointment, and sadness that had been underlying his angry outbursts. Early in our joint sessions I asked Ben to work on two things: to never get angry and to apologize every time he did. He smiled and said that it seemed impossible to meet my assignment, but he wanted to try. He came back the next week reporting that however hard it was to admit how angry he was, he found it almost impossible to apologize to Janice for getting angry.

Why was it so hard for Ben to apologize to his wife for his having been angry? Because this act of contrition is humbling and a part growing a pair. Reminder: a maturing man is both confident and humble. The more you admit to errors, the more you move towards self-confidence and genuine humility.

A mature man becomes more comfortable with apologizing, even though it might remain hard to do. They recognize apologies as a form of confession or admitting to error. At the time of that pivotal situation with Ben and the shopping cart, he didn't communicate what he felt whatsoever. Recognizing his shortcomings prompted him to come back into therapy and to continue working on being more honest with his feelings instead of sliding into anger. He has since learned that he can successfully communicate himself when he dares to state himself, both his successes and his failures. If that same incident happened now, I believe Ben would have said something like, "Oh, you forgot the TP. That means we will need to stop again. You know what, that's okay. Let's hurry on to the luncheon and we can pick it up later." He would have simply been more *honest*. He knew he was disappointed because of a time crunch (sad). He knew he loved Janice (joy). And he knew that forgetting something like toilet paper was a minor bother (sad and joy). Hopefully, Janice would then have said something like: "Thank you for being kind about it. I am sorry. Yes, let's worry about it later and just go enjoy the choir luncheon." With this simple kind of honesty, both Janice and he would have understood each other. They would have communicated.

Keeping Your Feelings to Yourself

"Keep your feelings to yourself"? Wait, isn't that what we are working against? Haven't I been suggesting that men need to speak more of their feelings, particularly joy and sorrow? Why would I suggest it is ballsy to keep feelings to yourself? As you get better at knowing how you feel and communicating how you feel, you will discover that you don't always need to express your feelings because it is good enough for you to know them. Knowing your feelings is the groundwork for maturity, which is the groundwork for having balls. It might be good for the other person *not* to hear your feelings for some reason. Perhaps your friend is in an emotional state himself that precludes his being able to hear your feelings. Perhaps you and he are not in a private enough place for you to say what is on your heart and mind. Perhaps there are kids around for whom it would not be appropriate for you to express something that could be harmful for them to hear. Perhaps you have felt through your feelings enough and no longer need to say what you previously intended to say. All of these reasons for not expressing your feelings have to do with the context of the moment.

There is great wisdom, grace, and manliness in containing your feelings and saving your feelings for a better time. The wisdom to know the difference between when to express your feelings and when not to is a part of having balls. This advice isn't much different from the Serenity Prayer—"God grant me the serenity to accept the things I cannot change, the courage to change the things I can, and the wisdom to know the difference"—or the core of the book of Ecclesiastes in the Jewish Scriptures: "For everything there is a season, and a time for every matter under heaven" (Eccl 3:1, NRSV). There is a time for everything, and the mature man can exercise wisdom to know when it is beneficial to speak his feelings and when it is best to not speak his feelings. It's never wise to speak feelings that lead to an argument.

Never Argue

I advise my male patients to never get angry, which seems impossible to most men. Now, I'm going to say you should never argue. How possible is that? I once told a therapist of mine that Deb and I never argue. He promptly told me that "arguments are necessary in any good relationship." I couldn't disagree more. Arguments are not necessary. Disagreements are necessary, and difficult emotions are necessary, but arguments are not. An argument is the combination of two things that do not belong together: emotion and information. You can express emotion, ideally the love-based emotions of sadness and joy, or if necessary, the defense-based emotions of fear and anger, but the people to whom you express emotion have to know that you are *expressing* emotion. Deb and I often begin talking to one another with the statement, "I'm going to make an emotional statement," which means that she or I will then say something that might sound outrageous, extreme, and *not logically true*. An emotionally based conversation might go something like this:

Deb: Ron, I think that we should just quit this whole business of psychotherapy and open an Italian restaurant.

Ron: That's crazy! What are you thinking? We love our work. We don't know anything about running an Italian restaurant.

Deb: Why are you so critical of me?

Ron: I'm not being "critical." I'm just being reasonable.

Deb: I'm trying to tell you my feelings and you're attacking me.

Ron: I'm not "attacking you." I might be attacking this crazy thought.

Deb: I just want you to listen to me.

Ron: I can't listen to craziness.

Deb: You're telling me that I'm crazy?

Ron: Maybe. The thought of opening an Italian restaurant is certainly crazy.

Deb: Maybe I'll do it on my own. You can do what you want. You can work forever seeing difficult patients.

Ron: We've been doing this for fifty years. What's happened to you?

Deb: Maybe I've grown up. Maybe you haven't.

Can you see how the whole essence of this unfortunate theoretical conversation is based on Deb's "feeling" that was expressed with "information" and full of emotion? I didn't see the feeling, much less the emotion. Rather, I was taken off guard, offended, and then defended myself. In my "defense of myself," I did what people do when they are "defensive": I became offensive.

In speaking herself, Deb is not saying that we actually do either thing, but rather she is saying that she has been overcome with the difficult clinical work she was doing on that day. How might the conversation have gone if I had been able to understand that Deb is making a feeling statement that has emotion in it even though this feeling is wrapped around both emotion and information:

Deb: Ron, I think that we should just quit this whole business of psychotherapy and open an Italian restaurant.

Ron: That sounds important, Deb. Tell me more about your feelings, please.

Deb: I don't know, Ron. I've been a bit overwhelmed with all the things we have to do with our business. I hate having to mess with insurance companies so we can get paid, for one thing.

Ron: You're right on that one.

Deb: I don't know. I'm seventy and you're eighty. I wonder how long one of us will live. I want us to live well and live long.

Ron: I'm with you on that one, too.

Deb: The "Italian restaurant" thing is just what came to mind because it is so far from what we are doing. Sometimes, I just get tired working with people.

Ron: The work can be challenging, that's for sure.

Deb: Maybe a French restaurant instead.

Ron: Both the French and Italians serve good wine.

Note how I do not get caught in the "information" of the Italian restaurant or quitting psychotherapy. More importantly, I don't insert my ideas because I know that this is a feeling statement that has both information and emotion in it. Undoubtedly, I am taken off guard and might feel defensive but I keep this feeling to myself. Do know, reader, that I am far from perfect when I hear emotional/informational statements and often miss the feeling underneath. I am still a work in progress.

People make informational/emotional statements all the time, but the essence of these statements is neither the information nor the emotion but the feeling underneath. When a woman is in labor and says "I can't do this," you don't argue with her. It is valuable for a woman to make such a statement that is emotionally true but factually false. There are many places where it valuable to make such outrageous and seemingly irrational statements. The listener needs to be capable of accepting the emotion without debating the fact. Emotional statements are not rational. When men say to me, "I don't want to live," this is an emotional statement. I am privileged (and burdened) to hear such statements that men dare say only to me. I am reminded of a statement from a very deeply religious man who said, "I would rather die than go bankrupt." I think he really meant it even though he didn't want to die. Who can hear such a statement? Not his wife, not his doctor, and not his friends. Yet, he really needed to say this "feeling statement" that was emotionally laden but not rationally true. He didn't want to die and he certainly wasn't suicidal; he just didn't want to live in his current financial distress. Life had become so burdensome for him that he couldn't see how he could live with the shame of going bankrupt.

Arguments are a mixture of emotion and information. Purely rational statements have to do with information. We can have a friendly debate or a heated debate that can be fun if we stick to the data. This is a rare occurrence. You can have an emotional discussion or an informational discussion, but you can't have both at the same time. To have an information-based discussion you will have to be aware of your emotion and govern the expression of your emotion. You might, for instance, make a statement in favor of stronger borders between Mexico and America, but if you do, know that you will likely run into someone's emotional response to your statement. If it is possible for you and your friend to have a friendly discussion of the pros and cons of a strong border, you might both learn something and maybe be of some service to America and Mexico. If you know what you feel emotionally, you can know when it best to express your emotion and when it is not. To avoid the fruitless arguing, you need to clearly state yourself and stabilize yourself, which fosters actual communication. There is a huge difference between expressing feelings and communicating them.

Communicating Feelings Is Difficult

In our book *I Want to Tell You How I Feel*, we admit that we can never communicate our perfect feelings perfectly. That fact, however, does not excuse us from getting better and better at communicating by working diligently on how we say what we feel and being aware that no words perfectly reflect our feelings. In fact, the more you work on communicating, the better you will get at it, and the better you will be known. We don't expect you to find the perfect words when you express your thoughts, but you have to know that words expressed are not the same as words received. What I have said may not be what my listener hears. For example, if you say to your son, "Where did you put the hammer?" and he gets defensive, what has happened here? He is reacting as if he had been criticized; possibly because you have previously scolded him for failing to put tools away, possibly because he feels ashamed of having forgotten to replace the hammer, possibly because he threw the hammer in the woods after he hit his thumb with it. But in this case, you might simply want to know where the hammer is and think that your son may know its whereabouts. There are many examples of this miscommunication that occur every day—sometimes because of the words we use, sometimes because of some kind of history of having been hurt in the past, sometimes because a word you used implied something critical, and sometimes because your listener simply didn't hear you.

I advise men that they need to take responsibility for "miscommunicating" rather than going to avoidance, anger, or addictive behavior. It is a very wise thing, a very ballsy thing, but a very hard thing to take responsibility for having miscommunicated. In all of these cases you need to simply say, "I'm sorry. I'm not communicating here" rather than saying, "You're not listening," "You don't have to be so defensive," "You're twisting my words," or "That's not what I said." Indeed, you may have said something that was perfectly logical in your mind, but it was not understood by your listener. It will take some practice, but saying, "I'm sorry, I'm not communicating" puts the burden on you and gives you another chance to communicate. This too, is a form of confession. I make it sound like this is easy to do, but it is no such thing. The difficulty is that you think that you have spoken clearly, which in your mind means that your listener has heard you and understood your words and your intention. Rarely is that the case. Words used and intentions behind the words are often universes apart. When you can change your words from "you're not listening" to "I'm not communicating," you are accepting the responsibility for not communicating. You are stabilizing. Secondly, you will convey to your listener a genuine humility that is based on your foundation of self-esteem, not on some misguided thought that people should be able to understand everything you said the way you meant it to be understood.

The only way you can get better at communication is to get better at understanding how people feel when they state themselves. Knowing that your own feelings can never be perfectly expressed leads you to realize that everyone has the same challenge. Because you have gained confidence in your own feelings, you are more generous with others in their feelings. You get to the point where you can listen, know that what is being said is emotionally based, and encourage your partner to keep on going until they believe they have expressed themselves the best they can.

Summary

1. An emotionally mature man is aware of his feelings.
2. He knows when to speak his feelings and when to keep them to himself.
3. He knows that sadness and joy are the most important emotions because he loves things and loses things regularly.
4. He expresses his feelings in words and action.
5. He is confident in himself and in his feelings while being humbled by times when he does not adequately communicate.
6. He apologizes for his mistakes.
7. He knows that any expression of his feelings will stimulate other people's feelings.
8. He gives careful attention to other people's feelings.
9. He is ready to engage in discussion and action when all feelings have been expressed and understood as much as that is possible.
10. He knows that mature communication is reciprocal.

POSTSCRIPT

Dos and Don'ts

You have read a lot about men, a lot about feelings, a bit about the differences men and women have, a bit about leadership as a man, and ultimately how men can more effectively communicate. We have studied the four "W's" that affect men: words, work, wine, and women. Now, let's be as practical as possible. In these final chapters we dare to suggest a few things that might be useful as you find your way into dealing with what it means to be a man.

CHAPTER 11

Dos and Don'ts for Women

I DARE TO SAY a few things to women about how they can relate to us men. I think women might profit from these suggestions and be ballsy in the process. Isn't that an odd statement, a "woman being ballsy"? My wife says that it isn't, but it is for me as a man to think of a woman being "ballsy." Remember, being ballsy is not about testosterone; it is about honesty and courage. Some of the suggestions I offer are quite important, while others might be trivial. Read them, think about them, feel about them, and trust your intuition as to whether you use them or not. The most important things I want to say are what you can *do* to improve your relationships with men. You will note that some of my suggestions, especially the *don'ts*, might seem to go counter to the way you have been taught to relate to people or even against advice well-meaning therapists have suggested. The essence of these suggestions lies on the foundation of knowing how you feel and effectively communicating how you feel towards the man in your life. I hope you notice that these suggestions are made in the spirit of you loving your man and seeking the essence of truth between the two of you, not on criticizing or complaining, which always lead to hostility and resentment. I assume that you want the man in your life to be a better person and in so doing make your relationship better. You will see that your attempts at improvement almost always have to do with something that you say. As you peruse these dos and don'ts, recall how I have suggested that we men are not primarily words-based people and as a result are not as efficient and experienced as you are with saying how you feel. We men want to be seen just as much as you want to be seen, but we are seen largely in what we do, not so much in what we say. Governing what we say and garnering what we hear is the hardest task you have with us men.

Dos: Speak to the Man About You

Communicate Your Feelings

Without a doubt, this is the most important thing that you should do with a man. But to ask you to *communicate* your feelings is much more than *expressing* your feelings, and it takes a lot of work. You might say, "I have been expressing my feelings for years and it doesn't go anywhere. The man in my life doesn't seem to care about what I feel." I was working with a couple recently, focusing particularly on helping the man express his feelings. His wife said that she was quite good at expressing feelings, so I asked her if she could give me an example. She said this: "We were in the car yesterday pulling out of the garage and Irvin was driving. He turned the driver's side car seat warmer on but not the passenger's seat where I was sitting. I told him exactly how I felt." I asked, "What did you say to him?" "I told him he was an asshole." Jackie believed she told him how she felt but she didn't. She thought she had expressed her feelings, but she hadn't actually told him how she felt. What might she have said instead of calling Irvin an asshole? Something like this: "Irvin, I feel disappointed that you did not turn my seat warmer on." Likely, Irvin would have made some excuse for neglecting her seat warmer, or he might even have been angry, or he might have gone silent. I suggested to Jackie that she should have gone further with expressing her feelings, perhaps something like this:

> *Jackie*: You know, Irvin, my greatest hope is that we are more generous and thoughtful to one another. The seat warmer is not really important here, but when you didn't turn it on for me, I felt neglected. I want to be special enough to you so that you would think of me and turn on my heater, too.
>
> *Irvin*: I'm sorry. I just didn't think of it, Jackie. I was looking in the rear-view mirror to be careful not to scratch the car. It is really that important?
>
> *Jackie*: No, Irvin, the heater is not what is important. My hope is that I can think more about you and you think more about me. I don't want to bitch about the seat warmer. I just want to say that I want to love you better and have you love me better.

Irvin: Jackie, I am really sorry that I neglected turning the seat warmer on. I just didn't think of it. Thanks for telling me your feelings. I agree with you: I hope we can think about each other more and love each other more.

Saying how you feel is saying something about you, like Jackie did here. The real task in expressing your feelings is knowing that there is never anything wrong with your feelings, but the words that are expressed are often wrong. When you express your feelings, try to keep the love factor central because love is always at the core of any feelings. Remember: when you have something you love, you feel joy; when you lose something you love, you feel sadness. You might say things like:

- "I felt sad" or "I felt really joyful."
- "I felt disappointed" or "I felt wonderfully surprised."
- "I felt worried" or "I felt great hope."
- "I felt discouraged" or "I felt really encouraged."
- "I felt sick" or "I felt really well."
- "I felt angry" or "I felt a situation of injustice."
- "I felt afraid" or "I felt particularly safe."
- "I missed your kissing me this morning" or "I went through the entire day wishing that we could have started the day with a kiss."
- "I felt resentful" or "I felt particularly appreciative."

Be Careful How You Express Your Feelings

There are great dangers in expressing your feelings. Some of these dangers are using the word "feel" when you really are making a judgment. If you say to the man, "I feel like you are abusive (or angry, or lazy, or work too hard)," you have not spoken your feelings. Rather, you have rendered a judgment about him, what he does, and what he says. Much better to use basic emotions like sad, afraid, happy, or even angry, like Jackie did in our previous discussion. It is better to say, "I am disappointed (sad, hurt) that you are late," thereby giving the guy something of how you really feel, not what you think of him. This is terribly hard to do because no one has taught you how to express your feelings like this, and certainly no one has taught the man in your life such things.

Admit That You're Wrong Sometimes

Just about every man I have ever seen has said something like "she never admits that she's wrong." Likely, this statement will offend my female audience, so let me explain what "she never admits that she's wrong" actually means. As with all important statements, it is a feeling statement, not a factual statement; i.e., the man "feels" that the woman doesn't ever admit that she's wrong. You know that you are wrong from time to time, but it is possible that you rarely say it. Consider saying something like this:

- Jim, I thought about what I said to you last night about your being overweight. I was wrong to say that. I am sorry.
- Jack, I was wrong to insist that we buy that new couch. I think I pushed too hard to get what I wanted. Maybe we should take it back.
- Greg, I made a mistake today at work. I misquoted Betsy to the rest of the team. I recognized what I did and apologized to Betsy. She was quite upset with me. It was a hard day.

Acknowledge Your Limits or Insecurities

Freud was the first psychologist in modern times. The first person in any field is usually wrong about a lot of things, just as were Aristotle, Galileo, Newton, and Abraham Lincoln. Freud noticed the frequency of insecurity with women and concocted his unfortunate theory of penis envy as a reason for this insecurity. The insecurity that he saw in women may, indeed, have been due to the cultural restrictions on women at his time of life. I think that both men and women have insecurities. We would all be better if we admitted to them, especially to our partners in life.

We men tend to feel inferior to other men in regards to the money we make or the professions we have. It might be good to carefully state something about these feelings at the right time and in the right place. For example a woman might say:

- Rog, I like this dress and I feel good in it, but I am scared that I might be kidding myself.
- When I make love with you, sometimes I am scared that I am not pleasing you as much as you please me.
- Gloria received recognition at a meeting today. I know she works hard and deserves the praise. Since I was moved to this department though,

I feel inferior and am embarrassed to admit I find it hard to appreciate Gloria.

Do Your Best to Hear How You Have Hurt the Man

At the beginning of an improving relationship, you will have to remember that anytime the man in your life is angry, avoiding, or engaging in some addictive behavior, he has been hurt in some way. You will not hear the "H" word from him when you have hurt him in some way until he gets better at using it, but most of us men don't actually know that we are hurt. You can be of immense help to a man who is avoiding feeling hurt by realizing that you have hurt him, hopefully unintentionally. Consider saying something like,

- "Jim, it seems that I have offended you by what I said. Please tell me what got you mad."
- "Sam, I'm sorry for what I said. I didn't mean to attack you, but it seems that I have hurt you. Please tell me how I attacked you."
- "Frank, the words that came out of my mouth weren't the best words. Please tell me your thoughts about what I said."

Apologize for Hurting His Feelings

Apologizing for hurting someone's feelings is not necessarily claiming that you said something wrong. We discussed this issue in chapter ten, where we distinguished different kinds of apologies. You may have said something that was dead-on true and needed to be said, but this fact doesn't preclude that your statement, however true, hurt the guy's feelings. Recognize that a truthful statement can still be hurtful. When you hear the typical male response of silence or anger, you have to read between the lines, knowing that the man is hurt. A conversation might go something like this:

Alice: Tom, I told you to get green beans instead of the black beans that you bought. Now, I have to run to the store and get what I told you to get.

Fred: What's the difference, for goodness' sake? Beans are beans.

Alice: I'm so sorry for snapping at you, Fred. My bad here. I shouldn't have barked at you.

Fred: Thanks for that, Alice. I will go back to the store and get the right beans.

Alice: No need to go back to the store, Fred. It is a minor disappointment. You are more important to me than the beans. Let's have some chili.

Initiate Important or Challenging Discussions at a Good Time

This means a time that is unencumbered with children, other responsibilities, fatigue, or alcohol. We men can't just start talking about feelings when the kids are around, late at night, when we're busy doing something or thinking something, when we're really tired, or perhaps even when we're watching a football game or playing a video game on a cell phone. It takes a great deal of patience, and a great deal of love, to look for a time when the man is available for intimate conversation.

Initiate Conversation about Something Good

It is way too easy in our current culture for people, whether men or women, to talk about what is wrong. When a man hears you say, "We need to talk," he becomes immediately defensive because he is prepared for you telling him something is wrong with him. This is not your fault. You might just want to talk about what color you would like to paint the basement office, but when he hears "we need to talk," most men think, "what have I done wrong this time?" Making spontaneous positive statements can be about work, the neighbors, the kids, the house, or anything else. Even better is some kind of compliment you make to him about what he has done or a favorable comment about what you have done.

Give the Man Something That You Really Want to Give

There is perhaps no greater joy than to give something to someone that I really want to give. Such gifts are acts of grace and serve both the giver and the receiver. Shakespeare said in *The Merchant of Venice*, "The quality of mercy is not strain'd. It droppeth as the gentle rain from heaven . . . It is twice blest: It blesseth him that gives and him that takes" (Shakespeare, 1600). Give all that you have to give. Give money, give time, give your left arm, or give your life. But don't give a penny, a second, agreement, sexual activity, or anything else that you don't really want to give. Give but don't give in. Giving in is not an act of grace, and it is not an act of love. It is an act of fear. Instead of giving in:

- Respond to his sexual gestures when you want to have sex. Just as important, initiate sex when you want to.
- Listen to the man in your life when he is complaining about work, but don't listen to the point where you become frustrated with him.
- Go out for dinner when you want to go out, and go to the place that you would really like, rather than giving in to going to his preferred places.
- Watch football if you enjoy it, or watch it for a few minutes now and then, but don't sit through a four-hour football game that is boring to you.

The dos are so much more important than the don'ts in life. They are easier to consider. The don'ts require more time and effort. Bear with me for these next several pages. Keep in mind that I do not intend to change you, how you feel, or what you believe but rather try to help you communicate better. Hopefully, these don'ts will give you some tools to know him better so you can love him better and in so doing help him become a better man.

Don'ts

Don't Tell the Man What to Do

Don't tell him how much to drink.
    Don't tell him what to eat.
    Don't tell him how to drive.
    Don't tell him how to care for his body.
    Don't tell him that he works too much.
    Don't tell him what clothes to wear.

When you tell a man what to do, you are trying to make him a better person. You know that, but the man in your life doesn't know that. At the core of these statements about what the guy should do, you have a *feeling*, but the way you express this feeling communicates to the man that you are criticizing him. You need to know that what you feel and think underlies your statement about him. I suggest that you communicate the feeling that erupts in you rather than expressing a judgment of him. For example:

Drinking:

- "Brian, I like you when you think and speak clearly. You have such a good brain! When you drink to excess, I miss you." Or . . .
- "Brian, you know how to introduce and carry on a conversation with just about anyone. When you drink to excess in public, I feel sad that others might think less of you." Or . . .
- "Brian, you are so fun, energetic, and intelligent when you are at your best. When you drink to excess, these qualities just don't show up as well as they should."

Eating. If the man in your life eats too much or eats food that is bad for him, see if you can find ways to carefully encourage him rather than telling him what he should eat. You might say:

- "Jim, you have a really good body. I am proud of how you have done so well over the years. I like how you take care of yourself." Or . . .
- "Jim, I've decided to do my part in our both eating better. I'd like you to join me in this effort so we can have a long life together."

Driving. Try one of these options:

- "Max, I know that you are a good driver and haven't had any accidents, but sometimes when you drive fast, I don't feel safe. I know that you are safe in your own eyes, but I would like to feel safer when you are driving." Or . . .
- "Max, sometimes when you are driving, perhaps a bit faster than I would like, I don't feel safe. When I don't feel safe, I keep to myself and feel separated from you, which is something I don't want to do."

Body care. Comments you might make about body care:

- "Trent, I noticed a bit of halitosis in your breath. It's not awful, but I thought you would want to know before you leave for work." Or . . .
- "Trent, I have noted recently that you sometimes have a bit of food stuck in your mouth that you try to get out with your fingers when we're in public. Could you delay the irritation or go to the bathroom for privacy." Or. . .
- "Trent, you have great teeth. I've always liked your smile. I've seen you occasionally feel some kind of pain when you eat. It seems that you might have a cavity that needs to be taken care of. I'd like you to keep your smile. Maybe a quick trip to the dentist would be in order. I think I'm up for an exam myself."

I have been running quite a bit since my heart event and I noticed that my running shoes might be wearing out. Deb and I went looking at shoes at a discount store and I found a pair for about $42 that I thought might work. Then . . .

Deb: They might work, but let's keep looking."

(We go to another store)

Deb: You know, Ron, I want you to continue to be healthy because I want you alive and able to do what is so important to you, like seeing patients and writing books. I think it is important for the both of us to do our very best to stay healthy.

Ron: You mean I should buy a good pair of running shoes rather than the cheap ones, right?

Deb: Right. That's a good idea!

Ron: Perfect."

Working too much: Here again, I can speak personally about this need because I tend to work too much, which may have contributed to my heart attack. Deb has mentioned this to me several times, but finally, I came to realize that, indeed, I do work too much. Deb has been kind in her comments, and I've heard things like this:

- "Ron, you are so good at working and you are good at your work, but I have noticed that you are frequently tired lately. I wonder if we could work together to find a way for you to work less." Or . . .

- "Ron, I've noticed that you have spoken of being tired a lot lately, which is not like you. I just want the best for you, and I know that work is your most important thing in life. I miss spending some time hanging out." Or . . .

- "Ron, the people you help in your work all appreciate what you do for them, and many of them couldn't do without you. I think we can find a way for you to do your good work, serve people, and keep healthy."

Clothes. Consider the following ways a woman could comment on a man's appearance:

- "Randy, you know that I think that you are really handsome. I like it when you look as good as you can look. Sometimes, when I see you wear those old baggy jeans, I think that you don't really show yourself off." Or . . .

- "Randy, when we went out to dinner the other night and you wore a sweatshirt, I felt sad. I just felt disappointed that we couldn't look our best at a restaurant."

Don't Tell Him What Is Wrong with Him

This is an adjunct to not telling him what to do, as well as the tendency we all seem to have to look for what is wrong with someone. Please, avoid telling him about his "issues" or the "pattern" of his misbehavior. Likewise, avoid any mental health diagnoses. Diagnoses, issues, and patterns are implicitly critical and put you in the position of trying to fix him. It never works. When you see the man falling into anger, avoidance, or addiction, consider saying something like:

- "Jack, I want to tell you something about me that you may not know. It is important to me. I get scared when you get angry. I know you're not trying to scare me but I need to tell you when I feel scared. I wonder if we could work together to find a way for me to be less scared, and perhaps for you to be less angry." Or . . .
- Max, it's wonderful that you want to take care of us, our property, and your job, but sometimes you are so concerned about these things that I feel a bit left out. Sometimes, I just miss you. Or . . .
- "Sam, you must know that you are the most fun person I know. I love that you are often the life of the party. Sometimes, however, your liveliness leads to your saying something that embarrasses me. I wonder if we could find a way for you to be just as much fun and be a little more careful with what you say." Or . . .
- "Jim, I know that you are generally an internal (introverted) person, and I know how important your privacy is. Sometimes, when I don't hear from you, sometimes for hours or days, I feel lonely and I miss you. I hope you can find a time and place where we could actually talk and listen to one another. I'll try to do more listening than talking.

Even if you carefully talk this way to a man, it is likely that he will become defensive because he will discern the displeasure you have with him. But over time, if you begin to talk this way, your feelings will begin to show through. Moreover, you will avoid the tendency of tolerating behavior that is harmful to him or offensive to you and others and help him become a better man.

Don't Complain about Him to Family or Friends

There is a huge danger of getting "support" from someone who doesn't love the man in your life the way you do. I have seen many women's friends advise her to leave a man because all they hear is what is wrong with him. Too many therapists suggest divorces as the only solution to relationship difficulties. Trust your feelings and work diligently to speak of your feelings, hopefully in a way that he can understand. It might be helpful to say one of these things:

- "Peter, you know that we've been struggling recently, and both of us are trying to find our way in our relationship. We have to do this together. I want you to know that I never speak to anyone negatively about you." Or . . .

- "Frank, a couple of my friends and my sister have often asked how we are doing, possibly because they see that we are struggling. I know they mean the best, but I have chosen to never speak to anyone about us, particularly something that is challenging." Or . . .

- "Dave, you know that I have never spoken to anyone about the challenges we have with one another. I would like us to speak to a professional counselor of some kind so we can find a way to succeed in our life together."

Don't Complain about People at Work

When men hear women complaining about their work, they are inclined to say something like, "If you don't like it there, just quit and find something you like," which of course does no good for the woman or the man. If work is difficult for some reason, consider saying something like:

- "You know that it has been a struggle for me at work for a long time. I have been feeling less than good at work, or going to work, for that matter. Some of it is the work environment, and some of it is particular people. I want to do my best, enjoy what I am doing, and receive a little appreciation for what I do. That hasn't been happening for a long time. I'm not asking for advice here but I do appreciate your hearing me out on this because I really want to be happy in work." Or . . .

- "Allow me to tell you what I heard from some people today. It was difficult to hear and I didn't know how to handle it. A person with whom I work closely shared with me that she is having an affair with the boss.

This put me in a difficult situation because she confided this information to me and evidently no one else knows about this situation. I had a hard time not rendering some advice. It's good to be able to tell you because I can't tell anyone else."

Don't Yell at the Man

I don't think women yell at the men in their lives any more than men yell at women, but yelling is never good for anyone, man, woman, or child. I put the largest burden on men to avoid anger in their female relationships, but that having been said, women also come to anger too quickly and need to find ways to express their hurt, offense, disappointment, or disapproval in ways that are not spoken primarily with anger. Recall that I have suggested that anger is a secondary emotional reaction after a person has been hurt and then becomes afraid of being hurt more. Find words that express your hurt, disappointment, or sadness, remembering that sadness is a "love problem," while anger is a defense.

Don't Overuse the "Hurt" Word

I work diligently with men to get the "H" word into their vocabulary. It is not natural, or perhaps more accurately, it is not culturally natural for men to say that they are hurt. This is not the case with women who have been privileged to feel hurt, to say that they are hurt, and to attend to other people's hurt. When a man hears the "H" word from a woman, he is nonplussed. He doesn't know what to do. He doesn't know what to say. He really doesn't know how to express his own feelings, which are something like, "I have done something wrong in your eyes and you are going to shame me for it." If you use the term "hurt" frequently, it loses its power and feels like a weapon instead of a tool in a relationship. Guard against saying elaborate statements of hurt like, "I feel SO hurt," "I feel hurt all the time," or "you keep on hurting me all the time." These statements create a feeling of shame in men and the underlying fear of rejection. They do not help a man understand his own hurt, much less yours. Try something like:

- "Jack, when you yelled at me, I felt something that is very important. I felt hurt. Let me try to say what this hurt is about. First, I love you, which is most important. Secondly, when you yelled at me, I felt pushed away from you, like you didn't like me or didn't want me around, or even that you didn't want me in your life. Perhaps these thoughts sound crazy, but I can't help thinking them when you yell at me."

- "Pete, I'm glad to see you. I was worried about you. You usually get home around six, but now it's almost eight, and I began to worry that you might have been in some kind of accident. There is another feeling I have when you're late like this and don't call me. I feel that I'm not important in your life. I'm sure that there was something important you had to do at the shop, but that thought doesn't help me when I start worrying about you."

- "Chuck, you know yesterday was our anniversary. I know such things are not terribly important to you. You don't really care much about your own birthday, much less anyone else's. But such things are important to me. I'm not looking for a $100 dinner on our anniversary or a new car or something, but I would feel loved if you gave me a card or a flower, or perhaps just if you wished me a happy anniversary and told me that you loved me."

Don't Interrupt the Man When He's Speaking

This is terribly hard for women because you know that when you and your friends get together, everyone talks at a fast pace, and you even override one another with what you think or feel. Recall the difference in the corpus callosum that makes it possible for women to speak and listen at the same time, something men cannot do. Men simply cannot speak and listen the way you can. When you're *adding* to what the guy has said, he feels *interrupted*. You need to give him a lot more time to speak himself than you would give a female friend. It's a chore, but you have to do it if you're going to communicate to him and really understand how he feels. This is a typical conversation that could happen if you "add" to what he is saying:

Ben: Mary . . . I don't know . . . I've been thinking . . . I don't know . . . thinking that we should . . .

Mary: Just spit it out, Ben.

Ben: Nevermind. It's not important.

Or . . .

Ben: Mary, I had a difficult time with Jack yesterday. He got mad at me for some reason, and I don't know what it is.

Mary: Ben is right-wing on politics and you're left-wing. He doesn't have the same values you have.

Ben: Maybe that's right. (Ben goes into his cave because he didn't get a chance to work out his feelings about Jack.)

In all of these circumstances the woman is trying to be a help to the man, but her quick responses or interruptions are essentially critical or diagnostic. More importantly, she is not demonstrating interest in his feelings. If a woman is to avoid the trap of speaking when the guy is speaking or making interpretations, she will have to wade through the man's trying to say something like,

Ben: Mary . . . I don't know . . . I've been thinking . . . I don't know . . . thinking that we should . . . I don't know. I feel all mixed up.

Mary: I'm listening. I'm not in a hurry. This seems important.

Or . . .

Mary: That must have been very difficult. What's on your mind?

In my asking you to listen in this way, do you feel like you're dealing with a child? Yes, you are dealing with a child if we see a man's childlike way of speaking his feelings. Yes, he doesn't really care about your feelings at this moment because he is trying to express his own feelings. You just need to be a silent listener, hear all kinds of irrational, emotional, and contradictory things from him while you sit patiently listening to him. This is an act of love and it is very hard to do.

Don't Talk When the Man Is Urinating . . .

It pisses him off. More seriously, don't talk to him when he is washing his hands, brushing his teeth, drilling into metal, talking on the phone, reading a book, or upstairs changing clothes. When the guy is doing these things, he is going about his business and he can't attend to what you say. He may not even hear you, much less be able to consider the value of what you say or meaningfully respond to you. All these silly things have to do with the fact that the guy wants to do one thing at a time and can't think of two things the way you do.

Don't Ask the Man Questions

This is really hard to do for everybody, but it is particularly challenging for women because they tend to gather information by means of asking questions. The great psychotherapist Fritz Perls said, "Underneath every question is a statement" (Perls, 1969), by which he meant that most questions are rhetorical, especially if they occur in a relationship. Consider how you might make a statement instead of asking questions:

- "Why were you so late last night?"
  - Meaning: I didn't like that you came home late.
- "How much did you drink at the party last night?"
  - Meaning: I think you drank too much.
- "Why don't you ever talk to me about your feelings?"
  - Meaning: I wish you would talk to me more often about feelings.
- "What is your problem?"
  - Meaning: I think something is wrong with you.
- "Why do you get angry so often?"
  - Meaning: I am hurt and offended by your frequent anger.
- "Why did you have so many texts to Shirley?"
  - Meaning: I am afraid that you have something going with Shirley.

Note that I have suggested that you avoid such questions and dare to say something about yourself, particularly how you feel.

Don't Believe What the Man Tells You

This must be the oddest instruction to give to a woman because it must sound like we men are all liars. We are not all liars, but we all lie. You have read that the primary ingredient of "balls" is being honest, and yet most men don't have that kind of balls. Asking women to "not believe anything the man tells you" follows straight from "don't ask questions." It is not your fault whatsoever that men might lie to you about something, and you can't correct a man's dishonesty by telling him that you can't believe anything he says. Recall that we men are not by nature verbal. Rather, we are physical by nature. We are not prepared for questions, criticisms, and challenges that naturally come with any female relationships. We enter any activity, particularly any relationship, from a physical/emotional standpoint rather than from a verbal/emotional standpoint. It is hard for men to be challenged about what they did, but it is ten times harder for them to be challenged about what they said. Sadly, men learn to lie, whether small lies to friends or profound lies with the women in their lives. If the man in your life grows a pair, he will be more honest. This is his work, not yours.

Avoid Inflammatory Language

Inflammatory language includes words like "abuse," "diagnosis," and any statement or rhetorical question that is shaming. Diagnoses should remain in the purview of a competent therapist who themselves often use them to a fault. In addition to avoiding abuse-like words and diagnostic terms, avoid using words that are abstract like "unacceptable," "irresponsible," "disrespectful," "intolerable," "disgusting," or "immature." All of these terms are shaming judgments and do nothing for you, much less for the man hearing such things. What is acceptable to you might not be to him and vice versa. What you think is irresponsible may not be so in his eyes. Again, work diligently to say how you feel, not the judgments that ensue from your feelings. He needs to hear your feelings, which is the best route to helping find his own feelings.

Women use the "D" word (divorce) way too frequently, or use cognates of the D word, like saying, "I refuse to put up with this anymore," "I can't live like this," much less more stringent demands like "get out" or cruder statements like "maybe you should go back to your indulgent mother." If you keep threats of divorce out of your vocabulary, you will be able to find ways to improve your relationship or actually find a way out of the relationship if it becomes clear that it is bad for you.

Don't Remind the Man of What He Did Years Ago

As a woman you have a better memory for feelings that are associated with things that happened in the past. You remember when the man in your life was dishonest, delinquent, or somehow unkind. The reason you tend to bring these things up is that you are still hurt by what he said or did. Instead of belaboring his past mistakes, which may be many, make a time when you can simply tell him about these hurtful things in the past, noting that you are just saying your feelings of hurt and accompanying sadness. Remind him you are not talking about him but about yourself in order to finish hurt and sadness. When you do this, you will eventually be able to forgive him for his transgressions, he will be able to apologize, know you better, and love you better. Then, you will be able to deal with what he says or does in the present without adding all of his other transgressions.

Summary

- Trust your feelings. Your feelings are never wrong.
- Do your best to express your feelings, but know that it is impossible to express feelings perfectly.
- Muse about your feelings until you can speak them carefully.
- Govern your emotional expressions.
- Know that you are much better with emotional words than men are.
- Avoid complaining and threatening.
- Listen to things that are wrong, not true, silly, or outrageous. Listen.
- Give, but don't give in.

CHAPTER 12

Don'ts and Dos for Men

The dos and don'ts for women are important, but far more important are the dos and don'ts for men. My focus in this book has been on what we men can do in order to be great men. Greatness, as I use the term, is not about being rich and famous, much less being tyrannical or even right. It is about being ballsy, about being a maturing man. If women do all the dos and don'ts outlined in the previous chapter, but we men fail to do our dos and don'ts, our relationships will most certainly fail. Ballsy starts with us and ends with us. If we can be ballsy in all of the aspects of life, we will be a great force for good. In the long run it is not about women nor about us men. It's not even about being ballsy. It's about being a force for good in the world. We find a way to do that, and we will do well in all our other day-to-day responsibilities like work, intimate partners, family, and property. Let's get started. We will start with the don'ts for men.

Don'ts

Don't lie

Not to yourself. Not to anyone else. Especially not to women. When we men get in the habit of lying, it has a very deleterious effect on our character and is ultimately equally harmful for everyone around us. Some men then fall into lying with impunity, while most of us just lie occasionally, sometimes about the most trivial things. There is the rare time when lying is the best thing to do. These are times of true danger, like if someone has a gun to your head. You might choose not to tell the whole truth when asked a very personal question or when you are in a public setting. You can tell "fish stories" for fun with a friend who knows you're embellishing. Aside from these rare times when lying might actually be the ethically or socially right thing to do, work on avoiding lying in most all circumstances.

Lying deteriorates any relationship, male or female, child or adult, employee or superior, friend or foe. Lying tends to cause other people to lie, just like your hurting someone causes them to hurt you. You might have developed a habit of lying, namely if you were raised in an environment where you had to lie to survive. If this is the case, you might find it profitable to explore your personal history of lying to see if there was a time in childhood when you found it necessary to lie in order to protect yourself from true danger or shame. What we did to survive as children is no longer necessary in the adult world. If you find yourself lying in your adult relationships, you have continued to operate in a mode of surviving rather than in a mode of thriving. So many of us men have lied to avoid disapproval, especially from the women in our lives. As Sir Walter Scott said, "Oh, what a tangled web we weave when first we practice to deceive" (Scott, 1808). If you get caught in your own web of lies, have the balls to get out as soon as you can.

Don't Get Angry

We discussed the epidemic of men getting angry several times in this book. We have grown up as boys where anger was too much a part of our lives, and it still is. We battled with other boys physically, athletically, musically, artistically, or academically. Our male voices are louder and lower, which scares women. You can yell or swear at another man, raising your voice or raising your hands in the air, but this kind of expressed anger scares women. I raised my voice the other day with Deb, and she kindly but confidently told me to lower my voice. I retorted that I wasn't "yelling" and again, she kindly but confidently reminded me that a man's raised voice sounds like yelling. Geesh. In this rare moment, I got caught expressing anger without even knowing I was feeling angry. Ideally, we should never get angry, but to do that we have to recognize the hurt that always precedes anger, the loss that precedes the hurt, and the love that has been lost in the first place. People do not see the hurt and the love when we are angry. They only hear the raised voice and the anger behind it.

Don't Give In

Giving is an act of love and leads to personal enhancement, relationship enhancement, and joy for both the giver and the receiver. One of my favorite Shakespearian expressions is "twice blessed," because both giver and receiver are better off when kindness or mercy is extended. You may not always want to give some form of love to someone, but if you give out of generosity, you will be better for it. *Giving in* is giving something to someone out of fear of their disapproval. Giving in always leads to resentment. Let me tell you what I told women in the last chapter:

- Give all that you can give.
- Give the shirt off your back.
- Give your left arm.
- Give your life if necessary.
- Don't give in.

Giving is generated by love and creates joy. Be a person who says "yes" and "no" honestly and genuinely instead of out of a feeling false guilt, which is fear of the other person's reaction. I know of many very happy marriages where giving predominates, and I know of many marriages where giving in occurs all the time, always to be followed by resentment.

Don't Stay with Something That Is Bad for You

The things that may be bad for you include a relationship, a job, a house, a town, a group, or a conversation. "Bad for you" means that you are worse off when you are with these people or places. You can't be at your best if you are surviving or tolerating. This suggestion doesn't mean that you do what you want all the time because there are things that you may not want to do but are good for you and good for your environment. Look to maximize the things that are good for you so you can be an honest force for good in the world. If you make an honest assessment of what is truly necessary for you and what is truly bad for you, you will see that most things fall between these two extremes. I work out regularly but don't ever like it. I like candy, but it is not good for me. More importantly, I have left things, places, and people because they were truly bad for me, and I have established relationships, found places, and bought things that were really good for me. It takes a bit of wisdom to know the difference between "good for me" and "bad for me."

Trust your feelings, which is tantamount to trusting your genuine intuition, and you will have genuinely good things in your life and reduce the genuinely bad things in your life.

Dos

Be Honest with Yourself

Being ballsy starts with being courageously honest with yourself. This means looking at what you do, how you think, and especially what you feel. Being honest means working to find a package of words that approximately describes what you feel, which is much harder than examining what you do or what you think. Remember, you will not succeed at finding exact words for thoughts, and it is even harder to find words that represent your feelings, so give yourself a lot of liberty to find approximate words for what you think and feel.

You might find that you feel . . .

- Something physical, like a pit in your stomach, cold hands, increased heartbeat, eyes watering, a cough, or even a mild headache.
- Really good for some unknown reason. Remember that joy is a natural part of being alive.
- Something emotional, like sadness, fear, or anger.

It is important to establish a foundation of trust in what you feel before you speak your feelings. As much as I want men to learn to speak their thoughts and feelings, I always recommend they feel first, think second, and speak third. Once you have given yourself enough time to feel the physical and emotional aspects of feelings, you will be able to think about these feelings.

Think Before You Speak

Allow yourself time to think this, think that, and re-think things. This stage can be seconds but for most men it is minutes, and may even be hours for you if you are unfamiliar with the physical-emotional-cognitive-verbal process of experiencing and expressing feelings. This period of time can be one where you give yourself a wide berth of thoughts accompanied by approximate words or even some kind of picture in your mind. This is a very important aspect of being ballsy. It is okay to find yourself saying things to yourself that seem weird, outrageous, stupid, or even wrong. No one should hear the words that you say to yourself in this stage. This feeling through so you can think clearly includes an element of containment until you are ready to speak what it is you have been feeling.

Speak Carefully and Kindly

As *Desiderata* has it, "Speak your truth quietly and clearly and listen to others, even the dull and ignorant for they too have their story" (Ehrmann, 1948). As we have learned, having balls doesn't mean any kind of dominance, male superiority, or authority, much less any statement that is demeaning or derogative. Remember, you might need to start talking with an admission that it is difficult to communicate your feelings like:

- "I need a moment or two, please, to think about what you have said. I'm feeling a lot of things when you say what you said. I need to sort them out in my own head before I respond to you."
- "That seems to be a very important discussion that we need to have. I need some time to think about it before we talk further about what you've said. I will get back to you as soon as possible."

All of these statements are ballsy because they are honest admissions of your limitation in finding words for your feelings. Such statements indicate that you have heard what your wife (girlfriend, mother, friend, coworker, or boss) has said, but these words also suggest that you want to connect with the person, be better known by them and know them better.

Make Declarative Statements About Yourself

Remember that the foundation of being ballsy with all these dos and don'ts is honesty. If you can be honest with yourself and then selectively open with other people, you will become a better man. The following three situations illustrate how a man must first be honest with himself before he can make declarative statements to others.

Situation 1: Father and Child

Fathers are really important in the life of a child. A father (or father figure) ideally serves as a transition from the safety of a mother figure to the opportunities and dangers of the rest of life. This means that the father needs to encourage, challenge, and sacrifice (himself) for his child. Consider the following situation where the daughter, age thirteen, has posted a revealing photograph of herself on her Facebook account, and some other parent informs Dad about this. Note how you, yourself, might feel, think, do, or say if this happened to your daughter:

- You are hurt.
- You are hurt because your daughter has (apparently) done something that seems unwise and possibly unsafe.
- You are afraid for your daughter's reputation and safety.
- You are afraid that this posting might stay with her for a lifetime and be an impediment to her entering the adult world.
- You don't know what to say.
- You don't know if you should even tell her mother.

Being hurt and afraid, you might say something like this to your daughter:

Dad: Lisa, I heard from Mrs. Gray that you posted a nude photograph on your Facebook account.

Lisa: I did no such thing.

Dad: Perhaps not. But I would like to talk to you about it, please.

Lisa: I told you, Dad, that I didn't post a nude photograph on Facebook. I posted a picture of myself . . . but, geesh, I wasn't nude.

Dad: (He understands that Lisa is defensive about whatever photo she posted and knows not to challenge her statement. So, he goes carefully, knowing that he can't get angry nor can he approve of what she's done. This asks Dad to be honest with himself and then find a way to be selectively honest with his daughter. He knows not to ask questions because questions will only make Lisa more defensive and then probably lie or get angry or stomp out of the room. He keeps all these thoughts to himself and decides to share his feelings.)

Lisa, so let's put aside the photo thing for the moment because this is not about a photograph or what someone else thinks about it. I don't give a hoot about what Mrs. Gray or anyone thinks of your post.

Lisa: That was supposed to be a private post to Shelly, not Shelly's mom. I don't know how Mrs. Gray got into Shelly's private account. Parents are always snooping around our cell phones. I don't like it.

Dad: I don't like it either. I wouldn't want someone to snoop around my private life, whether it was on my cell phone or a private email I sent to someone.

Dad: I'd like to tell you the most important thing in this matter . . .

Lisa: (interrupts Dad and says) . . . I know what you're going to say, that there are dangerous people out there, and that I shouldn't be having any kind of revealing photograph of me. Like I said, I didn't do that.

Dad: Actually, Lisa, I wasn't going to say anything about the photo or other people seeing it. I just wanted to tell you that the most important thing about this incident is that I love you.

Lisa: Geesh, I know that, Dad.

Dad: I'm sure you do, but let me go on and tell you a bit more about my love for you. I love you more than you can possibly imagine. There is nothing and no one that I love more than I love you. You know, of course that I love all the members of my family, but the love I have for you is special, maybe because you're my daughter. You are very special to me.

Lisa: That makes me feel a bit weird. Don't you love mom and the others just as much as you love me?

Dad: Yes, certainly I love you all the same amount, but the love I have for you is different and very special, maybe because you're the oldest or maybe because you're my only daughter. It's special whatever that means.

Lisa: What does this have to do with the photograph?

Dad: My love for you doesn't have anything to do with the photo or whatever you posted. My love for you involves seeing you as being very successful with people and school, and eventually everybody else in life. I want you to be very happy in your future life.

Lisa: That feels good, Dad.

Dad: So, let me get back to the photo post thing. When I heard about the Facebook post, I just felt sad. I didn't feel angry. I just felt sad, hurt, and a bit afraid. I felt sad and afraid because I love you. I felt sad because I look forward to you being successful in life and I thought this Facebook thing could hurt you being happy in life.

Lisa: How would that happen?

Dad: I don't know if it could happen, but I just thought things like someone, maybe the wrong person, might see some picture of you and hurt you in some way.

Lisa: How could someone hurt me by seeing a photo of me?

Dad: I don't know, Lisa, but I just thought maybe the wrong parent, the wrong guy, the wrong girl in class could use this photo against you in some way. I didn't go through the middle school years and high school years with the drama that you girls usually go through. Your mom has told me about what she went through, and it was awful.

Lisa: It is awful. The girls can be so catty. Boys can be so stupid.

Dad: I believe I understand girls' cattiness and boys' stupidity. I'm very sorry, Lisa, that you have to go through this time of life with gossip and cattiness. I can only imagine that it is awful. So, when I heard about the photo thing, I just felt sad. I felt sad because I love you and I don't want you to be hurt even though I know you have been hurt by people. I just felt sad. That's all.

Lisa: I'm sorry for making you sad, Dad.

Dad: Lisa, the only reason I felt sad is because I love you. That's the bottom line. Lisa, I will never tell anyone about this photo thing, and I won't ever bring it up again. It's a done deal. It happened or it didn't. It doesn't matter to me. What matters is that I love you and want you to be happy. Maybe you could profit from talking to your mom about the drama at school. She must have gone through it too and probably understands more than I do.

Lisa: Thanks, Dad.

Note the care that Dad used in talking with his daughter:

- He knew what he felt, he accepted what he felt, and he thought deeply about how he could communicate his feelings to his daughter.
- He kept Mom or anyone else out of the discussion.
- He didn't focus on the "problem" but rather, focused on the real issue: he loves his daughter.
- He didn't shoot his mouth off.
- He didn't ask any questions.
- He didn't agree with what she (apparently) did or didn't do.
- He didn't chastise her.

- He spoke of his love for his daughter and the sadness that he felt singularly because he loves her and wants the best for her.
- He felt deeply but kept his emotions of fear and anger primarily to himself.
- He made a declarative statement about himself.

Situation 2: You Have a Job That Is Not Good for You

Maybe you're under qualified for the job or over qualified for the job, or maybe the job is just boring and doesn't have any meaning for you. You have known that this job is not good for you, but you make a good income, and you can't think of another job that will match it in pay. In fact, this is more of a job than a profession, even though you're good at it. You want to be doing something that is more exciting and interesting to you and maybe something that is important in the world. Consider this way of being ballsy regarding your job:

Being ballsy with yourself:

- You've been thinking about this job situation for a long time, but you haven't been able to come to a decision because you've been caught with the practical things like money, logistical things like what other job might be available, and emotional matters like feeling scared and excited. You decide to face the scared part first.
- You admit that you're scared. You ask yourself, "What am I scared of?" You are scared of making a mistake. You're scared of being unemployed. You're scared of what other people think. You're scared of staying with your job and continuing to be unhappy.
- You allow yourself to be scared for a while, but then you remember that all fear is based on the possibility of losing something. What you might lose comes down to losing money and safety. You realize that you made some very good decisions when you were younger to prepare yourself for a life of work, play, and relationships. You realize that this is a time in your life where you need to look at the "second half of life," meaning what you're going to do for the rest of your life. You realize that while your decisions were good for reasons of establishing yourself and having safety, you feel that there is more to life than safety.

- These thoughts lead you to feel into the possible loss you might experience if you leave your job. This realization brings you to feel simple sadness, which you know is anticipatory loss. You realize this potential loss is because you love safety and have always "played it safe."

- You muse further. You realize that while you still need safety in life, you need something more than just safety: meaning. You muse further about your needing more meaning in your life, and these thoughts bring you back to the fact that your present job does not provide meaning for you. You admit that you have very few ideas of what kind of job or profession might be meaningful for you.

- After this bit of self-examination, you continue to assess your value system, i.e., what is important to you. Immediately, you note that quality is important to you. You also realize that being with people, ideally one-to-one, is important. You realize that being of some kind of direct service to people is important. You realize that you need a fair bit of stimulation in your day, and that you don't do well with too much routine. Most of all, you realize your work needs to be meaningful.

Note that all of this is done largely in private. This kind of thinking and feeling is not necessarily done in one setting or one time of meditation. Rather, it is done over a period of time when you give yourself the freedom to wander around your thoughts and feelings without being pressured into saying something to anybody about these things. You need time to think through on your own so that you can "take the stage" with confidence as we discussed in Chapters 4 and 8. You might talk to a friend.

Being ballsy with a friend

You: Jim, I'd like to share with you some thoughts and feelings I have about work.

Jim: What's the problem at work?

You: Actually, I don't have a "problem" as such. I'd just like to share some feelings and thoughts about work. Mostly, I need you to listen to me as I think out loud because I can't say these things to anyone yet, not even to Mary.

Jim: I can do that. Shoot.

You: In general, I'm not happy at work. There are a lot of things that are good at work, like my boss and my salary. But I've had an overall feeling that this job, maybe even this profession, is not right for me at this time in my life.

Jim: What other job could you get?

You: That's an understandable question, but I don't know what other job I might get because I'm not actually there yet. I'm still musing, thinking, and wondering more than planning or looking for another job.

Jim: Don't you want to have something in place before you quit your job or change your profession?

You: Again, that's a very reasonable question, Jim, but I'm not actually there yet either. Bear with me, if you can, as I try to say what's on my mind and heart with this whole thing.

Jim: I'll do my best, but you know I'm a "do it now, do it wrong, fix it, and go forward" guy.

You: I know this about you, and it works great for you, but I'm not quite like that. I need to think and feel and muse before I pull the cord.

Jim: I'll do my best. Shoot.

(Then you proceed to muse out loud. You might have to hold Jim back from his tendency to make suggestions.)

Now that you have been ballsy with yourself and with one other person, you can consider other options, like changing careers, going back to school, or starting your own business. You might even find yourself staying with your present job, at least for the time being, to see how you feel for a few days or a few weeks. You don't rush right into something. You don't spend time complaining about work. You don't threaten to run off to Tahiti. You feel and think.

Situation 3: A Personal and Private Matter About Yourself

There are many personal and private matters for us men. We struggle with our faith, our sexual desires, our political persuasions, or even our simple pleasures that could seem odd to other people. For many men personal and private matters can lead to addictive behaviors. You might gamble too much, get lost with too much sexual fantasy, eat too much, drink too much, play video games too much, watch TV too much, or work too much. All of these things are ones that cause you difficulty in some way and probably cause other people difficulty in some way.

Being ballsy with yourself

- Admit to yourself that you are not satisfied with what you are doing.
- Admit that you have been unable to stop what you want to stop.
- Realize that it will take discipline to overcome this behavior.
- Realize that you don't want to stop this behavior. You don't want *the process of stopping something that has become addictive* because it has given you a certain amount of pleasure for a long time. No one wants to stop smoking, overeating, or gambling; they want to *have stopped* and to *not have the desire* anymore.
- Start small: eat a bit less, drink a bit less, play video games a bit less.
- Notice that your brain is fighting your mind because your brain thinks immediate pleasure is good. Nothing wrong with your brain. It is doing one of the two things it does well: safety and pleasure. You have to override your brain's desire to maximize your immediate pleasure.
- You recognize that it is just hard to reduce the addictive behavior. You might be able to find a bit of solace in knowing that you reduced your addictive behavior just slightly.
- You recognize now is a time to talk to someone else about the challenge you are facing.

Be ballsy with someone else

Ideally, your partner or a close friend. You have to take control of the conversation. You don't want advice or direction, much less some kind of diagnosis or recommendation.

You: Mary, I want to tell you what I'm trying to do with my drinking.

Mary: I'm glad to hear that. Are you going to that AA meeting I told you about?

You: Mary, I'd like to tell you what I have done, not what I'm going to do.

Mary: OK.

You: I've decided to cut down on my drinking a bit and see how it goes.

Mary: Aren't you supposed to be entirely sober like AA suggests?

You: I've decided to find my own way in this project.

Mary: But doesn't AA suggest complete sobriety?

You: I think that approach is correct for some people, but I'm going to try to find a way that fits me.

Mary: So, you're not going to AA meetings and giving up all alcohol?

You: That is correct. I'm going to start small and see if I can get a handle on my drinking.

Mary: I don't think that will work.

You: Mary, here is where I really need you to listen to me and stay with me on this project. I'm sure this is very hard for you. I also know that my drinking has been hard on you for a long time. I am truly sorry for that, and I won't excuse my excessive drinking whatsoever. But at this time in my life I need to face this in my own way.

Mary: I'm not sure that I agree with your approach.

You: I'm not sure myself, Mary, but this is where I really need your support. I don't need your agreement. Indeed, you may ultimately be right, that I should go to AA and go completely sober, but this is not how I am going to handle this challenge.

Mary: What are you asking of me?

You: I'm actually asking a very important thing: to love me, to be on my side, and to observe me while I try to find my way in this drinking thing. I don't expect you to agree with me. Quite importantly, I'm asking you to support me in what I am doing without agreeing with what I'm doing.

Mary: How can I do that?

You: Primarily by hearing me as I talk to you about my drinking. I'm not sure if I can carry through with this, but I'm going to try hard in my own way to correct my excessive drinking. I want to tell you how I'm doing, what I'm doing, and what I'm feeling. I want to be honest with you about how much I drink and maybe why I drink. I need you to listen. I ask a lot because I am asking you to refrain from suggesting anything or correcting anything I tell you.

Mary: But I have a lot of feelings about your drinking. How am I going to handle those?

You: This is probably the hardest thing I am asking of you. I'm asking you to know how you feel about my drinking and keep your feelings to yourself.

Mary: But what if you get drunk and angry the way you have done in the past?

You: That's a completely different thing. Hopefully, I will find a way to conquer that kind of behavior. But if I get nasty, I don't expect you to put up with it. The best thing you can do is to leave me alone for a period of time. When I'm drunk, I'm not rational and I'm not kind. I'm not expecting you to put up with that sort of thing, nor am I asking you to do so. I'm asking you to hear my day-to-day report of my drinking, my limiting my drinking, my not drinking at all, or that I drank too much. I want to feel comfortable telling you about the struggle.

Mary: I can do that.

You: I will keep you informed. So, for instance today I . . .

This proposed conversation is one in which you stay in command of the conversation, stay with your thoughts, feelings, and desires, and stay away from any kind of argument or even discussion about how, when, and if you should drink. It is very hard to do without being defensive but rather sticking with what you want, what you feel, what you think, and ultimately what you say.

Listen to Everything People Say About You

Many of the things people tell us are dead-on right. They just shouldn't tell us their judgments, like how to live, what to do, what to think, what to feel, and worst of all: what they think is wrong with us. This is particularly true for women who think they are helping you when they say such things. Hearing someone's assessment of you puts you in a very difficult position. You may agree with what they are saying but simultaneously be irritated at being judged. The problem with someone telling you something about you is that they are not telling you about themselves, like how they feel. "I feel that you should . . ." is not a statement of how they feel. It is a judgment. Unfortunately, most people talk this way. Hear their statements about how they "feel," know that these are judgments, allow yourself to be hurt, and keep your feelings to yourself and then privately consider whether you should take any kind of action.

Understand That It's Hard to Be a Man

We men all feel the burden of the words, the work, the wine, and the women in our lives. It's hard to feel the responsibility every one of us experience as we engage the various aspects of life. We talked about this in chapter two, noting that responsibilities are burdensome and most men keep the burden to themselves. We feel responsible for the women in our lives, our children, our grandchildren, our property, our money, and what our friends think of us. To be ballsy means you have to face up to the responsibility of taking care of various aspects of your life. It is unavoidable. It is natural. It is part of being a man. We feel the burden of things close to us: when an infant cries in the middle of the night, or our teenage daughter says that she is pregnant, or a brother is dying of cancer. We feel the burden of things more distant from us: environmental damage, sex trafficking, wars, racial inequality, or maybe just the lack of ballsy politicians. We can identify with what President Truman first said: "The buck stops here," or what President George W. Bush said: "I am the decider." It is not an easy place to be.

What do we men do with this awesome burden of responsibility that lies on our shoulders? If you face the burdens of responsibilities in life you will initially feel quite lonely because no else feels exactly what you do: certainly not the women in your life, but equally importantly, not the men in your life. Much of what we have discussed in this book has to do with men finding, facing, feeling, and finishing feelings like loneliness that we experience in life. When we learn to do this, we then find the solace of people who understand how we feel, at least to the best of their abilities. When you find the right person, place, and time to share the burden of responsibility of being a man, you are ready to make a difference in the world. You are ready to get beyond yourself and *generate*.

Be Generative

I began this book with an apology to women, LGBTQ people, and anyone else offended by the use of the term "balls" because of its crude-sounding nature. There is a symbolic element to the use of the term balls that might just be the most important ingredient for good men who want to be mature men. The Latin origin of the term "genitals" has the same element as the words generation, gentle, generator, genesis, generosity, and generalship (Merriam-Webster, 2022). All of these words suggest a kind of "giving birth." In other words, being ballsy is to start something. When a man starts something, he gives the people around him an opportunity to respond to this starting by adding, subtracting, or otherwise enhancing what the man started.

In the long run being ballsy is not about being a male. Being ballsy is not about you and it is not about me. It is about bringing something to the world that the world desperately needs: courage and honesty. Balls-forward men.

Summary

1. Don't lie.
2. Don't get angry.
3. Don't give in.
4. Don't stay with something that is bad for you.
5. Be honest with yourself.
6. Think before you speak.
7. Speak carefully and kindly.
8. Make declarative statements about yourself.
9. Listen to everything people say about you.
10. Understand that it's hard to be a man.
11. Be generative.

Bibliography

Barrett, L. F. (2017). *How emotions are made: The secret life of the brain*. New York: Houghton Mifflin.
Beauregard, M., & O'Leary, D. (2007). *The spiritual brain: A neuroscientist's case for the existence of the soul*. New York: HarperCollins.
Berridge, K. C., & Robinson, T. E. (2016). Liking, wanting, and the incentive-sensitization theory of addiction. *American Psychologist 71*(8), 670–679.
Bloom, P. (2016). *Against empathy: The case for rational compassion*. New York: HarperCollins.
Bly, R. (1990). *Iron John: A book about men*. Philadelphia: Da Capo.
Brock, D. (2004). Comparisons of personality type and temperament and psychopathological indicators between evangelical and mainline denomination women seeking counseling. [Doctoral dissertation, Breyer State University]. Madison, WI: Midlands Psychological Associates.
Brock, D. (2016). "The Feminine Spiritual." In J. H. Ellens (Ed.), *Feminism and spirituality* (pp. 235–248). Santa Barbara, CA: Praeger.
Brock, D. (2016). "Faith and Feminism: Resolving the Gender Issue Through Mythology and Archetype." In J. H. Ellens, (Ed.), *Feminism and spirituality* (pp. 277–292). Santa Barbara, CA: Praeger.
Brock, D., & Johnson, R. (2011). "Narcissism and Evil." In J. H. Ellens (Ed.), *Explaining evil*, Vol. 1: *Definitions and development*. Santa Barbara, CA: Praeger.
Carmody, J. (1989). *Towards a male spirituality*. Mystic, CT: Twenty-Third.
Chapman, G. (1992). *The five love languages: How to express heartfelt commitment to your mate*. Chicago: Northfield.
Clark, S. B. (1980). *Man and woman in Christ: An examination of the roles of men and women in light of Scripture and the social sciences*. Ann Arbor: Servant.
Coates, J. (1986). *Women, men, and language*. 2nd ed. New York: Longman/Pearson.
Cole, E. L. (1992). *On becoming a real man*. Nashville: Thomas Nelson.
Cook, E. P. (1986). *Psychological androgyny*. New York: Pergamon.
Csikszentmihalyi, M. (1993). *The evolving self*. New York: HarperCollins.
Dalbey, G. (1988). *Healing the masculine soul*. Dallas: Word.
Damasio, A. (1999). *The feeling of what happens: Body and emotion in the making of consciousness*. New York: Harcourt Brace.
Davidson, R. J., & Begley, S. (2012). *The emotional life of the brain*. New York: Hudson Street.
Doidge, N. (2007). *The brain that changes itself*. New York: Viking Press.

Ehrmann, M. (1948). *The poems of Max Ehrmann*. Boston: Bruce Humphries Press.

Ekman, P. (2003). *Emotions revealed: Recognizing faces and feelings to improve communication and emotional life*. New York: Henry Holt.

Fanning, P., & McKay, M. (1993). *Being a man: A guide to the new masculinity*. Oakland: New Harbor.

Federal Bureau of Prisons (2022). Incarcerated Americans by gender. Washington, DC: Department of Justice. bjs.ojp.gov.

Freed, J., & Parson, L. (1998). *Right-brained children in a left-brained world*. New York: Fireside.

Friederici, A. D. (2011). The brain basis of language processing: From structure to function. *Physiological Reviews*, 91(4).

Gardner, H. (1983). *Frames of mind: The theory of multiple intelligences*. New York: HarperCollins.

Gazzaniga, M. S. (2018). *The consciousness instinct: Unraveling the mystery of how the brain makes the mind*. New York: Farrar, Straus & Giroux.

Gilligan, C. (1982). *In a different voice*. Cambridge, MA: Harvard University Press.

Goldberg, H. (1976). *The hazards of being male: Surviving the myth of masculine privilege*. New York: New American Library.

Goldman, B. (2017). "Two minds: The cognitive differences between men and women." *Neurobiology*, Spring 2017.

Goleman, D. (1995). *Emotional intelligence: Why it can matter more than IQ*. New York: Bantam.

Gray, J. (1992). *Men are from Mars, women are from Venus*. New York: Harper Collins.

Gurian, M. (1992). *The prince and the king: Healing the father-son wound*. Los Angeles: Jeremy Tarcher/Putnam.

Gurian, M. (1994). *Mothers, sons, and lovers: How a man's relationship with his mother affects the rest of his life*. Boston: Shambhala.

Gurian, M. (2003). *What could he be thinking?: How a man's mind really works*. New York: St. Martin's Press.

Hall, J. (1984). *Nonverbal sex differences: Communication accuracy and expressive style*. Baltimore: Johns Hopkins University Press.

Hawley, J. (2023). *The masculine virtues America needs*. Washington, DC: Regnery.

Herbert, N. (1993). *The elemental mind*. New York: Dutton.

Hicks, R. (1991). *Uneasy manhood: The quest for self-understanding*. Nashville: Thomas Nelson.

Hillman, J. (1960/1992). *Emotion: A comprehensive phenomenology of theories and their meanings for therapy*. Evanston, IL: Northwestern University Press.

Hillman, J. (1971). *The feeling function*. Dallas: Spring.

Hollander, D. (1995). *101 lies men tell women and why women believe them*. New York: HarperCollins.

Hyde, J. S., & Linn, M. (Eds.). (1986). *The psychology of gender: Advances through meta-analysis*. Baltimore: The John Hopkins University Press.

Jewett, P. K. (1975). *Man as male and female*. Grand Rapids: Eerdmans.

Johnson, R. (2002). *Friendly diagnosis*. Madison, WI: Midlands Psychological Associates.

Johnson, R. (2004). "Psychoreligious Roots of Violence." In J. H. Ellens (Ed.), *The destructive power of religion: Violence in Judaism, Christianity, and Islam*. Vol. 4:

Contemporary views on spirituality and violence, (pp. 195–210) Santa Barbara: Praeger.

Johnson, R. (2008). "The Miracle of Psychotherapy." In J. H. Ellens, (Ed.), *Miracles: God, science and psychology of the paranormal*, Vol. 3: Parapsychological perspectives, (187–193). Santa Barbara: Praeger.

Johnson, R. (2010). "Neurotheology: The interface of neuropsychology and theology." In J. H. Ellens (Ed.), *The healing power of spirituality: How faith helps humans thrive*, Vol. 3: Psychodynamics, (pp. 207–229). Santa Barbara: Praeger.

Johnson, R. (2013). *Seen and not heard*. Madison, WI: Midlands Psychological Associates.

Johnson, R., & Brock, D. (2017). *The positive power of sadness: How good grief prevents and cures depression, anxiety, and anger*. Santa Barbara: Praeger.

Johnson, R., & Brock, D. (2020). *I want to tell you how I feel*. Madison, WI: Midlands Psychological Associates.

Johnson, R., & Brock, D. (2022). *What's your temperament?* Madison, WI: Midlands Psychological Associates.

Jung, C. G. (1971). *Psychological types*. Princeton, NJ: Princeton University Press.

Jung, C. G. (1989). *Aspects of the masculine*. Princeton, NJ: Princeton University Press.

Jung, E. (1957). *Animus and anima*. New York: Spring.

Karen, R. (1994/2024). *Becoming attached: First relationships and how they shape our capacity to love*. New York: Oxford University Press.

Keirsey, D., & Bates, M. (1978). *Please understand me*. Del Mar, CA: Prometheus Nemesis.

Kierkegaard, S. (1847/1943). *Fear and trembling and Sickness unto death*. Princeton, NJ: Princeton University Press.

King, F. (1978). *He: An irreverent look at the American male*. Briarcliff Manor, NY: Stein and Day.

Kipling, R. (1956). "If." *Kipling: A selection of his stories and poems*, Volume II. John Beecroft (Ed.). Doubleday & Company, Inc.

Kohn, A. (1993). *Punished by rewards*. New York: Houghton Mifflin Company.

Kurtz, I. (1986). *Mantalk: A book for women only*. New York: Beech Tree.

LaLiberte, Cormac (2022). UW-Madison has a binge drinking problem. *The Daily Cardinal*. November 10.

Lazoni, S. (2018). *Empathy: A history*. New Haven, CT: Yale University Press.

Lederer, W. (1966). *The fear of women: An inquiry into the enigma of woman and why men through the ages both loved and dreaded her*. New York: Harcourt Brace.

LeDoux, J. (1996). *The emotional brain: The mysterious underpinnings of emotional life*. New York: Simon and Schuster.

LeDoux, J. (2015). *Anxious: Using the brain to understand and treat fear and anxiety*. New York: Viking.

Levant, R. F., & Pollack, W. S. (Eds.). (1995). *A new psychology of men*. New York: Basic.

Lowen, A. (1972). *Depression and the body: The biological basis of faith and reality*. New York: Penguin.

Lutz, T. (1999). *Crying: The natural and cultural history of tears*. New York: Norton.

Maccoby, E. E. (Ed.) (1966). *The development of sex differences*. Stanford, CA: Stanford University Press.

Maté, G. (2000). *Scattered: How attention deficit disorder originates and what you can do about it*. New York: Penguin.

Money, J., and Ehrhardt, A. A. (1972). *Man and woman, boy and girl: the differentiation and dimorphism of gender identity from conception to maturity.* Baltimore: Johns Hopkins University Press.

Moore, R. L., & Gillette, D. (1990). *King, warrior, magician, lover.* New York: HarperCollins.

Narramore, B. (1984). *No condemnation: Rethinking guilt motivation in counseling, preaching, and parenting.* Grand Rapids: Zondervan.

Orstein, R. (1997). *The right mind: Making sense of the hemispheres.* New York: Harcourt, Brace & Company.

Peck, M. S. (1978). *The road less traveled: A new psychology of love, traditional values, and spiritual growth.* New York: Simon and Schuster.

Perls, F. (1969). *Gestalt therapy verbatim.* Lafayette, CA: Real People Press.

Pittman, F. S. (1993). *Man enough: fathers, sons, and the search for masculinity.* New York: Putnam's Sons.

Power, J. (1969). *Why am I afraid to tell you who I am?* Allen, TX: Tabor.

Reich, W. (1961). *Character analysis.* New York: Farrar, Straus & Giroux.

Reinisch, J. M., Rosenblum, L. A., & Sanders, S. A. (Eds.). (1987). *Masculinity/femininity: Basic perspectives.* New York: Oxford University Press.

Sanford, J. A., & Lough, G. (1988). *What are men like?* New York: Paulist.

Schore, A. N. (1994). *Affect regulation and the origin of the self: The neurobiology of emotional development.* Hillsdale, NJ: Lawrence Erlbaum Associates.

Schwartz, J., and Begley, S. (2002). *The mind and the brain: Neuroplasticity and the power of mental force.* New York: HarperCollins.

Scott, Walter. (1808/1911). *Marmion: A tale of Flodden Field*, Canto VI. London: J. M. Dent & Sons.

Seligman, M. (2002). *Authentic happiness: Using the new positive psychology to realize your potential for lasting fulfillment.* New York: Free Press.

Shakespeare, W. (1994). *The merchant of Venice.* Harlow, Essex, England: Longman.

Smalley, G., and Trent, J. T. (1992). *The hidden value of a man: The incredible impact of a man on his family.* Colorado Springs: Focus on the Family.

Sonderegger, T. B. (Ed.). (1984). *Psychology and gender.* Lincoln, NE: University of Nebraska Press.

Spence, J. T., & Helmreich, R. L. (1978). *Masculinity & femininity: Their psychological dimensions, correlates, and antecedents.* Austin: University of Texas Press.

Sternberg, W. (1993). *Masculinity: Identity, conflict, and transformation.* Boston: Shambhala.

Stotland, E. (1969). *The psychology of hope.* San Francisco: Jossey-Bass.

Tangney, J. P., & Dearing, R. L. (2002). *Shame and guilt.* New York: Guilford.

Tillich, P. (1952). *The courage to be.* New Haven, CT: Yale University Press.

Tournier, P. (1958). *Guilt and grace.* New York: Harper & Row.

Van der Kolk, B. (2004). *The body keeps the score: Brain, mind, and the healing of trauma.* New York: Viking Press.

Vitz, P., & Felch, S. (Eds). (2006). *The self: Beyond the postmodern crisis.* Wilmington, DE: Intercollegiate Studies Institute.

Von Fronz, M-L, & Hillman, J. (1971). *Lectures on Jung's typology: The inferior function and the feeling function.* Dallas: Spring.

West, M. (2007). *Feeling, being, and the sense of self: A new perspective on identity, affect, and narcissistic disorders.* London: Karnac.

Whiteside, M. F. (1998). Custody for children 5 and younger. *Family Court Review*, 36(2), (pp. 479–502).

Wolf, F. A. (2002). *Matter into feeling: A new alchemy of science and spirit*. Portsmouth, NH: Moment Point.

Zinczenko, D. (2006). *Men, love and sex*. New York: Rodale.